Charlie Connelly is a bestselling travel writer, award-winning broadcaster and the author of seven previous books, including *Attention All Shipping: A Journey Round the Shipping Forecast*, which was a Radio 4 Book of the Week. Charlie was a presenter on the *Holiday* programme and co-hosted Radio 4's *Traveller's Tree*. A former rock 'n' roll tour manager, mortuary assistant and, somehow, marketing manager for the *Complete Works of Lenin*, Charlie is the official ambassador to England for a breakaway Lithuanian republic, has been falsely accused of intending to invade Rockall and has duetted live on Uzbek national television with the country's biggest pop star. All by accident. He lives in Ireland with a large collection of ukuleles.

Also by Charlie Connelly

Stamping Grounds: Liechtenstein's Quest
for the World Cup

Attention All Shipping: A Journey Round the
Shipping Forecast

In Search of Elvis: A Journey to Find
the Man Beneath the Jumpsuit

And Did Those Feet

*Walking Through 2000 Years
of British and Irish History*

Charlie Connelly

ABACUS

ABACUS

First published in Great Britain in 2009 by Little, Brown
This paperback edition published in 2010 by Abacus

Copyright © 2009 Charlie Connelly

The moral right of the author has been asserted.

A CIP catalogue record for this book
is available from the British Library.

ISBN 978-0-349-12088-1

Typeset in Bembo by M Rules
Printed and bound in Great Britain by
Clays Ltd, St Ives plc

Papers used by Abacus are natural, renewable and
recyclable products sourced from well-managed forests and certified
in accordance with the rules of the Forest Stewardship Council.

 Mixed Sources
Product group from well-managed
forests and other controlled sources
www.fsc.org   Cert no. SGS-COC-004081
© 1996 Forest Stewardship Council
FSC

Abacus
An imprint of
Little, Brown Book Group
100 Victoria Embankment
London EC4Y 0DY

An Hachette UK Company
www.hachette.co.uk

www.littlebrown.co.uk

This book is dedicated to the memory of
Dominic Bussey
1974–2008

Contents

Introduction

The prospect of staying at the Norwich Travelodge is not usually one to set the heart a-flutter. There are more exotic destinations in the world. There are more exotic destinations in Norwich. But as my train pulled out of Liverpool Street station and the sunlit back gardens of the east London suburbs flitted by in a rapid silent slideshow of terraced domesticity – a child's tipped-over plastic tricycle, a mildew-darkened greenhouse with a smashed roof pane, a chained collie bucking and barking sound-lessly – I caught sight of my reflection in the sun-flashes that occasionally illuminated the window. I was smiling, and I was heading for the Norwich Travelodge. Clearly something strange was afoot.

As the houses and steel-fenced, prefabricated industrial units began to thin out in favour of more and more greenery, I looked up at the rucksack strap swinging from the overhead storage shelf where I'd wedged it after an inelegant sprint across the concourse for the train and tried to think about what lay ahead. I thought about how I would soon be making this journey in reverse, and how it would take me a lot longer than this even if, as inevitably came to pass, we sat outside Witham for an hour and a half due to a points failure. I thought about how, when I got to Norwich, I would be saddling up Shanks's Pony and walking back – that's *walking* back – with my rucksack strapped to me like a snazzier version of Dick Whittington's hanky-on-a-stick, a sturdy pair of boots on my feet and, hopefully, a song in my heart and a rainbow draped around my shoulders. I was setting out at the beginning of a series of journeys that covered not just distance, immense and daunting distance that would have me walking as far in about eight months as I had in about the last dozen years, but time too, following a chronology that would run into millennia. I wasn't walking from Norwich to London just for the sake of it. For one thing, that would be an odd thing to do and would cause people to edge away nervously if I mentioned it in conversation. No, from Norwich Travelodge I would be retracing the first of a series of great journeys from history, following a trail of righteous destruction instigated by a woman grievously scorned nearly two thousand years ago who has since passed into mythology, whose biography has been lost in the wispy caverns of time, leaving only shadowy half-truth and romantic fable. The only remaining certainty was the route I was about to undertake.

This would be the first in a sequence of journeys tracing routes taken by some of the most famous and not-so-famous figures in the history of these islands, journeys that had, and in many cases continue to have, an effect on the way we live now. We're surrounded by history. We can barely walk down the street without tripping over the stuff. We're so spoiled by the abundance of the past in our midst that it's easy to take it for granted. Not only that, with our still-too-common perception of history as an area for dusty, musty old academics poring over dusty, musty old books, we've lost a sense of the vibrancy that history hoards. The past has everything: wars, battles, power struggles, love stories, mysteries, murders, miscarriages of justice, heroism, cowardice, tragedies and the inexplicable popularity of the codpiece. It's not confined to earnest, learned books and stuffy museums with ancient, clanking central heating systems and attendants who all look like Deryck Guyler. It's everywhere, it's around us and it's alive: we can actually reach out and touch it.

Whenever I've been to the US, pitching up somewhere with an inquisitive expression and well-thumbed guidebook, a smiling, friendly person would skip out of the door, flash me a wide and perfect American smile and say, 'OK, let me tell you a little about the history of this place.' Then they'd pause, hold their hands up defensively, their palms facing me, as if I was about to wrestle them to the ground and bite off their nose, and add, 'But hey, of course we don't have history like *you guys* have history.' Now, we can debate the millennia-spanning chronology of the Native American tribes until the steers come home, but you know what they mean – and they're right. We guys do have history, wheelbarrows full of the stuff, and thankfully for the most part people wrote it down. A great deal of it was biased, subjective and often wildly inaccurate, but then cast your eye along the front pages of the national papers next time you're in the newsagent's. Thankfully, too, for the most part the material we have is often rollicking, gripping and hand-flying-to-mouth scurrilous, and, by jiminy, I love it.

When I was at university I shared a house for a while with a philosophy student. She was a bit bonkers at the best of times, but when she'd twirl her hair while Rosie, her pet rat, sat on top of her head and say, 'I think the reason I love philosophy so much is because, you know, it's just in . . . *everything*,' while I was trying to watch *Sportsnight* I'd have to restrain myself from calmly removing my shoe and taking Rosie out like a leather-uppered, rodent-exterminating William Tell. I'd gone to university to study Russian. Actually no, I'd gone to university to meet girls and drink until I was sick, but officially I was there to do Russian. After a year or two of failed exams and missed classes the university let it be known that they really didn't want me to study Russian any more and I'd have to do something else if I wanted to retain my right to meet girls and drink until I was sick. I sat sullenly in a meeting as various departments tried to suggest ways of keeping me there, to each of which I shrugged and harrumphed noncommittally. Eventually the history department took me under their wing and, my goodness, am I ever grateful that they did. Because, contrary to what my rat-loving housemate thought, it's history that's, you know, just in . . . *everything*. Politics, sociology, philosophy, biology, anthropology, literature, language – you name it, history's got it. And those lovely, lovely people in the history department set me right back on the road to historical epiphany even when I had yet to learn that girls rarely fancy someone mumbling insensibly with sick on their sleeve, who shares a house with a rat. Within weeks of beginning the new course I had remembered just how passionately I loved history, and how convinced I was that it's the key to just about everything. Girls still didn't want to know, though.

I've always been aghast when people in the course of a pub conversation have said, 'Actually I'm not all that interested in history, to be honest.' To me that's just like saying, 'Actually I'm not all that interested in absolutely anything in the world around me. I inhabit a vacuum, a sensually empty, silent, twilight world of nothingness in which I am impervious to anything and anyone, to be honest. Right, my shout, same again?'

OK, I might be being a bit disingenuous; of course, by not being all that interested in history they most likely mean they're not that bothered about being able to rattle off the names of the Tudor monarchs in order, or nail the date of the Battle of Prestonpans, or précis the outcome of the Bretton Woods Conference. Which is fair enough. But such textbook dryness is not what history is all about, any more than the fascinating, all-encompassing world of scientific discovery is encapsulated entirely within the periodic table.

Sitting in the pub with the person-not-interested-in-history, I'm looking around, wondering about the people who have passed through over the years. The air-raid warden discussing events at the front with the soldier on leave. The students excitedly debating the possible implications of the Bolshevik Revolution. The blacksmith staring wordlessly at his drink, worried for his livelihood owing to the relentless progress of industrialisation. The collier, merrily drunk and rosy-cheeked, unaware that he's minutes away from being press-ganged and sent to sea, never to return. All in this room, where generations of hearts have been broken, arguments have been settled, unbreakable friendships have formed, fists have flown and some unbelievable drunken bollocks has been spoken.

To me, history is alive, current and constant. Walk down your local high street, for example. Look beyond the homogeneous chain stores and you'll see, I don't know, the butcher's shop that's been there for generations run by the same family. Two men on ladders are replacing a sign over a shop front, temporarily revealing an old, beautifully hand-painted one dating back more than a century. A plaque on one building commemorates the birth of a famous poet. The clock chimes on the tower built to commemorate victory at the Battle of Trafalgar. Women sit chatting on benches either side of the obelisk that remembers the local fallen in both world wars. An old horse trough built to water the mail-coach horses is now filled with flowers. The 'Boys' and 'Girls' chiselled into the lintels above the doors of the drop-in centre reveal that it was once a school: who studied there, made lifelong friends there, spent an entire teaching career there?

The past is all around us, in the buildings, in the landscape, in the ground we walk on. It's not in lists of monarchs or dates of battles that it truly comes alive; it's in people and places. Everyone and everywhere has a story. I've been to some places that, on the face of it, promise nothing of the remotest interest and found myself riveted by the story of something that happened there. I grew up near Blackheath in south London; to the casual observer, just a great big expanse of grass sliced by a couple of roads. Yet it was a plague pit: during the Great Plague of 1665–6 hundreds of bodies were thrown into pits, scattered with lime and buried. In the Peasants' Revolt of 1381 it was a major rallying point for the rebels – Wat Tyler's Mound in the middle of the heath is supposed to be where the peasant leader addressed his followers. In Viking times, Ethelred the Unready's fleet moored at Greenwich and his men camped on Blackheath for the best part of three years while pillaging in the area. It was the site of suffragette rallies – Emily Wilding Davison was born nearby – and apparently also the place where golf was played in England for the first time. Dick Turpin used to ride across it. Beneath Blackheath are caverns and tunnels left by ancient chalk mines (part of the A2 collapsed into them in 2002, leaving a crater twenty feet across), and when a shaft was sunk in 1939 to see if the tunnels might be usable as a bomb shelter, the remains of an early Victorian masked ball were found scattered on the ground, as if everyone had left in a desperate hurry and the place had been sealed up ever since. For a bare patch of grass, that's not a bad record.

It's this passion for the past and my firm belief that history is alive and everywhere that resulted in me boarding the train to East Anglia. In *The History of the Decline and Fall of the Roman Empire*, Edward Gibbon wrote that 'history is, indeed, little more than the register of the crimes, follies and misfortunes of mankind'. He may well have a point. But for me it's much more than that: it's about individuals and their stories; how they contributed or otherwise to the themes of history and the great events of the past. I wanted to meet people from the past, sit them down in the corner of a pub with a couple of pints and ask them what it was like. I mean, what was it really *like*? When Julius Caesar and his ships appeared out of the fog, approaching the Kentish coast in 55BC, who were the locals who massed on the white cliffs and menaced him away? How did the word spread that something was afoot? How fantastical did the Roman vessels appear to them? Repelling one of the greatest military leaders in world history was some feat, yet we've no idea who those people were.

What must it have been like to slide around the Thames Frost Fairs, drunk on cheap beer? When London Bridge had houses and shops on it, who lived there? Who plied their trades there? Did the boggly-eyed, slack-jawed heads on poles give them the willies when they loomed out of the darkness on the way home from the tavern? When Sir Walter Ralegh came back from the New World, did anyone really give a toss about the potato? Was Charles II's relentless philandering the talk of the taverns, spoken of in tones of impressed reverence by the men, and of appalled condemnation by the women?

It also struck me that much of our history has been created and influenced by travel. There are the epic journeys of discovery by the likes of Magellan, Columbus and Amundsen, the expansion of empires, centuries of emigration and forced transportation. Closer to home the countryside has, over the millennia, been criss-crossed by journeys of people from all facets of society, from monarchs to minstrels, pilgrims to protesters, navvies to noblemen. Those journeys were conceived out of trade, rebellion, love, fear, necessity, greed, adventure, desperation, recreation and just plain old wanderlust. They are all soaked into the landscape; many were determined by it; yet more have altered it – ancient trackways becoming major thoroughfares, towns and cities springing up from stopping-off points on trade routes. Journeys of all kinds have helped to form the Britain we know today, undertaken by the itinerant musicians, the peddlers, the jugglers, the glee-men, the messengers, the quack doctors, the herbalists, the armies on the move.

I wanted to travel those routes too. As I looked out of the train window while we flashed through the little station of a village so quickly that I couldn't even read its name, I reflected that my chosen mode of transport was the right one. That village we just passed had its own history: it grew up on a trade, generations of families had called it home, it'd had its boom years and its slumps, its scandals and its crimes, and I'd just shot through it in seconds without even knowing its name. I was glad that I'd chosen to walk.

There can surely be no better way to ease your way to a healthier mind and body than by walking. It's leisurely, it's good for you, it's easy. You don't need any special equipment; you don't need any particular skills or training. Walking is a scandalously underrated and ill-appreciated human trait. Ever since our ancestors first stood on their hind legs, started moving about, quite liked the sensation and the higher view, and turned to their friends and said whatever the Mid-Pleistocene for 'Hey fellas, look at me! Woo hoo!' was, we've scored over other mammals thanks to our sheer upright ability. As children, arguably the most significant moment in our development, the crucial parental 'I was there' event, is when we take our first steps. The first time we, in similar fashion to our ancestors millennia ago, planted our feet flat on the ground, nappied bottoms rampant, and raised the top halves of our bodies to an angle roughly perpendicular, put one foot slightly in front of the other, wobbled precariously and then brought the other one level to the loud applause of those privileged to witness baby's first steps, we were setting out, literally, on the journey of a lifetime.

An average person, if such a thing exists, will take more than twenty-two million steps in their lifetime. I have to confess I probably lost count of mine pretty soon after the first one, but just imagine: twenty-two *million* steps. Breathing aside, is there anything we do so often without really appreciating its significance? Now, I'm probably too easily impressed by things like this. Electric windows on cars still inspire awe in me. But, for heaven's sake, walking – ain't it something? When you stop and think about it, ain't it really something?

The process of moving from one location to the other on foot has also earned itself wider significance than merely moving from A to B. When there's a widespread social grievance leading to a mass outpouring of displeasure against authority, what do we do? OK, apart from signing an online petition and then going back to poking random strangers on Facebook. What we do, from the Peasants' Revolt through the Pilgrimage of Grace and Martin Luther King's Freedom Walk right up to the Buddhist monks in Burma, is we go out and we walk en masse. Take the monks: their dignified progress through the streets in their scarlet robes was one of the iconic images of this fledgling century. It's the most basic way we can possibly make our presence felt. Walking makes us all equal; it's something pretty much everyone can do and as a mass action is an incredibly eloquent display of united opinion. Sometimes the walking protest can be taken to extremes. In 1953 a former Philadelphia socialite named Mildred Norman Ryder set out to walk around the US for world peace and didn't stop for twenty-eight years, until eventually her real name was entirely forgotten and she became known simply as Peace Pilgrim, the name she had adopted when she set out. She relied on charity – she never asked for accommodation or food – and had covered thousands upon thousands of miles when she was killed – get this – in a car crash after agreeing to be driven to a speaking engagement. Walking is resolutely democratic: it's easy to do, and it shows that a whole bunch of aggrieved people is truly not to be messed with.

Talking of pilgrims, when we want to show our religious devotion, to prove it goes far beyond just reading prescribed texts, praying and generally being nice to people, we go on a pilgrimage. We walk. From Croagh Patrick to the Hajj via the Camino de Santiago de Compostela, we use walking as an expression of our devotion. The further we walk, the more devoted we are. Indeed, Arthur Blessitt has carried a twelve-foot-high, forty-pound cross for more than thirty years of walking, in what is believed to be the longest continuous journey ever, taking in more than three hundred countries and approaching some forty thousand miles. And there was me thinking the bloke who shouts about Jesus through a megaphone at Oxford Circus was dedicated.

I would have a long way to go to approach Arthur Blessitt territory, but the more I thought about walking the more excited I became by it. Certainly, in the past lengthy journeys on foot had never really bothered me. I used to walk the four-mile round trip to school every day with no qualms whatsoever. The only time I've ever been stopped by the police was in the late eighties, when I was walking home from the main local library, a distance of around four miles that necessitated passing through some of the swankiest streets for miles around. Clad as I was in an old green bomber jacket with frayed sleeves and a tatty baseball cap pulled low over my eyes, it's no wonder that my carrier bag and I aroused the suspicions of passing plod. When I told them whence I was walking, and opened the bag to reveal nothing more than a Happy Mondays LP and a couple of Aldous Huxleys, rather than the video recorder and selection of credit cards they'd been hoping for, the two policemen looked at me with first suspicion, then amazement, then pity before offering me a lift, which I declined. I preferred walking.

These days, however, my life has become a little more sedentary. I work from home. My days usually involve getting up, making tea, showering and then parking my rear end on a chair for the rest of the day. I don't even walk to a bus stop or railway station. Thanks to modern technology I can work, listen to music, watch the news, chat to friends, write to people, book tickets for a gig and even order lunch without ever getting off my arse. OK, I'd have to get out of the chair and answer the door in order to get my lunch, but one day I'm sure even that hardship will be taken care of somehow. Nearly every apparent technological advance seems to be designed to make us move around less. It started with the car, progressed to the television remote control and now involves just about everything. Every new gadget might as well run a marketing campaign that says, 'Sloth: isn't it the nuts?'

I was well into my mid-thirties. I was getting undeniably podgy. I could go days without leaving the house. If I ran out of milk I'd often drink black tea or coffee rather than walk to the corner shop a hundred and fifty yards away. I wasn't so much a couch potato as a whole sack of immobile sofa-top Maris Pipers.

The more I thought about it, the more I could see that there were no drawbacks to walking. Everything about it is good for you, not to mention self-improving. All that fresh air and thinking time – it had to be a good thing. After all, many great writers and thinkers have praised the intellectual stimulation of a good stroll. Henry David Thoreau was of the opinion that 'the moment my legs begin to move, my thoughts begin to flow'. Jean-Jacques Rousseau agreed with him: 'When I stay in one place, I can hardly think at all.' Indeed, it could possibly be argued that the road to the *Discourse on Inequality* began one evening when a fifteen-year-old Rousseau arrived back from a walk in the countryside later than anticipated and found the gates of Geneva closed for the night. Rather than hammering on the gates or attempting to scale a wall, the young thinker paused a moment, sighed, turned round and started walking. And walking. A walk that would take him as far as Italy and France. 'My body has to be on the move to set my mind going,' he said, presumably to the sound of his mind whirring like a turbine.

Aristotle is said to have taught and thought only while pacing up and down. Which is something we all do: think of times when you've had to think intensely and quickly about something. Rather than sitting there pondering and wishing you had a beard to stroke, you're out of your seat and you're walking up and down, right? Other devotees included John Stuart Mill, John Keats, Thomas Hobbes (who even had an inkwell built into the top of his walking stick for when mobile inspiration struck), Jeremy Bentham and William Wordsworth, who made almost an entire career out of walking. He wouldn't stop. 'I love a public road: few sights there are that please me more,' he wrote in *The Prelude*. 'Such object hath power o'er my imagination since the dawn of childhood.' He did most of his writing while walking up and down a gravel path at the back of Dove Cottage, whatever the weather. Thomas De Quincey calculated that by the time he turned sixty-five, Worsdworth must have walked somewhere between 185,000 and 190,000 miles. And even then he wasn't finished. Not by a long way. So, by the simple process of walking, of putting one foot in front of the other, I could expand my mind, possibly even find myself, learn loads about all kinds of things, all the while getting fit, losing weight and earning myself the pertest pair of buttocks I've ever had in my life.

More recently than the likes of Wordsworth and Rousseau, what was arguably the greatest and most iconic moment of the twentieth century? It was when man walked on the moon. Not Kennedy being shot, not the Berlin Wall coming down, not Everest being conquered, not even Clive Mendonca's hat-trick for Charlton Athletic in the 1998 Division One Play-Off Final. Not the first satellite going up, not poor old Laika the dog being shot into orbit, not Yuri Gagarin being the first human in space, not even the first missions to send back images of grinning astronauts floating around in zero gravity, spinning cutlery in mid-air and giving thumbs-ups to the camera. No, the moment that had most of the globe spellbound was when a man walked on the moon for the first time. When Neil Armstrong did just what all of us do more than twenty-two million times in a lifetime, but on the moon.

As Neil Armstrong, the American civil rights protesters and the Burmese monks proved, walking makes history. So what better way for me to explore history than by setting out through it on foot? By following some of the journeys that shaped the history of our lands and their people?

I set to work immediately, to identify some likely contenders. I spent day after day in the British Library, trying to plan my itinerary. I wanted to find a good spread of geography and chronology, covering as much of these islands as I could in as wide a historical timeframe as possible. I wanted to find a range of journeys, not just monarchs (and all too frequently that would be male monarchs), but regular folk too. Alas the nature of recorded history made the latter difficult – the best recorded journeys are inevitably those of the big cheeses, the royals and aristocrats with the means and education to keep an account themselves, or to have people do it on their behalf.

I found that many potential journeys overlapped. The Jarrow Crusade followed much of the same route as King Harold hot-footing it from Stamford Bridge to Hastings, while my plan to recreate the Shakespearean actor Will Kempe's *Nine Daies Wonder*, where he morris-danced from London to Norwich, was thwarted by it being the reverse of the Boudica route I was about to begin. I had hoped to follow the route of the bluestone from south-western Wales that makes up part of Stonehenge, which, I deduced with some excitement, might well be the earliest traceable journey in our history, but then I read that the stones were most likely moved by glaciation; had they actually been moved by humans they'd have probably gone by sea. But eventually I had my itinerary and then commenced many an evening of poring over road atlases.

I also thought about how authentic I'd need to be. While researching Harold's march from Stamford Bridge to Hastings I'd discovered the story of a man named Chas Jones, who walked from the site of the Battle of Fulford to Waltham Abbey to see how the messenger who delivered the news of the Vikings' success at Fulford might have made the journey. Not only that, he did it dressed in a woollen monk's habit over a linen shirt and what he mysteriously described as 'medieval underwear'. He slept in the open and did the journey in six days (although he did admit to thirty-five miles' worth of lifts when the route was too dangerous to walk). I considered at length whether I should try to make my journeys as authentic as that, but then wondered where I'd draw the line. If I was to follow Boudica to the letter, I'd have to burn down Colchester, London and St Albans on the way. While there might be a number of people who'd be vigorously in favour of this, it was probably more trouble than it was worth. Similarly, I didn't much fancy taking an arrow in the peeper at the end of the Harold journey; nor did I particularly relish the thought of dressing as some kind of down-at-heel Danny La Rue to emulate Bonnie Prince Charlie crossing the Minch disguised as Flora MacDonald's maid. No, total authenticity was unnecessary; the journey was the thing.

When I began to tot up the potential mileage I'd cover I soon twigged that to undertake these journeys, some of them running into hundreds of miles, I would have to go through some kind of training and make sure I had at least the basic equipment necessary. Taming my sedentary lifestyle, I began walking to places. Sometimes I'd walk somewhere even though I didn't need to go there. I was walking purely for pleasure and exercise. For the first time I began properly to explore my locality on foot, and by chance one day found an old abandoned railway line that was a gorgeous, tree-lined walk through long-abandoned stations and tunnels and platforms well on the way to being reclaimed by nature. That was certainly something I'd never have discovered at home with my feet up, watching *Curb Your Enthusiasm* box sets and eating Quavers. Eventually, rather than descending daily into the fetid Piccadilly Line I began walking to my research sessions in the British Library, a journey that took me the best part of a couple of hours. I'd read somewhere that humans walk at anything up to three or four miles an hour. Naturally I fancied myself at the speedier end of that range, and deduced that the distance I was covering to King's Cross was about six miles. Call it seven. And a half. The return journey meant that I was covering the best part of fifteen miles every day, which was quite something. It was only much later, when I consulted a pedometer, that I learned the real distance was almost exactly four miles. And walking both ways was very much the exception. My training mileage wasn't anything like as much as I'd convinced myself it was, but at least it was more than I was doing before.

It may only have been four miles to the library, but those early walks exhausted me. I kept finding myself nodding off over the books, proper head-on-desk snoozing that would leave me puffy-eyed, shiny-faced and with a flying buttress of hair sticking out from the side of my head when I woke with a start. One day I jerked upright from slumber to realise I'd left a big blob of dribble across two pages of a well-regarded history book. On another occasion, having woken up, lifted my head from what I'd been reading and decided to splash water on my face to help revive myself, I looked in the bathroom mirror and realised I'd just walked through a crowded floor of diligent readers with the *Independent*'s football results imprinted across the right side of my face.

One other legacy of my early training walks was learning, the hard way, that you really do need the right equipment for this sort of thing. As a lifelong proponent of denim trousers and casual sports footwear, I'd naturally assumed that I could do these epic journeys in jeans and a pair of trainers. If I threw some T-shirts, jumpers and underwear into a holdall and slung it over my shoulder that would see me right. After a couple of days of arriving at the library walking like John Wayne and sweating like G. K. Chesterton in a Turkish bath, I realised that I might need some specialist advice.

In this regard I sought out my old friend Polly. Now, Polly is the poshest person I know. She's also a born adventurer in the mould of the great Victorian travellers. Although she's one of my best friends, Polly frightens me slightly, not least because she can drink me under the table and thrash me at arm-wrestling. When Polly decides to do something she doesn't do it by halves. When she fancied a bit of cycling, there was no question of wobbling around the cycle path in her local park. No, Polly packed her panniers and cycled around Spain. When she realised she quite liked life on two wheels she decided to learn to ride a motorbike. Not for Polly a snail's pace slalom through traffic cones in the playground of a local primary school on a Sunday morning to the lawnmower accompaniment of a two-stroke engine. No. She went to New Zealand, donned leathers, bought a snarling two-wheeled beast of a thing and set off around the mountains. Polly is a formidable gal well versed in extremes. If anybody knew the equipment I'd require, it was Polly.

I met her in a café in London prior to my shopping spree. Despite having only recently returned from winning a yak-wrestling tournament in Siberia or something, Polly had come well prepared and went through a list of items that she considered I'd need. She used words I'd never heard before, words like 'wicking' and 'tog'. The list she'd made looked frighteningly long. My list hadn't really got beyond 'rucksack', 'cagoule' and 'biscuits'.

Fortunately, I already had a good, stout pair of walking boots. A couple of years earlier I'd decided to go to Reykjavik for new year and, thinking Iceland might be a bit snowy and slippery underfoot, deduced I'd need something more than trainers on my feet. At my local travel store they saw me coming. From miles away. I am a shop assistant's dream because I find it so hard to say no. I think, they've taken all this time and trouble to help me, it would be rude not to buy all four pairs of shoes, even though two of them are the wrong size and one pair is for women. There's one born every minute, and it's usually me.

Two knowledgeable assistants soon had my flanks covered, sensing a sucker ripe for the fleecing. 'Iceland, eh?' they'd said when I told them why I was there. 'You'll be doing some trekking then?' Now, my plans for that long weekend stretched no further than strolling between welcoming bars for beer, steaks the size of dustbin lids and whatever the Icelandic for 'Auld Lang Syne' might be. I categorically would not be doing any trekking, not by any stretch of the imagination. But there I was, confronted by two sinewy, weathered men experienced in the outdoors. I wanted them to think I was like them, not the good-for-nothing layabout I really am. In the split second after the question, my brain must have hit the button marked 'psychological emasculation' and set off the sirens. Macho autopilot kicked in. 'Yeah, I'll be doing a bit,' I lied, nonchalantly. I may even have shrugged slightly, to give the impression that a thirty-mile yomp across volcanic permafrost was the sort of thing I'd do before breakfast. This pathetic bravado led to the purchase of a lightweight, slipper-comfortable pair of Brasher walking boots for about five times as much as I'd intended to spend. Which served me right, of course. Especially when I arrived in Iceland to find that the Reykjavik pavements are thermally heated, and hence no more challenging than a stroll to the chip shop after a bit of light drizzle.

But at least I had the boots. Now I just had to work from the ankles upwards, and, my goodness, Polly was rising to the task. She pushed a piece of paper across the plastic chequered table-cloth. It contained terms I'd never even imagined existed. 'Hyper-' this and 'breathable' that. And what on earth are internal storm flaps? It turned out that Polly had e-mailed a man she'd met a few weeks previously, while she was driving a dog sled across the Yukon. I pictured this guy in a tin shack, head to toe in furs, a laptop balanced on his knees while the odd cloud of snowflakes blew into his face like W. C. Fields in *The Fatal Glass of Beer*, little realising that the recipient of his equipment expertise was someone whose idea of a winter trek was catching the bus to Oxford Street for a bit of Christmas shopping. The advice, of course, was fulsome and expert and made me feel even more of a useless big girl's blouse.

It was then that I was distracted by a vintage advertisement for Newcastle Brown Ale on the wall behind Polly. It reassured me, chiming as it did with the way I wanted these journeys to turn out. It was from the thirties, I guessed, and showed two happy-looking coves outside a tent, one lying on the floor with his shirtsleeves rolled up but his tie still neatly knotted while his friend sat in a camping chair in shirt, tie and sweater, pouring out a glass of ale from a bottle. Both looked supremely contented, as if there was no greater combination in the world than the outdoors, plus-fours, manly conversation and strong drink.

'When you are "under canvas",' read the ad, 'you can always keep in touch with civilisation by including a few bottles of Newcastle Brown Ale in your camping equipment. When sultry days in the open air bring a thirst that must be quenched, or when the weather lets you know whether your tent is really waterproof, in either case Newcastle Brown Ale meets the occasion.'

Although in the event of discovering a leak in my tent my first thought might not be, bloody hell, what I wouldn't give for a bottle of Newcastle Brown Ale right now, this was my kind of advice, and at nine shillings for a dozen pints I wasn't going to argue. Polly was still running her finger down the items of equipment I'd need, her eyebrows knitted with all the determination of Madame Defarge with a cardigan to finish. I was about to suggest adding a dozen bottles of beer to the bottom of the list when Polly said, 'Right, now the thing to remember is to keep your pack as light as you possibly can.' Righto, I'll just take the ten bottles. 'You're going to be carrying everything you need on your back, so you've got to take lightweight equipment and even then keep it to an absolute minimum.' Half a dozen bottles, then? My shoulders began to droop. 'We'll get you the lightest clothes, probably a maximum of two items of each. There's nothing else for it – if you're away for a while you're going to smell.'

This wasn't really going how I'd thought it would.

'Are you going to camp?' she asked. 'Will you need a tent?' I hadn't really thought about that. An image of me standing proudly next to a freshly and expertly erected tent flickered into my mind. Seemed plausible. Then I remembered that I am the least practical person there is. Getting a cork out of a bottle is a major operation, let alone slotting together poles, lining up eyelets and bashing in tent pegs. Plus I am a yellow-bellied scaredy-cat. Sleeping outdoors was not something I'd done or really even contemplated since the time my younger sister and I had decided to spend the night in her Wendy house in the back garden, when I was about ten. We were both terrified of the slightest noise, even the summer breeze gently tugging at the plastic, but neither of us wanted to let the other know until our mother came out and made us both go in anyway. It was probably about nine o'clock. And still light.

No, a much more appealing image was of me strolling, ruddy-cheeked and healthy, into a village as the sun began to set, presenting myself at the bar of an ancient thatched inn and being shown to a well-appointed bedroom with clean sheets and an en suite bathroom before returning to the bar for steak and kidney pie and a pint of Grunston's Old Funtbuggler, or somesuch. Weighing up that against the image of me wrapped in a damp sleeping bag, shivering in the darkness of a half-assembled tent convinced that at any second an anaconda would slither out of the undergrowth and inhale me, the tent and my rucksack into its slimy, acidic belly, there was no contest, even if I wasn't quite sure whether they actually had anacondas in Lincolnshire.

'No, I won't need a tent,' I replied, and Polly crossed some things off her list.

After lunch Polly marched me to a large outdoors shop and within seconds had the staff running around at her command. They learned as quickly as I did that you're best advised to do what Polly says. I, meanwhile, stood there like a bewildered, whiskery mannequin. All sorts of phrases whizzed around as Polly and the assistants earnestly consulted each other as if I wasn't there. A sixty-litre rucksack or forty-five, they discussed. Litres? I'm going to put clothes in the thing, not fill it with diesel. But no, rucksacks are measured in litres. They're also known to people who take this kind of thing seriously as packs rather than rucksacks – I'd need this kind of lingo when meeting fellow walkers out in the sticks. Now I'd know that a passing nod and 'nice pack' wasn't some kind of proposition. The time began to pass in a blur of micro-fleeces, water bottles and the latest developments in waterproof textile technology (which had apparently moved on considerably, even in the few days since Polly's Yukon friend had penned his advice). My shopping basket was filled to the brim. I had walking trousers and waterproof overtrousers. I had fleeces. I had socks of different thicknesses. I had strange little clips, the purpose of which I would never discover. I had a water bottle with a Swiss flag on it. At one point I was convinced that Polly was telling me how important it was to have a good bass player. Before I could remind her that I was in fact going walking, not forming a funk band, Polly put her hand in the small of my back and propelled me towards a rack marked base layers.

When I thought I could carry no more and was about to saddle up and head for the tills, Polly stopped dead in her tracks, closed her eyes, clicked her fingers and bellowed, 'Underpants!' I presumed this was some kind of adventurers' swearword substitute, but no, she had me by the elbow and was leading me towards a display of special walking underwear. Again, these were blessed with the magical gift of wicking and were guaranteed not to chafe. These were the most special, hi-tech undercrackers that had ever been parked against a human posterior. At this point even I, the biggest sucker going, began to suspect that I was being hornswoggled; I mean, whoever heard of special pants for *walking*? Hadn't I walked in every pair I'd ever owned? Clearly I was being taken for nothing but a mooncalf and a jabbernowl, and even dear old Polly was in on the racket. It was then that I remembered taking nearly ten minutes to sit on a chair at the British Library thanks to chafing that later required so much baby powder around my nether regions that I spent two whole days effectively walking around waist deep in a cloud. Yep, Polly knew best, as usual.

'Only two pairs,' advised Polly. 'You'll just have to rinse them out at the end of every day.'

Two pairs of pants soon balanced on the top of the basket. I would be going away for weeks on end and taking only one change of underwear. Whatever you do, don't tell my mother. I heaved my purchases to the till, waited as each item was scanned, was informed of the total price, passed out on the floor, was revived with smelling salts, handed over my credit card, had it processed and handed back to me glowing red hot between industrial pincers, and made my way gingerly out of the shop, pale, wan and suffering from my first walking ailment, namely a definite lightness in the wallet region.

Meanwhile, my itinerary was slowly coming together. Many a satisfactory evening had been spent with a road atlas on my lap and a large Jameson's in my hand. I got the traditional atlas game of looking up amusing place names – Cocking, Bell End, Twatt – out of the way quickly and got down to the serious business. A gaggle of great journeys was researched, traced and either discarded reluctantly or added to the shortlist. Finally, after many weeks of poring over books and websites, and watch- ing DVDs, not to mention actually leaving the flat and walking about, I settled on a selection that I thought provided a good range of geography, chronology and rattlingly good stories, packed my new gear into my new rucksack (sorry, pack), and headed out of the door for Liverpool Street station. I had a date with a warrior queen and I was about two thousand years late.

Chapter One

AD60–61: Boudica's revolt

It was very early on a Norwich autumn morning and I was standing naked in a hotel room. An unnerving image for which I apologise, but it doesn't last long, I promise. On the bed, warmed gently by a stream of strengthening post-dawn sunshine, lay my new walking clothes: pairs of light cotton walking trousers, pairs of expensive pants at the cutting edge of undercracker technology, assorted base layers, fleeces and waterproofs; all items of clothing I'd never owned before but would spend the next goodness knows how many weeks wearing nothing but. I had a good – and recklessly optimistic – twenty-five miles ahead of me that day, a plan that plunged me right in at the perambulatory deep end. It was much farther than I'd ever walked before, but I had all the right gear and a curiously unfamiliar, yet not unwelcome, sense of bravado with me. I mean, it's only walking. I've done it all my life. How hard can it be?

I put on the pants, curious to see if they lived up to the hype. I stretched, I squatted, I lifted my knees in an exaggerated marching movement; I even tried an ill-advised star jump that rattled the cups on the tray on the other side of the room. I was, frankly, amazed. This was by far the most comfortable item of underwear ever to pass my kneecaps. I slipped a base-layer T-shirt over my head and it fell down my torso as light as silk. Trousers next; again so light I barely knew I had them on. Then the walking socks and lightweight fleece, followed finally by the boots. These took several attempts to lace properly, but I got there in the end. I wouldn't need the waterproof overtrousers – a relief, when I saw how many zips would be involved in getting them on and off and the potential for being found later by the cleaner, apparently trussed up and trapped in some self-abusing S&M practice – so I slipped into my lightweight waterproof jacket, packed everything else back into my rucksack, heaved it on to my back and headed for the door. I caught sight of myself in the mirror on the way out, and I confess that I was more than a little impressed by what I saw. I never, ever give any impression that I know in the slightest what I'm doing. But there, nodding back at me with the kind of self-satisfied expression of a man in a razor advert who's just had a really amazing shave, was a switched-on guy who clearly didn't just know his onions but was au fait with the whole grocer's barrow. I all but made pistols of my hands and pretended to fire them at my reflection. Man, I was hot stuff. I left the room, descended in the lift and strode out through the lobby and into the street.

Then things started to fall apart a bit. I stood with my back to the door of the hotel, facing a busy main road, and realised that I didn't actually know which way to turn next. I rummaged in the pocket of my waterproof jacket and pulled out my map, the north Norfolk page of my road atlas torn out and – how's this for sensible – placed inside a clear polythene folder in anticipation of inclement weather. Unfortunately for me the Norwich Travelodge, like the car park to which it was attached and the bathroom shop on which it sat, wasn't marked. In fact, as far as the map was concerned, Norwich was nothing more than an olive green blob criss-crossed by yellow and white arteries. I knew I needed to head south, almost directly south, but I had no

idea which way was south. Of course, while I had the best clothing available to man and even a pedometer to keep me abreast of
my step-by-step progress, I didn't have a compass.

Fortunately, a booklet in a rack inside the door of the hotel
detailed every Travelodge in the country, complete with a little
location map. I found Norwich and discovered that I was in fact
facing the right way. It was an auspicious start. I crossed the
busy road, employing my well-served holistic technique of finding my way: I set off in a chosen direction with a determined
stride and confident, tight-lipped expression. I find with remarkable regularity that this somehow makes it more likely to be the
correct way than if I purse the lips and take a few hesitant steps.
Hence within an hour and a half I was strolling into the sun-
drenched village of Caistor St Edmund, where my journey
proper would start, and where I would take up the trail of my
first historic fellow-traveller.

We know very little about Boudica. For a start, we don't even
know whether her name really was Boudica. We have no coins
featuring her image, no archaeological evidence as to where
she lived, no personal artefacts, nor even any contemporary
references to her existence. What we do have are the accounts
of two Roman historians, Tacitus and Cassius Dio, who both
relate the extraordinary story of the Iceni queen who came
as close as anyone to driving the Romans out of Britain, fired by
vengeance, injustice and the cruellest sense of grievance induced
in any mother from any period in history. Even these accounts
were written long after the events that made the Boudica legend –
up to a century later, in fact. Hence the story of Boudica is
one lost in myth and half-truth, with fact and fiction difficult
to separate.

We do know that the Iceni tribe, whose lands covered most of
what is now Norfolk, Suffolk and Cambridgeshire at the time of
the Roman conquest, was a wealthy one. We're not sure why

they were so wealthy – most of the Iceni seemed to be self-sufficient farmers – but many archaeological finds reveal fine clothing and jewellery, suggesting they were big on ostentatious displays of opulence, just as in centuries from now East Anglian archaeologists might turn up hoop earrings, sovereign rings and thick gold chains. Many of the finds relate to horses, which were major status symbols, so we can be fairly sure that the Iceni were a rich bunch that almost certainly played polo while the rest of the tribe watched wearing primitive panama hats. Actually no, I made that last bit up. We know too that in AD60 the Iceni king was Prasutagus, a client king recognised by Romans and Britons alike, who was permitted to retain his status as long as he remained on side with the Roman occupiers and didn't resist Roman rule. There had already been a small uprising by the Iceni when the Romans tried to forcibly disarm them, but they'd been allowed to keep their client status once the rebellion had been put down. It's possible, probable even, that Prasutagus had reigned as king since the successful Roman invasion of Britain under Emperor Claudius in AD43, although it was his predecessor Antedios who would have agreed the tribe's client status. The Romans would have been pleased with the deal, as much of what is now Britain was bubbling with resentment and rebellion at these toga-wearing, Latin-speaking interlopers. For such an influential tribe to accept Roman rule would have been viewed approvingly by Rome, particularly as the Iceni lands were within striking distance of their administrative capital at Camulodunum, now Colchester.

It seems that around AD60 – nobody's sure of the exact date or that of the subsequent rebellion – Prasutagus died suddenly and the trouble began. The king left a will, something he would have regarded as a legally binding document given his client-king status and the fact that he would have been granted Roman citizenship as part of the deal. In that will Prasutagus left half his estate to his two daughters and the other half to the Emperor

Nero. Why Boudica is not mentioned in the will isn't totally clear. Maybe the king wanted to ensure the safety and provenance of his offspring and hence his bloodline; maybe Boudica wasn't as readily compliant with Roman rule as her husband; who knows. As it turned out, the events that followed would render the will worthless, but not before it triggered a sequence of events so extraordinary that we're still talking about them nearly two millennia later.

When news of Prasutagus's bequest reached Catus Decianus, the Roman procurator of Britain, he didn't exactly greet it with a hey-nonny-nonny and a high-five for the messenger. He was furious, in fact, incandescent with rage at this presumptuous dead king. As far as Catus was concerned, the Iceni lands were not Prasutagus's to bequeath to anyone other than the Roman Empire itself. Clearly Prasutagus regarded his relationship with Rome as one of equals, while Catus Decianus saw the Iceni as a vanquished tribe under an impotent figurehead of a monarch granted empty privileges just to keep them quiet. Either way, Catus overreacted to a quite unbelievable degree, sending soldiers into the Iceni lands to pillage the property of their nobles. The Iceni had already been forced to give up their weapons after the previous revolt, and this was further humiliation for the proud tribe. Tacitus reported that 'the chief men of the Iceni were stripped of all their ancestral estates as if Rome had been given the lands as a gift, and slaves were made of the king's relatives'.

For the late king's family in particular, things were to get much, much worse. In a dreadful and, on the face of it, most un-Roman turn of events, Catus had Boudica, the queen of the Iceni mourning the death of her husband, flogged while her daughters were raped in front of her by Roman soldiers. It was an inexplicable act: Boudica, by virtue of her marriage to a client king, would also have been officially a Roman citizen, and any corporal punishment of a woman was almost unthinkable in

the Roman Empire. Rape was an offence punishable by execution; the rape of virgins abhorrent in a society that prized moral
rectitude. In the accounts of Tacitus in particular (who is known
to have been less than enamoured with Nero's flouting of
Roman moral codes), we can discern a genuine sense of anger
and disbelief at Catus's actions. Certainly the burning sense of
injustice felt by Boudica and her people was so intense you can
almost sense it today – this was one of the most despicable
episodes in the history of these islands. Almost immediately, the
resentment that had festered against Roman rule for the best part
of two decades exploded into angry rebellion. The Iceni began
to graduate from the countryside, gathering into a huge, seething
mass of people to rise up against the oppressor that had taken
away their freedom and violated their queen – a queen who, as
far as the people were concerned, had been chosen by the gods –
and wreak merciless vengeance. Under Boudica's leadership, the
Iceni and their neighbours the Trigovantes would set off for the
Roman capital at Camulodunum – modern Colchester – for an
orgy of destruction and murder.

Today we don't know where the rapes and flogging took
place, nor from where Boudica's ragged army set out, and the
location of the Iceni royal residence has never been established
beyond doubt, if indeed there was a single royal home. There is
evidence of a major settlement at Thetford, also at West Stow,
Needham and Saham Toney, and it's likely that the massed ranks
of Iceni set off from many locations, uniting on the Roman
road to Camulodunum. There was no obvious starting point
for my journey, so I had chosen the village of Caistor St
Edmund.

The English summer of 1928 was particularly fierce, with a
severe drought. At the height of the heatwave an aeroplane was
flying over Caistor St Edmund, around four miles south of
Norwich, when the pilot noticed what appeared to be a large

rectangular grid of bleached lines in an already parched barley field. The scorching weather had betrayed the exact location of the Roman town of Venta Icenorum, the remains of its walls and streets clearly visible thanks to the unusually dry conditions.

Excavations were begun in 1929 and continued until the mid-thirties, when it seems funding ran out. The findings of the dig were never actually published, but in 2007 new technology was used that revealed Venta Icenorum to be one of the most significant Roman sites in the UK. By using something called a caesium vapour magnetometer – which sounds like witchcraft to me – archaeologists have been able to discern a detailed plan of the town, at its peak the size of forty football pitches, right down to the iron rings joining water pipes way below ground level, without having to turn a single clod of earth. The fact that Venta Icenorum was, unlike most Roman settlements, never destroyed or dismantled is enough to have archaeologists salivating like sniffer dogs over Pete Doherty's guitar case.

Venta Icenorum translates as the 'marketplace of the Iceni'. After Boudica's rebellion, the major Iceni settlements were flattened and rebuilt as Roman towns, a clear demonstration if one were needed that, whatever had happened under Boudica, the Romans were back in charge now, thanks very much. Given their liking for the grand symbolic gesture, the fact that they turned Venta Icenorum into such a major town – theatre, temples, forum, the lot – could suggest that it had been Boudica's home.

I'd considered all the Iceni locations but Caistor St Edmund seemed to be the most appropriate. While it might not be the location of the degradation of Boudica and her daughters, the fact that the village was acknowledged by the Romans in its Latinised name as a place where the Iceni would gather suggests it was a likely muster point for at least a substantial part of Boudica's forces. It was also very close to the main route to Camulodunum, and while that may not have been a fully developed Roman road this early in the Empire's occupation of

Britain, there's little doubt that it would have been an important thoroughfare even then. Caistor St Edmund would certainly have been a place Boudica knew well.

Today Venta Icenorum lies outside this small, dozing village, and when I arrived from Norwich that morning there wasn't a soul around. I found the site easily enough and walked along the grassy mounds that cover the walls of the town. On such a peaceful, sunny morning it was hard to imagine this field, where sheep grazed contentedly beneath the shadow of the church tower, as the site of a busy Roman settlement, let alone the probable departure point for one of history's greatest uprisings. The lush green serenity as I sat on a bench looking across towards the church made it hard to associate this place with the events of two thousand years earlier. Starlings chirruped in the hedgerows, the trees rustled in the breeze and the sound of the distant A47 drifted across the fields, the sun flashing off the odd car windscreen in the distance. Certainly the scene in front of me didn't chime with the description of Boudica herself given by Cassius Dio in his history of Rome.

'She was very tall in build,' he wrote, 'most terrifying in her demeanour, the glint in her eye most fierce, and harsh of voice. A great mound of red hair fell to her waist, around her neck was a large golden torc and she wore a tunic of many colours upon which a cloak was fastened with a brooch. This was her general attire.' The begrudging old chauvinist also added that Boudica 'was possessed of a greater intelligence than is usually found in women'. This is the only recorded description of Boudica's appearance, and although Cassius Dio was writing many years after the events of AD60–61 there is no reason to doubt that they are significantly correct. Certainly it's spawned every depiction of the warrior queen since, from Thomas Thornycroft's statue on the Embankment in London to Alex Kingston's appearance in the frankly awful feature-length television version of the Boudica story (if you're going to refer in the script to

Colchester as 'Camulodunum', why then have the characters refer to Londinium as 'London'? And as for the hilariously ham-fisted attempt to make the film, you know, *contemporary* by having Roman characters refer to the Iceni repeatedly as 'harbouring terrorists', just don't get me started.)

Given such scant source material, it's hard to place Boudica anywhere, let alone in an idyllic English countryside scene. Even her name might be wrong – the word Boudica comes from an old Celtic word for victory, so may have been a ceremonial or inspirational name given to their leader at the time of the rebellion or even posthumously. For centuries the mistranslation by a medieval Latin scholar of Boudica as Boadicea meant that until relatively recently we even got that wrong. Already then, as I sat on the bench watching the sheep mooch about above the buried Roman streets, Boudica was proving elusive. My only chance of getting any closer to grasping the wisps of fact within the myth lay in following the route of her trail of destruction.

I popped a square of chocolate into my mouth, took a few gulps of water from my bottle, shouldered my rucksack and set off for the A140 and the sleepy town of Diss. I strode off up the lane, crossed a bridge over a stream and saw on the horizon the traffic racing along the road I would be following for the next five hours or so. I'd prepared my route uncharacteristically carefully in order to trace the modern route of the old Roman road, and backed this up by using an online route-planning website that, as well as telling car drivers the best way to go, also had an option for walkers. This supported my initial sofa-based fingering of the road atlas, in that the A140 was the most direct route, as well as the one that followed the authentic road constructed two thousand years earlier by the Romans themselves. Eventually the lane opened out into a large and busy roundabout and the signpost on the first exit pointed me towards Diss, Ipswich and one of the most stupid and misinformed things I've ever done in my life. Which is, in the words of Bananarama, really saying something.

The A140 is a very, very busy road. It's also dangerous: in the last twenty-five years there have been more than seventy deaths along its length. Large lorries thunder along it. Cars are nose to tail even at high speed. Walking along the pavement adjacent to the road, I was already unsettled by my proximity to the traffic when, barely five hundred yards beyond the roundabout, the pavement came to an end. I found myself walking among muddy ruts and grassy clumps, jagged branches tearing at my clothes as I stepped around unidentifiable lumps of metal, bottles and discarded road detritus. My ankles twisted on the uneven ground and there was barely a foot either side of the white line that divided my increasingly terrified slow progress and the seventy-mile-an-hour parade of messy death whooshing past my right ear.

This couldn't be right. When the website had given me a walking route along the A140 I'd envisaged a wide tarmac path with a fulsome expanse of well-tended grass between me and death by haulage. It wouldn't have sent me down this road unless it was safe to do so, would it? Would it? Stupidly, I persevered for about half a mile. I expected to hear horns of varied timbre sounded by drivers informing me of the sheer dangerous idiocy of my situation, but I imagine they were just too astounded to react in time, too busy shouting 'What on earth is that twat doing?' to reach for the hooter.

Eventually I accepted the mortal danger of my position, conceded that not everything on the internet might necessarily be correct and headed back the way I came. When I reached the roundabout my legs were shaking. I went back to Caistor St Edmund, where I'd have to take out the map and find another way, one that wouldn't leave me smeared over a large part of Norfolk. I flopped on to a bench on the outskirts of the village, dumping the printout from the website into a nearby bin. I was on the first morning of my walk through time and I was already thoroughly fed up, a good hour or two behind schedule and feeling the gnawing, helpless loneliness that doing something as startlingly stupid as I just had usually engenders. The sensation of the world speeding by at close proximity to your ear and the fact that everyone, but everyone, within a radius of several miles knows much better than you do isn't good for the confidence. I pulled out the crumpled page from the road atlas (it would still be a while yet before I'd realise the obvious folly of this method of navigation, even before acknowledging the lunacy of not packing a compass) and tried to find a route south that would-n't have me killed. In addition, the sun had gone in, the sky was beginning to bruise and the wind was beginning to pick up. Some battling between the map and the wind ended with my uncovering a route that ran parallel enough to the A road, but it was still one that would add time and miles on to my already tardy itinerary. I set off along the back lanes, darkened by over-hanging trees, with the startling preponderance of squashed woodland animals in the road doing little to lighten my gloomy self-pity.

I passed through a number of villages with pretty names – Stoke Holy Cross, Saxlingham Nethergate – and my mood eventually began to brighten, along with the weather. In one village I sat for a while on a bench at the crossroads and three different people called out a morning greeting. I mean actually called out, from a distance, not even just a cursory dip of the head owing to unavoidable proximity. I'd already noticed that when I stepped off the road into the hedgerow at the approach of a car the driver would wave. Living, as I had, my entire life in London, I was used to the only gesture employed by someone at the wheel of a car being a single raised middle finger, but these were people waving thanks. As I progressed through the lanes I saw birds jumping around in the hedgerows and the odd white flash of a rabbit's rear end as it darted away from my approach. I may have been as far as possible from a rampaging pack of wild-eyed Britons hell-bent on revenge, but already this was so much better than dicing with death on the A140. Even if there had been a footpath all the way, the monotony of the featureless miles and the deafening roar of traffic would have put me in a terrific funk, authenticity of the route notwithstanding. No, this was a far, far better option.

Self-congratulation is always a bad thing. Once you start feeling pleased with yourself about pretty much anything, your hubristic downfall is guaranteed. Hence with only a torn-out page from a road map for guidance, and already way, way behind schedule, I took a grievous wrong turn and found myself emerging from some trees back at the non-stop pedestrian deathfest of the A140. I crumpled. I slipped my pack off my back and flopped down on to it. I held my sweaty head in my hands and stared at the ground. Suddenly, I noticed that everything hurt. The tops of my thighs were complaining vociferously about their mistreatment. The balls of my feet were throbbing. My shoulders ached where the rucksack straps had been and there was an ominous pain developing in my right knee. I looked at the map and saw that I was way off course. It was lunchtime now; I'd been walking for six hours and I'd covered barely a quarter of the distance I'd planned for the day. How could I have possibly expected to cover twenty-five miles on my first day? How on earth was I going to complete all these journeys when, on the very first morning, I'd messed up in spectacular style? How was I expecting to live on my wits when I was clearly only half-equipped?

Although I was displaying all the classic traits of the big girl's blouse, I knew I'd have to press on somehow. I was out here in a strange place, alone and with no prospect of easy salvation; I'd have to carry on. I was about to turn back the way I came when I noticed, about fifty yards up the road, a pub.

The bowl of tomato soup brought a bit of colour back to my cheeks, while the steak pie at least took my mind off the throbbing in my feet. Even the whoosh of passing vehicles barely five feet from the pub door stopped unsettling me with flashbacks to the morning. I reached into my trouser pocket and pulled out the pedometer I'd already christened Pedro, which proudly informed me that I'd walked twelve miles. Granted, about half of those miles were wholly unnecessary, but already this was the furthest I'd ever walked in one go. I felt restored, and with a newly squinting eye of cynical experience worked out where I was and traced a new route. All I needed to do was cross the A140 outside the pub, head out through some small streets and I'd be on a back road south that would take me to Diss. I'd have walked closer to thirty miles by the time I got there rather than the anticipated twenty-five, but hey, wouldn't that be some achievement for my first day astride Shanks's Pony?

If I was learning nothing – and the morning's events had already suggested that I was in fact learning nothing – I was beginning to realise how when you're out on your own all day, walking, the mood swings can be quite spectacular. Already my mood had swung more often in the space of six hours than in all my years as a hormonal teenager. The slightest setback can bring cumuli of doom upon your head, and a chink of hope can have you dancing down the street with a rainbow around your shoulders. I drained my drink, donned my rucksack and set out again with a glad and happy heart.

Within half an hour my mood had swung again. I'd crossed the A140 without mishap and plunged into a network of suburban crescents full of timbered modern housing – that all seemed to lead me back to precisely where I'd started. I studied the map, failed to see where I'd gone wrong and headed in again. The fact that the streets and houses all looked the same, even down to the shrubbery in the front gardens and the silver cars in the driveways, didn't help and again I ended up right back where I'd started. Yet again I traced with my finger the route that irrefutably led to the road to Diss and walked back into the maze of streets before irrefutably arriving right back where I'd started. I tried twice more, same result. Never mind, I thought, I'll wake up in the Norwich Travelodge in a minute and this will all have been a big, snuffling, sweaty anxiety dream. I waited patiently to wake up, but the realisation soon dawned that the absence of a naked Nicole Kidman meant that this wasn't a dream after all. I trudged back to the main road and its relentless traffic. I looked south. Somewhere down there was Diss. I looked back towards the groundhog suburbia I'd just left, sighed, shifted the rucksack, took half a dozen reluctant steps and then saw it. On the other side of the road. About two hundred yards away. The bus stop.

I couldn't possibly. Could I? I consulted the map again. It was still a fair few miles to Diss, the best part of twenty in fact. My laps of the estate had meant the clock had ticked round perilously close to mid-afternoon. Surely I couldn't give in and take the bus, not on the first day. I came to an agreement with myself. If there was a bus due shortly, I'd think about getting on it. If there wasn't, I'd press on. That, at least, postponed the decision for the next couple of hundred yards during which I weighed up the pros and cons. It seemed a bit of a cop out, hopping on a bus on my first day. I'm sure Boudica wouldn't have approved. Mind you, she probably had a chariot. My feet hurt. My thigh muscles hurt. My knee was persistently sore. I jangled the change in my trouser pocket. I'd probably even have the exact fare. But if I took the bus on the first day it would make doing the same even more tempting in the future. I'd have lowered the cheating bar from the outset. I heard a faint 'pock' from somewhere. Then another. Then a 'pockety-pock-pock'. It was a sound that would become horribly familiar in the coming months, the sound of raindrops landing on my waterproof jacket. I looked up at the sky to see scudding grey clouds. A raindrop landed next to my right eye; a tiny detonation of cold wetness. The bus stop was feet away now. There might not be a bus, not for ages; this is the countryside, after all. I can still make it to Diss on foot: imagine the feeling of accomplishment. Imagine the sense of shame if I took a bus, even just for a mile or two. I checked the time and looked at the timetable. The time and the timetable matched with an imminent bus all the way to Diss. I looked up and there was a yellow single-decker looming up at me with DISS in big letters above the windscreen. I jangled the coins in my pocket again. The doors opened with a wheezy hiss. I had exactly the right change.

The journey took just the right amount of time for me to slump into a very real funk of ashamed disappointment. We passed through villages of varying size and postcard prettiness; I watched through glazed eyes as a procession of pensioners in woolly hats boarded and disembarked. Before long I was stepping off and into the light drizzle that was wetting the pavements and rooftops of Diss. Apparently taking its name from a Viking word for the 'village of the dancing horse', Diss is, I was delighted to learn, a member of a movement promoting 'slow towns', where citizens enjoy life in their town in a 'relaxed and pleasant way'. Before I could explore the town in a relaxed and pleasant way, however, I had to find a relaxed and pleasant bed for the night. I extracted the address and phone number of a nearby bed and breakfast from the tourist office – the only B&B likely to accommodate a scruffy, hobbling character gibbering wildly about the A140, it seemed.

I walked along the main street, passed a grassy expanse on which a fairground was preparing for the evening's shenanigans, found the turning and matched the house number to the piece of paper in my hand. It didn't look like a bed and breakfast, and there was no sign outside to confirm it as such. I rang the bell. No answer. I rang again. Still no answer. I walked back towards the fairground and it started to rain again. I stood under an oak tree, a suddenly fierce wind blowing splatters of rain at me and dislodging larger globs of water from the leaves above. I rang the phone number of the bed and breakfast and got an answering machine. I left it ten minutes and rang again. Again, no answer. My immediate prospects didn't seem promising. I'd had a pretty dismal first day, and now there seemed to be a night under a tree at the end of it. I stared into the drizzly middle distance as the lights of the fairground began to wink. The pattering of the rain on the leaves provided a percussive soundtrack to the closing credits of a largely miserable day. I felt as far from Boudica as it was possible to be. She'd have been pitching tents with her army now, their families with them, carts loaded with possessions and supplies. The Iceni barely planted any crops that year, so certain were they that they'd be gone a long time, perhaps never to return. It wasn't so much an army on the move as a mobile town, not unlike the fairground away to my right with its caravans and lorries and rides and stalls. It's possible that Boudica passed through here – just a couple of thousand years too early to have the chance of taking away a goldfish in a polythene bag or an enormous synthetic SpongeBob SquarePants to lash to the front of her chariot – and I wondered what her mood would have been on her first night on the road.

It seems that she set off without much in the way of a plan beyond wreaking revenge on the Romans by sacking Camulodunum. As the wind flapped at the walls of her tent and she heard the noises of the night outside, the stamping and snorting of horses, the hubbub of conversation, what was she thinking? Did she doubt herself the way I was doubting myself now? As well as a highly justified sense of grievance and thirst for revenge she also carried the hopes of her people. She may even have realised that the hopes of the entire land rested with her. Was she thinking as far ahead as driving the Romans from Britain? Or was she thinking no further than vengeance for the wrongs done to her, her daughters – doubtless waking nightly with nightmares alongside her in the tent – and her people? What did she dream that first night? Could she even sleep at all, or was she so consumed with anger and anticipation that she tossed and turned until the glow of daylight appeared on the horizon?

At that moment my phone began to ring. 'Oh, hello there,' said a friendly male voice, 'it's the Cobwebs bed and breakfast here. I've just done 1471 and your number came up. Can I help at all?'

Within a couple of minutes I was ringing the doorbell again and being shown to a big, warm, comfortable room by a lovely smiling couple; certainly it was a far cry from a calfskin tent in a field of hairy-arsed, blue-painted warriors. Or so I presumed: I hadn't looked at the fairground that closely.

After a very welcome cup of tea made by my hosts, and a lie down that proved to be just the right length of time for my leg muscles to stiffen up irrevocably, I could do no more than hobble into the town, have a curry while listening to a couple at the next table arguing animatedly about having the pointing done on their house and realise that I was completely exhausted, hobble back past the now fully operational fairground where some teenagers laughed at me, climb into bed and fall into a deep, deep sleep. All before nine o'clock.

The alarm went off early the next morning. I switched it off, sighed, rubbed my eyes, opened them, forgot where I was, remembered where I was, swung my legs out of bed and headed for the shower. Actually that's not quite true – I did all that, up to but not including the bit about swinging my legs out of bed. When I went to move my legs searing pains shot up my calves and into my buttocks. I stopped. That couldn't be right. I tried to manoeuvre my legs out of bed again and the same thing happened, as if someone was inserting red-hot skewers into my rear end. This wasn't good. I'd consulted Pedro before hitting the hay and despite the bus ride had walked more than fourteen miles. Not bad for a first day, even if it fell considerably short of the twenty-five I'd blusteringly budgeted for on my itinerary. But if my legs were in this state after fourteen miles, what would they have done had I blundered through the twenty-mile barrier and beyond?

After ten minutes of psyching, persuading and a little bit of praying, I managed to get out of bed. I half crawled, half hobbled to the bathroom and showered gingerly. Even my arms were aching. How could my arms be aching? Washing my hair was an operation so painful and awkward I possibly deserved a benefit concert. Dressing was a sore and slow process, while my feet were aching like never before: thankfully I was totally blister-free, but the balls of my feet felt as though they'd been repeatedly beaten with a broom handle. I tackled the stairs one at a time, about five minutes at a time, and made my way into the breakfast room.

'Are you all right?' asked my host.

'Fine,' I lied through clenched teeth. 'Just a bit stiff, that's all.'

It was just as I was finishing breakfast that I remembered something. Just before I'd left for Norwich, Polly had phoned me. 'Just a quick tip,' she said. 'Make sure that when you get to where you're staying every night you do a really good stretching session. You'll be tired and won't want to, but your muscles will cramp up otherwise and you won't be able to move the next morning. If you can do it again just before you go to bed that's even better. You'll be right as rain the next morning.'

I set off back up to my room. About an hour later I arrived there. Stretching was now my only option. It wasn't so much shutting the stable door after the horse has bolted as shutting it after the horse has emigrated and sent back a series of amusing postcards, but I'd give it a go. Placing my feet shoulder-width apart, I straightened my legs, placed my hands on my hips and leaned forward. My muscles creaked like a wooden ship at anchor and when I tried the same thing leaning back I swear there was a twanging noise like when Jerry stretches a sleeping

Tom's whiskers and lets go. It hurt, oh boy did it hurt, but I could certainly feel movement coming back.

Eventually I was mobile enough to set out for the road, and with encouraging words from my hosts set off gingerly down the road, turned right, crossed a bridge and passed almost immediately from Norfolk into Suffolk.

In contrast to my first day on the road, this turned out to be a much better experience. The sun shone and in a short while I'd walked off much of the remaining discomfort in my leg muscles. I passed through a number of villages, all of which seemed to be taken straight from the pages of coffee-table books of ye beste of olde England. By late afternoon I'd reached the outskirts of Debenham, a village so beautiful and friendly that I decided, on the spot, to spend the night there. I'd arrived just as the local school turned out, and apple-cheeked children in uniforms swung their satchels happily as they accompanied their parents along the street. Most of them smiled at me too, despite my being a sweaty, scruffy, whiskery stranger. I would become used to approaching villages like in the opening scene of *Rambo*, expecting that at any moment Brian Dennehy would pull up in a police car and escort me through to the other side making it plain that drifters weren't welcome, but so far my progress through some of East Anglia's finest villages hadn't been hastened by pitchfork prods to the posterior.

I called at the post office to see if they knew of anywhere to stay, and arrived just at the tantalising end of a conversation between the postmistress and a customer. When you walk into a room and hear '. . . so I asked them if he'd died in a car accident, but they said no, it was an elephant', you know you've just missed a belter of a story. There were no bed and breakfasts as such in the village, the postmistress told me, but two of the pubs had rooms. I bought a couple of postcards and retired to a bench on a grass verge to write them.

'Hello there,' said a female voice after a couple of minutes. 'I was in the post office just then and heard you asking about accommodation. The two pubs are both very nice, but the Cherry Tree is probably cheaper than the Angel.'

I thanked her very much.

'Where have you walked from?' she asked.

'Diss,' I replied with a smile.

'Crumpets!' she said, eyebrows rocketing skyward. She asked how far I was going, and I replied St Albans, via London.

'Crumpets!' she hooted again, before wishing me all the best and leaving me to my postcards.

I found the Cherry Tree at the bottom end of the village. It was a large pub with one of those children's slides outside that's disguised as a tree, with a big face on it that gives you night-mares. I plunged inside, which, coming as I did out of the sunshine, was rendered immediately almost pitch dark. I felt my way to the bar, and as my eyes adjusted found myself faced with a smiling barmaid called Zoe. 'I'm selling the Adnams at a pound a pint,' she said. 'There's nothing wrong with it, it's just we've had a temperature problem in the cellar and I need to get rid of it quickly.'

I was beginning to think that on the way into Debenham I'd been hit and killed outright by a truck and was now in heaven. I handed over a mere pound coin in return for a pint of Suffolk's finest and asked if they did accommodation.

'I do,' came the reply, 'but I haven't done it recently. To be honest, you'd probably be better off trying the Angel, but if they can't put you up I'm more than happy to. It wouldn't exactly be luxurious, though. In fact, tell you what, I'll give the Angel a ring for you now if you like.'

Twenty-four hours earlier I'd been standing under a tree in a damp and drizzly Diss thinking these historical journeys were a really bad idea, certainly without the aid of a tour bus containing its own Jacuzzi and well-stocked bar. Now here I was in a sun-drenched village where people said 'crumpets' as an expression of surprise, drinking fine beer at a pound a pint while a guardian angel looked after my accommodation for me. Yes, I was definitely dead. It had clearly been mercifully quick as I didn't remember a thing, not even a screech of brakes. I sat at a table, listening as Zoe not only established that the immaculately named Angel had a room but even negotiated a cheaper rate for me, giving me a theatrical wink with every negotiative gambit. Eventually she hung up looking pleased with herself. I decided that I quite liked being dead.

'That's sorted then,' she said, before telling me the rock-bottom price she'd confirmed for me and asking where I was heading the next day. My first thought was to have a quick spin around the Elysian Fields before popping back to Earth to give a few people I didn't like a bit of a haunting, but I stuck to my original itinerary and told Zoe that I was due to hit Ipswich – news that didn't on this occasion elicit a response based on toasted snacks.

'Ooh, which route are you taking?' I wasn't sure so produced my map, which seemed to have died with me, as had my rucksack. Zoe slid into the seat beside me and studied it, before calling out to a man across the bar: 'Richard – best way to Ipswich from here, walking?'

A middle-aged man with curly grey hair thought for a moment before picking up his pint and joining us at the table. He was a commercial driver and knew the highways and byways of East Anglia well. From the way he spoke, I was starting to suspect that I might not be dead after all. I put the haunting hitlist on hold for a bit and listened.

Before I knew it my route had been planned, I'd been invited to a charity concert that evening and I had drunk four more pints of outstandingly cheap ale. I felt practically local. I felt practically pissed too. I wasn't dead after all, this was just a terrific place full of terrific people – a scruffy stranger with a rucksack mooches in and within minutes feels like he's the prodigal son.

Eventually I realised that darkness had fallen and it was high time I headed off to the Angel to drop off my stuff and get cleaned up ahead of the concert. I wobbled off up the street, found the Angel – a delightfully ancient inn – and was shown to my room along undulating creaking corridors. I put down my rucksack, lay on the bed, heaved my clean trousers out, ready to wear to the concert after a quick shower, and then woke up seven hours later, clean trousers still next to me on the bed and a mouth as dry as the Sahara.

Despite my disturbed drunken night I was up and away early the next morning, to cover the eighteen or so miles to Ipswich. I called in at the village shop for some water and found that on passing through the doorway I'd stepped back about forty years. Old-fashioned jars of sweets lined the shelves, ancient greetings cards lounged higgledy-piggledy on a rack. There was not a square inch of space wasted; every surface was covered with confectionery, stationery, books, newspapers and magazines. Behind the counter, just her head and shoulders visible, sat a lovely, lovely bespectacled old lady, who seemed so tightly packed among the wares that it was entirely possible that the shop had been built around her. We chatted for about ten minutes, she telling me about how she used to cycle the local lanes as a young girl and picnic with friends in the summer. 'The summers seemed to go on for ever then,' she said in a soft Suffolk accent before tailing off, suddenly back astride her bicycle, the wind in her hair, the breeze flicking at her summer dress, a picnic wrapped in a chequered tea towel in the basket of her bike.

She was such a delightful lady I could have pulled up a chair and chatted to her all morning. I felt a little guilty that she'd brought such sunshine to my day and all I was buying from her was a bottle of water. I cast around for something a bit more expensive, and my gaze fell upon a small rack of Ordnance Survey maps. I picked up one marked Ipswich, Felixtowe and

Harwich and placed it next to the bottle of water, on top of the piles of newspapers on the counter. 'The essential map for out-door activities' it boasted on the cover. I'd got my road atlas pages of course, and smirked slightly at the OS map's claim of indispensability. What would I need with an Ordnance Survey map? I was going long distance, requiring a big-scale map. Still, I handed over the money, said goodbye to the lovely old lady and left the shop. I sat on a bench outside, decanted the water into my bottle and opened out the new map.

In that moment I knew my walking life would never be the same again. The heavy paper dropped from its folds and opened out like an accordion. The map almost peeled apart and, rather than the jumbled grid of roads I was used to seeing, an entire landscape opened out in front of me. For the first time ever the roads were secondary to everything else. Where my roadmap showed anything that wasn't a road as a white nothingness save for the olive blobs of built-up areas, on this map wavy contours swam gracefully across the paper in formations that occasionally clustered together to indicate higher ground. Areas of woodland had little trees on them to denote just which type of woodland it was. In Ipswich itself, individual houses were marked. Further out, farmhouses had their names printed above them (I'll admit that Gobblecock Cottage did elicit a guffaw that undid the awe inspired by the nearby World's End Plantation, but come on, Gobblecock Cottage.) Strange, unfamiliar words in gothic script loomed up at me, like 'tumulus'. Suddenly my journey had acquired another dimension. I was seeing the map in layers, in relief. For the first time, I wasn't just looking at a map, I was reading it.

The church clock struck eight and brought me out of my mercatorial reverie. I folded away the map and set off again as the morning sun burned off the mist hanging around the grave-stones in the churchyard. I passed the Cherry Tree, umbrellas neatly furled on the tables outside, and pressed on. My progress was good and fast over the flat landscape. My feet seemed to be becoming hardened to the unfamiliar rigours of road walking. By lunchtime I was on the outskirts of Coddenham, having already clocked up nearly ten miles. As I walked along a tree-lined road where the filtered sunshine made patterns on the tarmac, I became aware of a van slowing up next to me. On a couple of occasions I'd had people pulling over and offering me lifts, and I thought this might be another such occasion. I glanced across and saw that the driver was looking at me and gesturing with his arm extended and digit upraised. I prepared my middle finger and was propelling it in an upward direction in reply when I noticed that the driver had a big smile on his face. Then I realised that it wasn't a middle finger I could see, but a thumb. It was Richard from the previous evening at the Cherry Tree, grinning at me and giving me a huge thumbs-up. Before my now wholly inappropriate gesture reached the extent of its parabola I managed to fan out my other fingers and turn it into a strange backhanded wave. With that he was gone, away into Coddenham with a rev of the throttle and a cloud of exhaust.

It was a beautiful day to be walking. The sun shone from a clear blue sky while a breeze kept me at a perfect temperature. More postcard-perfect villages saw me pass through them until I finally stopped for a sandwich at a pub in Henley. I'd made such good progress that I allowed myself an hour's rest before making the final push into Ipswich. I set off sufficiently recovered, fed and watered to make the last five or six miles a doddle. Yet for some reason things soon began to fall apart. I couldn't seem to find any kind of rhythm. Every step seemed to be an effort in itself. The sore knee I'd felt at the start of the journey began to throb in an increasingly painful way. Although the terrain, like much of eastern England, was almost perfectly flat, I felt almost as if I was walking up a substantial hill. My rucksack was suddenly very heavy, as if it was pulling me downward. The sun seemed to beat stronger than before; my feet ached and complained from boots that felt twice as cumbersome and weighty as before. The road was unforgiving too, with high banking at its edge and trees right against it making it impossible to find softer ground to walk on or rest. Ipswich refused to appear on the horizon. My pace slowed, my breathing became increasingly laboured.

Eventually I reached the outskirts of Ipswich, by which time my stride was barely one boot length. I actually caught myself whimpering as I hobbled through the outer districts of the town until I finally reached the centre. It was a Saturday afternoon and the place was packed with shoppers. I had no idea where I was going, but I had to find somewhere to stay and fast. All I wanted was to heave off the boots, crawl out from under the rucksack and flop down on a bed. I had already decided that I'd stay two nights here if I could; clearly I needed a rest. The question was, where? I limped around but couldn't find a hotel. I was starting to feel a bit giddy among the crowds. The faces of the shoppers loomed up in front of me as they passed; it was almost as if I was looking through a fish-eye lens. Finally I saw a sign for the tourist information office and decided to throw myself upon their mercy.

The tourist office was in a converted church. At least that's how I remember it – it could have been some kind of exhaustion-induced hallucination predicting my own imminent funeral. As I remember it, my entreaty for a room was met with pursed lips and the response, 'Hmm, it could be tricky, the town's nearly full.' Full? Full? How could the town be full? Who on earth goes for a weekend break in Ipswich? Please, please don't tell me Ipswich is full. I can't move. I can't go anywhere. If the town's full I'll just have to lie down here and die quietly among the postcards and brochures. I'll be no trouble, I'll expire with the minimum of fuss.

Several phone calls elicited a 'no vacancies' response. Things really weren't looking good and the girl behind the desk was on the point of giving up. 'There is one last place I could try . . .' she said, picking up the receiver and tapping in the number. The usual exchange took place, before suddenly she departed from the script. 'You have? Oh brilliant. And how much will that be?' They could have replied 'four grand in cash, a new car and full conjugal rights to any future daughter you may have' and I'd have agreed. Half an hour later I was being shown into a newly furbished room in a wonderful recently opened bed and breakfast whose owner had trained as a chef at the Dorchester, and offered evening meals accordingly. I booked in for two nights without the slightest intention of leaving until I absolutely had to. There were candles in the room, proper toiletries in the bathroom, a coffee maker and fresh milk in a jug. There was a flat-screen television and a big, soft, comfy double bed. In the midst of my suffering earlier in the day I couldn't have come up with a more perfect place. So salubrious was the room that it was with a definite feeling of guilt that I began the daily process of washing out my pants and socks in the pristine sink.

I dined that evening with the only other residents, an elderly couple staying there while the council replaced their kitchen and bathroom. Over liver and bacon they praised the owners to the heavens for their hospitality and cuisine, to such an extent that I began to suspect that their own house up the road had been finished weeks ago – they just didn't want to leave. And I couldn't blame them.

It was with some reluctance that I finally left early on the Monday morning, heading for Colchester. Since leaving Caistor St Edmund I'd not really felt much connection with Boudica and her army. There's no way they passed through sleepy, sun-drenched villages, pausing briefly for a cheese roll, a pint and a pleasant chat about local property prices. Colchester, the Camulodunum of Boudica's ire, would present the first opportunity to really gain a sense of those times, and would also present the first piece of tangible evidence that the rebellion actually took place, in the layer of burnt earth. Although I was following the route of the rebellion as closely as I could, the landscape of the area had changed so much that Boudica would have recognised practically none of it. The fields had been enclosed since her time, whole areas of woodland had gone, communities and even major towns had sprung up (Ipswich barely existed back then) and the rutted, bumpy track down which her chariots, carts and footsoldiers travelled and camped beside had been replaced by a four-lane highway that could take you from Norwich to Colchester in a couple of hours rather than the several days it would have taken the Iceni.

I had to pass through the centre of Ipswich on my way south, just as the lights were flickering on in the shops and the 'closed' signs flipped round to 'open'. Café owners placed tables and umbrellas outside; the clack of unbolting doors accompanied the gentle sounds of a town yawning and stretching its way into the day. I clumped into a bookshop and purchased a clutch of Ordnance Survey maps, having been converted to them with evangelical zeal. I crossed the street to a coffee shop and planned my route with a luxury of anticipation. It promised to be a good day – for once I wouldn't have to find accommodation as I'd already arranged to stay with relatives in Colchester. I sipped my coffee and plunged into the maps: what had previously been a two-dimensional chore was now something I regarded as a bit of a treat.

As I sat there, however, the sun disappeared, the sky darkened and the heavens opened with monsoonic determination. The umbrellas outside the coffee shop bulged in the suddenly strong, gusty wind, tipped over and went bowling down the street. Caught-out commuters dived headlong into shop doorways while massive raindrops hurled from the sky exploded on the cobbled road like the white-tipped waves of a stormy sea.

For the first time, and with some excitement, I donned full waterproofs – only my eyes were visible – put the map in my pocket, hoisted my pack and headed out into the maelstrom. I splashed through the town centre and over the railway line, then sloshed through the suburbs as passing traffic sent up great fountains of spume. Most of the Roman road along which Boudica would have passed is now the A12, but I'd noticed on the map that there was a stretch marked 'Roman road' running parallel to the main thoroughfare for a good distance just south-west of Ipswich and I was heading for it with the zeal of someone who knows just where his map is and exactly where he is on it.

Once I was through the suburbs I'd have to cross what looked like a retail park and pick up the ancient road there. The bright lights of a vast Tesco supermarket soon shone out of the rainy gloom. After some aimless criss-crossing of a car park the size of a small county, during which time the rain eased and stopped as quickly as it had begun, I followed signs for the park and ride, descended some steps, passed beneath the A12 through a foot tunnel and emerged on the old road. Clearly this had once been the main road south from Ipswich; there were still faint road markings on the neglected leaf-strewn tarmac. Nothing came up here any more, it was a dead road. Some plastic bags whipped around in circles in the wind as watery sunshine began to leak through the clouds. It was quiet; I was all alone. For the first time I felt like I was peeking through the curtains of time. For the first time I could be certain that I was actually on the same route as Boudica and her army. The creaking, trundling carts passed along here. The Iceni, grimly determined and driven by vengeance, would have walked along here with Boudica at their head, a vast, noisy procession of men, women, children and horses spread wide across the road and beyond into the surrounding fields, knowing that with every step, every turn of the cart wheel, they were closer to justice, or at least their version of it.

As the sunshine grew stronger and drew sparkling starflashes from the wet tarmac, I too felt the sense of determination that the Iceni shared, that proud people who'd been emasculated by subjugation and seen their queen, their divinely appointed leader, and her offspring violated by an invading army of aggressors. They would have felt nothing beyond a desire for vengeance: there was no political plan behind their revolt, no agenda other than retribution; but walking in their footsteps I could feel the butterflies in my stomach, the nervous excitement, the feeling that every step was into the unknown.

The sun became stronger as I walked the dead road. I removed my waterproofs in an old bus shelter, and walked for a good couple of miles along the same road as the Iceni. At Brantham the Roman road joined the modern road and I left the tarmac in favour of a footpath across country. Instantly I noticed how much easier on the feet the soft ground of the footpath was and how much more relaxed I felt in the knowledge that there was no danger of being swiped by a passing Lexus. I climbed over stiles and sidestepped cowpats baking and steaming in the sunshine. Then, after I'd swept gracefully over one particular stile, I suddenly became aware of several heads swivelling towards me. Bovine heads. Lots of them. Directly between me and the next field. I'd never encountered cattle at close quarters before, at least not without potatoes and mustard. Do cows attack? I flicked through my mental card index to see if I could recall any 'couple mauled by angry cow' or 'man suffocated by udder' headlines. Nothing came up. I couldn't risk it, though. Polly would know: she's wrestled polar bears, probably. I sent her a text asking as nonchalantly as possible whether cows ever go for you. She replied immediately. The answer I'd been hoping for was, 'No, of course they don't. I mean, just look at them.' The answer I got was, 'Occasionally they do, and they can be bloody scary.' Ulp. Then another message followed: 'There's nothing wimpy about being scared of cows.' That was some consolation but it still didn't get me to the other side of the field. Bravely I took a couple of steps forward. So did the cows. I stopped. So did the cows. I stepped forward again. So did the cows. I stopped. So did the cows. It was clear that the only way to solve this was via a bore-off. I wouldn't move until they did – whoever gave in to sheer tedium first would lose. I stood there for what seemed like an age. Glaciers came and went. The cattle and I just looked at each other until eventually one of them cracked, its gaze moving to the other side of the field. Something appealing must have appeared there as the cow began to trudge towards it. The other cows turned their heads to look, thought it seemed as good a place to go as any and almost as one mooched over to the other side of the field. I all but punched the air. I'd won. I'd outsmarted some cows. I hotfooted it across the field, over the stile and on towards Colchester feeling like I'd qualified as a real, live, genuine outdoorsman. I took Pedro from my pocket to check my mileage and he looked proud of me.

After the morning rain the sky had become a deep blue, with the odd little fluffy cloud. I realised what a stroke of luck it had been buying that first OS map in Debenham. I'd never otherwise have been walking through such beautiful, peaceful country-side. I passed between fields along a narrow path lined with tall gorse that eventually opened out by an old house on the River Stour. As I approached, there was something familiar about the scene. I'd never been here before, yet something nagged at me that I knew the place. When I got to the building and read the signs the penny dropped – I was at Flatford Mill, the location of Constable's *The Hay Wain*. The trees were a bit bigger and there was no hay cart in the river or spaniel at the water's edge as there had been in 1821, but it was the strangest feeling to be walking through a scene that I knew so well from a painting. It was like walking around the corner and embarrassing Botticelli's Venus into grabbing a towel, or knocking into a cavalier and asking what he's laughing at.

Eventually I reached the outskirts of Colchester without managing to wander into any more great works of art – as I walked along the river I kept an eye out for the Lady of Shalott, but she must have moored somewhere for the night. As I passed through the northern suburbs the sun began to set, spreading a spectacular deep orange fire across the western sky. It was as if I was approaching the town just after Boudica's arrival, finding it in flames as the sky darkened. My aunt and uncle were out when I arrived so I retrieved the key from where they'd left it, let myself in and went straight upstairs to run a hot bath. As I settled beneath the water to soothe my aching muscles I reflected on what Boudica and her cohorts did to the Roman capital.

Camulodunum had been an important Iron Age settlement with earthwork defences before the Romans arrived. The name derives from Camulos, the Celtic god of war. It's clear that by the time of the Iceni revolt Camulodunum had become a properly Romanised settlement of classical buildings and wide streets set out on the same sort of grid pattern as Venta Icenorum. As the administrative capital of the British outpost of the Empire, it had all the trappings of a major Roman town – a senate building, shops, a theatre and, most strikingly, a huge temple dedicated to the late Emperor Claudius, who had succeeded where Julius Caesar had failed by adding the inhospitable islands to the north of Gaul to the Empire. The temple was enormous, and the cause of much local resentment: large taxes were levied on the populace and many were forced into slave labour to help with its construction. For a conquered people, it probably didn't get more humiliating than having to build and pay for a huge temple to the man responsible for your subservience.

It's therefore probable that by the time Boudica's forces came within striking distance of the town the rising was beginning to turn into a proper rebellion, as much as being the product of angry vengeance. As the Iceni trundled through the East Anglian countryside, aggrieved Britons must have poured out of villages and settlements to join the cause, adding further grievances to the roster and swelling Boudica's ranks into many thousands.

We don't know what kind of role Boudica actually played, whether she was the leader in the sense that she made the decisions and planned the strategy, or whether she was the symbolic umbrella under which leaders from the East Anglian tribes discussed their plans and tactics. Either way, if the descriptions of Tacitus and Cassius Dio are to be believed, Boudica would certainly have made a brilliant figurehead for the rebellion.

For a capital, however, Camulodunum was curiously lax in its defences. It was home to hundreds of army veterans who, having completed their twenty-five years of military service, were given plots of land to farm into their dotage. In a notably fortunate piece of timing, most of the Roman military forces in Britain were about as far away as they could possibly be, engaged in a concerted attempt to wipe out the druids on Anglesey. Hence Camulodunum had at best a skeleton defence force of retired veterans and a paltry number of serving soldiers. When news of Boudica's travelling hordes reached the town the locals pressed Catus Decianus, the man responsible for triggering the uprising in the first place, to provide military assistance. He mustered barely two hundred troops before hitching up his toga and hot-footing it to Gaul before Boudica could get hold of him.

The Ninth Legion, based in the East Midlands under Petilius Cerealis, did set off in an attempt to meet the rebels at Camulodunum but was ambushed en route and absolutely hammered – some three-quarters of the two thousand or so troops were killed, with the remainder limping back to a fort near Peterborough and barricading themselves in until the heat was off.

Boudica's forces approached Colchester meeting no opposition. Given the fact that their progress from Norfolk would have been slow – even with horses they would most likely have taken longer than I did, possibly covering only ten miles a day – the residents of Camulodunum would have had plenty of opportunity to pack up their belongings and leave. The proximity of the coast and the River Colne, as well as the main road south, would have made it fairly straightforward for those who could to get away, but it's not known how many people remained by the time Boudica arrived. Certainly Catus Decianus's couple of hundred grunts would have been there, their ranks swelled by veterans willing to take up arms against the uncivilised hordes about to rampage over the horizon and trample their allotments. Maybe some shopkeepers and traders stayed behind in foolhardy attempts to protect their livelihoods, but it seems likely that Boudica's forces approached what largely amounted to a ghost town.

Nevertheless, they fell upon the place in a storm of aggression and destruction. The property left behind was looted and systematically burned to the ground. The soldiers would have provided only token resistance to the thousands of screaming, blue-painted warriors descending on the town with the rage of years of pent-up grievance. Nothing and no one would have been spared. According to the accounts, those that remained barricaded themselves inside the Temple of Claudius. They may even have been in there for a couple of days, protected by the thick walls until the Britons scaled them and began to dismantle the roof, dropping on to the survivors and killing them where they stood. The statue of Claudius outside the temple would have been smashed down. Indeed, a young boy picked the face of the statue out of a river in Suffolk about a hundred years ago. Not realising what it could be he took it home, painted it white and stuck it in his parents' garden, from where it was eventually retrieved by the British Museum. How it got to Suffolk nobody is entirely sure, but it seems probable that given its symbolic significance Boudica's people would have carried it with them as a trophy – perhaps it was tossed into the river by Iceni returning after the final defeat, aware that to be caught carrying such hot goods in a climate of Roman indignation at having their ears boxed would take some explaining.

★

As I lay in the bath looking up through the window at the stars, I tried to imagine what it would have been like the night before the carnage. The remaining soldiers in Camulodunum must have known deep down that they had no chance. They would have sat up late, sharpening their swords and fingering the blades, tightening the straps on their shields, a cold feeling in their stomachs. A last few traders would have been burying their wares in the hope that there might be a business to return to once they'd left the town. The old and infirm, those who couldn't leave, would have prepared themselves for the inevitable while nurturing a desperate hope that the small band of trained soldiers would have the expertise, discipline and experience to outwit and defeat the Boudican hordes.

Outside the town, maybe even on the very spot where I lay, Boudica's people would have bedded down for the night, falling into a nervous, disturbed sleep, excited by what was to come. The tribal leaders would have cast their minds forward to a time when the Romans had been driven out and they could return to their old ways and the old order.

Most of all, though, I thought of Boudica. Maybe she too had gazed up at the stars, still feeling the sting of the welts on her back, but mainly the pain and anger in her heart at what had been done to her daughters by the people occupying the town outside which she now lay, the beating, rotten heart of the invading culture, the home of the evil that was done to her and her family. She may not have expected Catus Decianus still to be there, but she could walk his streets, pass through his buildings and bring it all down in a merciless firestorm of revenge.

The next day I walked into the centre of Colchester, a town I know well as I lived there for four years when a student at the concrete monstrosity of a university that sits, ugly and defiant, on its outskirts. I reached the bottom of the High Street, where the castle stands. It's hard to believe now, given Colchester's irrevocable association with Roman Britain, but the town was only confirmed as the Camulodunum of history in the 1920s. The archaeologist and broadcaster Sir Mortimer Wheeler made a series of archaeological discoveries, perhaps the most significant of which came at the castle itself. Crossing the wooden footbridge and passing through the entrance I looked down a roped-off staircase into a dimly lit space below. It was Wheeler, an upper-class, military, 1920s Tony Robinson, who first twigged that these were not just the foundations on which the Norman castle had been built; rather it was the remains of a Roman temple, the Temple of Claudius where the remaining citizens of Camulodunum had attempted to sit out the destruction.

Colchester Castle itself has had an eventful history. It was besieged by King John during the turbulence that led to the drawing up of Magna Carta. Matthew Hopkins, the self-styled Witchfinder General, used the castle to interrogate women he suspected of witchcraft, and in one of the most unsavoury episodes of the English Civil War two highly respected royalist officers were executed in the grounds. So unjust was this incident that, apparently, nothing has grown on the spot to this day, and birds never sing there. The round tower and façade of the castle, as well as its red slate roofs, give it a curious, almost Tuscan look. This is because it passed, in the early eighteenth century, into the possession of a man named Charles Gray who, thinking the castle was Roman, 'restored' it at great expense to its, er, national glory. It was a bit like looking at the Tower of London and thinking, hmm, that looks to me like it was built by Native Americans, and plonking a totem pole on the roof.

The castle has an extensive display related to Boudica. As well as the burnt pottery, lumps of melted and fused glass, carbonised barley and material from what was apparently a pile of burnt mattresses, there is a display exploring how Boudica's image has been used in popular culture. My favourite was probably a car advert that looked to be from the early 1980s. 'It's

what Boadicea would have driven,' it claimed. 'She had a repu-
tation as a leader of men. A go-getter who inspired confidence.
The sort of woman who would find the Mitsubishi Colt 1800
GTI irresistible.' Of course she was.

I thought back to the night before the Britons sacked the
town. I could almost hear the conversation of two blue-painted
warriors, picking the last sinews of mutton from the bones as
they sat around the fire. 'You know what?' one might have said
between chews, 'the thing with Boudica is, right, she's got a reputation as a leader of men.'

'You're not wrong,' his mate might have replied. 'I've always
seen her as a go-getter who inspires confidence.'

'Exactly,' would come the reply, bone pointing at his friend in
confirmation. 'I'd even go so far as to say that, given a couple of
thousand years, she'd be just the sort of woman who'd find the
Mitsubishi Colt 1800 GTI irresistible.'

'This is it,' would come the reply. 'That rabbit done yet?'

I spent much of the day revisiting old haunts, not least the back-
street pub that had been my local as a student. Back then it was
a friendly yet run-down place, patronised by a small but fiercely
loyal band of regulars. Returning for the first time in some
fifteen years I was surprised to see it had been done up. I stood
outside and remembered some of my fellow drinkers. Peter, the
science fiction book illustrator with the roll-up cigarettes and
permanently wayward bed-hair. Old Ron with his grey beard,
sparkly eyes and dry wit. Gary at the pool table with his lank red
hair, misted-over National Health glasses and almost impenetrable Essex accent. The sticky floors, the ripped-open seating, the
surface lifting off the bar thanks to years of bleached-cloth clean-
ing. All that seemed to have gone, refurbished to look like any
other pub. There were even hanging baskets now. Inside it
looked familiar yet strangely alien, as if a crime scene had been
redecorated. On the wall, in the place where our certificate for

winning the Colchester and District Pub Quiz League had been hung proudly and with great, if drunken, ceremony, there was now a Blu-tacked advert for an alcopop. I walked back to the centre of town feeling suddenly old. It's strange: walking along the Roman road in Ipswich had made the events of two thousand years earlier seem current and alive; now, barely two decades seemed an irretrievable time away.

From there I revisited the Hole in the Wall, a popular Colchester pub that was placed, as its name suggests, in a breach in the Roman wall which protected the town that grew up after the Boudican destruction. A sign on the door proclaimed it a 'chav-free zone'. It was mid-afternoon and I had the place almost to myself. I sat in an armchair next to a section of unrendered wall, which I immediately realised was the Roman wall itself. The stones were dark red and black, smeared with patches of salty white. I wondered about the men who built it, touching one of the stones and trying to imagine the day it was laid there, as two workmen – slaves probably – mixed the cement and positioned the freshly hewn stone in place. What were they talking about when they sited the stone I was touching right now? Where did they go at the end of that day? What became of them? Who did they love? Who did they hate? These nameless, faceless men, who one day in history placed a stone on to wet cement and made sure it was firm without even thinking that it would still be there, as strong and sturdy as the day it was built, two thousand years later. Certainly it's more than can be said for our pub quiz league championship certificate, and I for one know which was the greater achievement.

I had one more pub to visit. The George Hotel sits near the centre of the High Street, all posh with its sofas, armchairs and focaccia. I ordered a drink and asked if I could see what I'd come for. After some huddled conversations I was invited down some stairs and into a cellar, where a pane of glass was fixed to one of the walls. Near the top was the first tangible evidence of

Boudica's revolt I'd seen – a reddish stratum about four inches thick; here, below ground, a layer that stood out from the rest of the earth because it was clearly the result of a major conflagration. Archaeologists have determined that the depth of the stratum corresponds almost exactly with the date of Boudica's rebellion. This is what she left behind.

On leaving Colchester I headed across country in the direction of Chelmsford. It's likely that Boudica's forces would have hung around Camulodunum for a couple of days at least, celebrating, praying and dividing up the loot under the smoke of the smouldering town, knowing that the Roman army was still a long way off. From Camulodunum, the rebels would head south to the new trading port of Londinium. Was that always the plan, even before the sacking of Camulodunum? By then Boudica would have been fully aware that the Roman legions were occupied on the other side of the island, still weeks away from any confrontation. Maybe she was advised that this was an opportunity to press home a unique advantage, a chance to rid the land of the invader. They'd picked up support and numbers all the way from the Iceni lands and the same would happen the further south they headed. Londinium was another focus of Roman power, less symbolic than Camulodunum but economically important to the occupying people. Boudica's forces had struck a fearsome blow against the Romans by destroying their capital – something that gave the rebels an enormous psychological advantage.

Whenever the decision was made to press on to the Thames, it wasn't long before the travelling mass of Britons was on the road again and heading south. The Roman road from Colchester to Chelmsford is again the A12, so I struck out parallel, delighted to find, at one stage, that I was crossing Boadicea Way.

The next couple of days were notable only for being caught in a sudden and fearsome hailstorm just outside Tiptree, and a curious encounter when I really was in the middle of nowhere.

I emerged from a long footpath through fields where I'd not seen another soul for hours, and joined a country lane. I noticed an old woman in a blue knitted hat on a bike up ahead. She stopped and seemed to be watching me. As I drew nearer I realised that she was shouting something at me. After a short while I realised she was shouting 'left, right, left, right' in time with my steps, something she kept up until I reached her. I smiled at her, a little confused. She grinned.

'You're a soldier, aren't you,' she said, more as a statement than a question.

'Er, no,' I replied, startled. Believe me, there can't be anyone on this earth less likely to be mistaken for a soldier than me.

'Yes you are, I can tell.'

'No, I'm really not, honestly.'

'You are.'

'Am not.'

'You are.'

'I promise I'm not.'

'You can't fool me, you know.'

I realised there was to be no convincing her. 'Oh, all right, you got me. I am a soldier, yes.'

Her smile turned into a toothless beam. She took one hand off the handlebars and stuck it out. I took it and shook it. She had a surprisingly firm grip.

'Well done,' she said, put her hand back on the handlebars, placed her furry-booted foot on the pedal and cycled off. To where, I've no idea. After she'd gone I took out the map, which confirmed that we were miles from anywhere. I couldn't even guess where she'd come from or where she was going, nor the provenance of the single tin of marrowfat peas in the basket of her bike.

I passed through Chelmsford then rejoined the Roman road, which went ramrod-straight through Margaretting and Ingatestone before eventually arriving on the outskirts of

Brentwood. After days in the countryside I'd finally hit suburbia. Huge mock Tudor mansions lined the road. Blonde women with big earrings drove past me in four-wheel-drive vehicles inversely proportionate to their own size. I passed along Brentwood High Street, still following the course of the Roman road, until suddenly I had my breath taken away from me. I crested a hill while looking at the map, and when I looked up there, spread before me, was the London skyline. I stopped in my tracks and let out a strange noise that was half laugh, half yelp. For the first time I realised just how far I'd actually come. I'd started in Norwich, for heaven's sake. And now, here, before me, the horizon was no longer a flat expanse of trees and the occasional steeple, it was the familiar grey silhouettes of the NatWest Tower, the Gherkin and St Paul's Cathedral. Boudica herself would have come over this hill. She wouldn't have squeaked 'Ooh, look, you can see the London Eye from here' of course, but I wondered whether she would have seen curls of smoke rising from the modest settlement of Londinium, and the sails of boats arriving on the Thames. Either way, the next target of her ire was now within striking distance.

Boudica, even if she'd seen the settlement as she came over the hill in the same way I had, would have known that the city still lay a good two days away. That first glimpse would have inspired her, however, and if she had spent the night in whatever the equivalent of the evocatively named Holiday Inn Brentwood M25 Junction 28 was in AD61 – and I'd recommend the chicken if she ever did again – she would have slept soundly in the knowledge that, having completely destroyed the Romans' centre of administration, a poorly defended trading post should present little or no problem. Naturally, she didn't expect to meet with no resistance whatsoever. The trundling progress of her motley procession meant that a major encounter with the Roman army, as far as she knew ankling it down Watling Street from Anglesey, was going to occur at some point in the near future. The destruction of Londinium, however, would strike at the heart of the Romano-British economy; not as symbolic a blow as the trashing of Camulodunum, but an important one nonetheless.

Suetonius Paulinus, the commander of the Roman forces, had arrived in Londinium with a small detachment of cavalry to try to work out what to do next. He'd expected a bit of a respite after chopping up the druids on Anglesey – maybe even getting the ferry over to Dublin and going on the lash in Temple Bar – but instead he was haring across the country because some woman was charging around burning things down. He wasn't happy, and nor were the people of Londinium. Word had reached the settlement about the destruction of Camulodunum at roughly the same time as it would have reached Suetonius, and many people would already have left for the safety of the countryside. The more determined would have remained, whinging in taverns about what this might do to property prices, and ships would still have been arriving, unaware of the impending carnage descending on the little town by the Thames.

Londinium was a fairly new settlement of some thirty thousand inhabitants. It would have been a cosmopolitan place, just as it is today, with traders and merchants from all over the Empire seeking to exploit the growing opportunities presented by this chilly island north of Gaul. Goods and slaves were exported here from as far away as Wales and Scotland, while imports were unloaded and distributed in what would have been a lively, noisy and thriving place. It would have been distinctly muted that day, though, as Suetonius stood at its centre. He had two options. The first would be to assemble as many soldiers as he could at such short notice to defend the town from the invaders. However, he'd heard about the devastation of Camulodunum and knew that the Britons would be arriving in even greater numbers and with morale sky high. The alternative option was to evacuate Londinium, leave it to the mercy of the Iceni and their allies, and muster a large Roman force to meet them at full strength somewhere down the road when the odds were more in Roman favour. Which wouldn't have pleased the Roman *Evening Standard*, but they'd have just blamed Ken Livingstone anyway.

He chose the latter option, something that would have left many of the remaining residents aghast, such as the trader who buried a hoard of coins near what is now King William Street, never to return for them. You could see Suetonius's point, however. While London was a key trading post it lacked the trappings of a major Roman town: there was no senate, no theatre, no major temple and no centre of administration. As far as Suetonius was concerned, Londinium could be sacrificed for the greater good of the Roman future in Britain and a greater opportunity to defeat the rebellion at a later date. Londinium, then, was doomed.

The next morning I crossed the M25 and soon left the countryside behind. It would be road walking all the way now as I followed the route of the old Roman road through Romford and Ilford and on beyond Stratford. When Boudica's forces arrived Londinium would have been practically deserted – it was probably the last time that London was ever truly quiet. Her forces would have entered the town unmolested and found it largely empty of people and lootable goods. Cassius Dio provides a gruesome account of what the rebels did to the locals that were left: women were impaled on wooden stakes in an horrific allegory of the rape of Boudica's daughters while some, he reported, had their breasts cut off and stuffed into their mouths. It is important to remember that Boudica's rebellion had no noble or honourable political cause at its heart; it may have developed political aims as the mobile riot thundered around the southeast but, as far as we can tell, this was a lashing out at authority inspired by anger and sheer naked vengeance. Boudica's forces, who would have been a large and disparate group impossible to instruct in a coherent manner, were as capable of atrocities as any other armed group with the smell of blood in their nostrils.

Again we have physical evidence of the havoc wreaked by Boudica and her forces in a stratum of burnt earth in the soil beneath modern London. The Museum of London has a small display of items clearly damaged by fire that date from around the time of the rebellion, including the coins mentioned above and some grain discovered near Fenchurch Street. London's most tangible Boudican legacy, however, is Thomas Thornycroft's dramatic statue at the end of Westminster Bridge, near the Houses of Parliament. Depicting the Iceni queen on a chariot, arms raised and a spear in her hand, with her daughters either side of her, it was placed there in 1902 long after Thornycroft's death and even longer after it was commissioned by Prince Albert. It's possible that Albert saw it as the maternal personification of the British Empire, with an obvious nod to his reigning missus. More Britannia than Boudica, perhaps. Either way, for such an elusive historical figure to have a substantial statue in such a prominent location in a place she destroyed is a measure of the place Boudica has in the history of England. And, having burnt down London, she wasn't finished yet.

Could there be a more inoffensive city than St Albans? The name itself seems to come with a benevolent smile, and the very thought of it makes you want to put your arm around it and go 'aww'. So why, then, after leaving Camulodunum and Londinium as smouldering ruins, did Boudica turn her ire on leafy, sleepy old St Albans? The answer possibly lies in the reasons why the rebellion was largely to fizzle out soon after the rebels sacked the place. St Albans sits on the site of an old Iron Age town called Verlamion, a major seat of the wealthy Catuvellauni tribe. The Catuvellauni had a long history of tussles with their neighbours to the east, the Trinovantes, who now made up a sizeable chunk of Boudica's forces. The coming of the Romans had managed to keep a lid on such tribal rivalries in much the same way as Tito's Yugoslavia did in the Balkans, but now, with the Romans seemingly on the back foot and the Britons feeling invincible, the old rivalries began to surface.

The Catuvellauni had taken to Roman life with great zeal. They felt great in a roomy, flowing toga and suddenly found themselves with unfettered access to olive oil to die for. They soon began referring to Verlamion by its Roman name of Verulamium, and probably spoke with cod Italian accents and began supporting AC Milan. So pleased were the Romans at this blatant grovelling that they gave the town a status that entitled its inhabitants to call themselves Roman citizens. Verulamium soon became the third-biggest town in Roman Britain, and with its quisling people and the doubtless effective lobbying of the Trinovantes about those feckless, flaky Catuvellauni, Verulamium became an obvious target for the Britons. In addition, the Romans had routed Watling Street, one of their major thoroughfares, through Verulamium. This was the road that would bring the legions back from Anglesey, so it's likely that Boudica and her fellow leaders would have been anticipating a large and inevitable confrontation, and thought it should come while morale and momentum were high. Hence once Londinium had been ransacked the rebels made for the road to Verulamium.

This road is now the modern A5, beginning at the bottom of the Edgware Road, and it's fairly certain that Boudica would have joined it where it met the road from Camulodunum. It's a spot now occupied by Marble Arch, and the place I found myself early one blustery morning among the car horns and police sirens that provide a constant soundtrack to life in the capital. Half a dozen tourists took photos of each other in front of the arch itself, probably commenting that 'it's no Arc de Triomphe, is it?' in their native tongues. Fittingly, John Nash designed it with a nod to the triumphal arch of the Emperor Constantine in

Rome. I descended into the underpass where a young homeless couple slept among a jumble of sleeping bags, cardboard and blankets, him behind, his arm protectively around her, both peacefully impervious to the rush-hour mayhem.

Having become used to the more leisurely pace of the countryside, the sheer busyness of my home city took me aback. When I emerged from the underpass and turned back to look at Marble Arch, several grim-faced suit-wearers tutted at me for forcing them to briefly break their stride. I smiled at one; he looked at me as if I'd just made a clumsy pass at his grandmother.

The junction of the roads is the site of the notorious gallows of Tyburn, and three brass triangles in the road mark the spot of the infamous Tyburn tree. Although the last person to be hanged there 'danced the Tyburn jig' in 1783 it's still a word associated with execution. It was busy enough, that's for sure – on one day in 1649 twenty-four people were hanged simultaneously – not least because it was occasionally used to execute people who were, er, already dead. When Charles II was restored to the English throne he had the three-years-dead Oliver Cromwell and two of his cohorts dug up and strung up at Tyburn. After that Cromwell was beheaded and his head put on a pole at London Bridge, where it remained for more than twenty years. After that it was passed around like a wrinkly old rugby ball until it was finally laid to rest in Cambridge in 1960.

Despite more than five hundred years of seeing off felons – the first recorded execution on the spot was in 1196 – there's little now beyond a plaque that I couldn't find and the brass markers to tell you of the horrors that took place here so I headed off north, along the arrow-straight road slicing between Marylebone and Paddington. It was around twenty miles to St Albans, a journey that would have taken Boudica and her cumbersome caravan two days, if not more. I was aiming to do it in one. To mark the end of my first journey in the footsteps of history I'd booked into a beautiful-looking pub for the night, where I intended to park myself in front of a steak and kidney pie of such diameter you'd think they'd used a gasometer as a pie dish. That was several hours away, though, as I sidestepped the commuters of the Edgware Road, the suits and raincoats darting in and out of the coffee shops and sandwich shops that, the further I walked from the centre, soon gave way to a procession of Turkish and Arabic emporia, the air filled with exotic musks and the glint of silver and gold from shop windows. I passed within a hefty six of Lord's cricket ground and then, at Maida Vale, the spot where the head-master Philip Lawrence was killed trying to break up a fight outside his school in 1995. At Kilburn I plunged into the heart of Irish London, past the pubs where for decades old toothless men in flat caps had sung songs of the country they had left behind. I passed a newsagent that had every Irish newspaper you could think of, from the *Cork Examiner* right up to the *Donegal Democrat*. It was then I realised that I was walking through a microcosm of London and its history; a city that grew out of trade and has as a result been home to people from every corner of the globe, from the spice traders of Boudica's day filling the streets with exotic aromas to the Polish builders disappearing into the Polski sklep for the cigarettes that taste of home.

On through Cricklewood and its synagogues, the imposing arch of Wembley Stadium away to my left, then Dollis Hill, Colindale and on to Edgware and, to my surprise, the hospital where I was born. Another synagogue disgorged its occupants as I passed what appeared to be an Orthodox wedding. The men were in their dark suits and hats, the women in their best floral print dresses, their hair kept neat by Alice bands, licking tissues in order to wipe the rosy cheeks of children looking uncom-fortable in their suits.

And then I reached the place where London ends.

I'd never really thought about it before, but the English cap-ital does, I suppose, have to stop somewhere, and I'd found that place. I'd reached the end of London, the point where the concrete and bricks and noise and people and rush and bustle and moneymaking and traffic and sirens stop. Just past the synagogue I'd come to a roundabout. I nipped through a break in the traffic, crossed the road and became aware that things had suddenly become very different. When I stepped out of the road on the other side I landed not on another cracked, uneven pavement but bare, worn earth fringed with grass. Ahead of me lay not shops, flats and offices, but trees and a flimsy-looking fence. It was quiet too. So marked was the contrast, so amazed was I to reach the end of London, that I crossed back and forth a couple more times. I felt like I'd reached the end of a rainbow – the end of London, a mythical place, the kind of place where you should find some kind of little bearded fella toting a pot of gold.

I pressed on and after crossing the M1 and passing through Elstree the road veered left, the only deviance from the straight Roman line between Marble Arch and St Albans. This, I realised, could have been where the road builders routed Watling Street through Verulamium as a big thank you to the flibberti-gibbets there for being such great plastic Romans with their lovely togas and insatiable thirst for olive oil.

By around six o'clock that evening I was in St Albans and walking towards the pub I'd booked for the night. I'd specifically chosen an historic-looking inn to mark the end of this particular journey, and intended an evening unwinding among the beams and horse brasses, getting quietly squiffy in the corner.

My suspicions that all was not quite as it seemed began when I couldn't get through what appeared to be the door. It wasn't just locked, it seemed permanently sealed. I walked around to the back of the pub, and there was some kind of glass atrium thing marked 'Reception'. Now, when I stay in a pub the usual routine is to mooch in, walk up to the bar, secure a room for the night, be ushered up a creaky back staircase and led down undulating corridors by the barmaid. In this case I entered a glass hallway and found a hotel-style lobby full of pot plants and chrome. I checked in and was shown to my room. Once I'd heaved off my boots, bounced on the bed a couple of times in an approving manner, opened and closed all the cupboard doors, switched on the light in the bathroom and looked in the toilet – all the traditional, territory-marking rituals of the new hotel room – I picked up the piece of paper I'd been given downstairs. The dinner menu: I'd been looking forward to this. I rather felt I'd deserved it. I had, after all, just walked from Norwich to London and then to St Albans; the opening day's bus ride aside, it was the longest self-propelled journey I had ever made, cover-ing two hundred-odd miles. I was starving, thirsty, and within minutes wanted to be doing some serious business with the soup of the day.

There didn't appear to be a soup of the day. In fact, the menu before me had to be some kind of spoof. For a start it had the day's date at the top, and the items on the menu had no prices against them. What had happened to the sticky plastic folder with the ketchup blob in the top corner? And what kind of lan-guage was this?

I have no idea what a 'wild mushroom cappucino [sic]' is, and I don't think I want to know. The same goes for pan-seared Black Pearl scallops, dressed pea shoots, citrus sea asparagus, roast shelfish [sic] foam, poussé spinach, vanilla bubbles, cardamom reduction and all the rest of the pretentious, badly spelled twad-dle that made up the bill of fare – which was, incidentally, only available as a three-course meal at one price. I would shortly be heading out for a Chinese. No matter, I'll pop downstairs for a quick pint. After a shower and a change of clothes I took three steps into the bar and stopped. I shook my head and rubbed my eyes. This couldn't be right. It just couldn't be. The beamed, brassed, cosy saloon I'd anticipated was nowhere to be found. Instead, the bars of this beautiful, ancient, characterful inn had been filleted, emasculated, torn apart, desecrated and turned into an open-plan, laminate-floored, beige-seated, dishes-of-pebbles-in-the-fireplace cavern of aesthetic barrenness. The place had been destroyed. It had been turned into a soulless, identikit rectangle, an insult to the history of the building and a crime against any kind of historical appreciation, a den of roast collop of Rougié foie gras iniquity. It looked like the soft focus final shots of a property makeover programme just before the estate agents arrive to purr appreciatively about how any sense of character or personality has been efficiently and vigorously removed. I almost sank to my knees. Instead, I backpedalled furiously until I was halfway across the car park and went somewhere else.

The next morning, still appalled, I made my way across the room for breakfast, where I dined alone and appeared to be the only guest. An expensively retro radio on the other side of the room oozed tuneless new-age noodling from its speakers. A patronising male voice cut in to announce the name of the station, of which I had never previously heard, before adding that it provided 't'ai chi for the ears'. Only the pillar between us saved the radio from being smashed into its component parts by a flying coffee pot.

How on earth are people allowed to get away with doing this to historic places? How many people do you know who have walked into a traditional old pub – hand pumps on the bar, hunting prints on the wall, pewter tankards hanging from nails, dark oak panelling, all cosy corners, warmth and character – and said, 'You know what this place needs? Ripping everything out, putting a laminate floor down and sticking a big dish of pebbles in the fireplace. Then they'd be on to something all right'?

I left the pub as quickly as I could and headed out to Verulamium Park, the site of the old town sacked by Boudica, desperate for a quick and restorative infusion of history. It was a glorious, peaceful morning, the sun glinting off the damp grass, the silence broken only by the occasional quack of a duck on the pond. It was early, and the only other people I could see as I warmed my face with the morning sun were a red-faced woman jogger doing wheezy laps of the pond and a mother and her young son feeding the ducks ('George, don't get close to the edge . . . George, you're too close to the edge . . . George, you're GOING TO FALL IN!'). The serenity of the scene, the deep blue sky behind the rich green of the trees, again made it difficult to imagine that anything as awful as the sacking of an entire town could have happened here.

By the time Boudica and her followers arrived, Verulamium was deserted. The word had spread about what had happened at Camulodunum and Londinium, and the locals had legged it, taking everything of value with them. The wind direction also made it harder to burn down the town, with some buildings remaining practically untouched. The destruction was still pretty much total – again there is a layer of burnt earth somewhere below the park – but there was probably a sense that the fun was going out of all this looting and burning business. Boudica's rebellion was becoming a victim of its own success. The lack of a 'real' battle was probably leaving some sections of the mob bored and unfulfilled. There was no longer any treasure to plunder, just empty houses to torch, and even that was losing its lustre. It's funny, I was probably imagining it, but having spent the past few weeks with just Boudica for company I began to feel a little disillusioned myself. The rebellion had destroyed the three most significant towns in Roman Britain – quite a hat-trick. But there was also the knowledge that they'd met no significant resistance and that was sure to change. Maybe the constant travelling along rutted, uneven roads in such vast numbers was taking its toll too. Keeping such a whopping great bunch of people fed, united and happy was a tall order, and I bet there was no wild mushroom cappuccino then. Old inter-tribal disagreements would have been reigniting, and the sacking of Verulamium would prove to be the Boudican revolt's last success.

By now the well-presented museum had opened, so I spent an hour or so wandering the exhibits. There was film footage of Sir Mortimer Wheeler, the man who had deduced that Colchester was the Camulodunum of history. He spoke from the site of the dig he conducted at Verulamium, his hair immaculately Brylcreemed above a neat moustache, one hand placed self-consciously on his hip and the other holding a cigarette as he described the progress of the dig in a clipped upper-class accent.

From the museum I made my way to the edge of town, wandering through the Roman theatre that dates from the reconstruction of Verulamium after Boudica's revolt, standing on the site of the dressing room and trying to imagine the nervous anticipation among the performers as they heard the hubbub of the audience outside – probably similar, in fact, to the humming of the thousands of insects in the hedge surrounding the site. I walked out to where the stage had been and pictured the comedies and tragedies, the recitals and gladiatorial bouts that enthralled audiences two thousand years ago in exactly the same way as they do in similar establishments today. I walked on through the sunshine towards a roundabout, along a well-tended boulevard with wide footpaths. I became aware that my step was slowing tangibly, that my first journey was coming to an end. I reached the roundabout and walked a short way along the exit marked Redbourn A5183, the continuation of Watling Street. This is where I would leave Boudica; where the historical trail goes cold.

We know from the accounts of Tacitus and Cassius Dio that she took her followers north along Watling Street, knowing Suetonius Paulinus was heading her way with the full might of the Roman legions at his command. The inevitable battle did take place, but nobody can say for sure where it was. Mancetter, near Atherstone in Warwickshire, seems to be the most likely location as it sits hard by Watling Street and the terrain seems to correspond with the historical accounts. Either way, the Britons were defeated by the superior tactics and discipline of the Romans, and Boudica was never heard of again. Many surmise that she chose to take her own life by drinking poison rather than suffer the ignominy of being taken to Rome and paraded through the streets as the previous British rebel king Caratacus had been. Nothing is known of what became of her daughters either, whether Boudica's bloodline continued. There was a strong but groundless rumour in Victorian times that Boudica is buried beneath Platform 8 at King's Cross Station, while in 2006 Birmingham archaeologists claimed they'd found her grave in King's Norton, just next to McDonald's.

I stood for a while, looking along Watling Street to where the road curved around to the right and out of sight, picturing a noble, charismatic queen standing proud on her chariot at the head of her mishmash of warriors, their carts rumbling along the track, heading towards her destiny.

After a few minutes I turned around, retraced my steps and began to walk forward almost a thousand years.

Chapter Two

1066: King Harold, Stamford Bridge to Hastings

'Well, it's a bonny day all right.'

'Aye, it is that. Cobwebs in the trees too. It's like everything's slowing down.'

It's a sleepy, sun-dozed autumn afternoon and the two men at the next table are right: it's a bonny day and everything is slowing down. Across the road from the pub some children are feeding quacking ducks that are mooching along the riverbank. Two mothers with pushchairs trundle towards the Co-op as a man cycles past them languidly, crossing their lengthening shadows as the sun pushes its autumnal warmth across the street and through the window, catching flecks of dust hanging almost motionless in the air. It's one of those afternoons where time stretches and everything adopts a dreamy quality. Briefly I wonder whether I'm actually in the right place, so incongruous is the scene to the reason I'm here. Could this really be the site of one of the most decisive and bloody battles ever to have taken place on English soil?

I can see the memorial from here. I've just been over to see it, in fact – a modern space enclosed by low brick walls, with benches flanking a small standing stone, on the edge of a sparsely filled car park dotted with the first tentative leaf fall of autumn. A bunch of dying but still vividly red carnations has been laid on the plinth, one drooping forlornly over the edge. Set into the wall at the back is a marble plaque, with two golden battleaxes crossed over the date 1066. It's a date familiar to anyone with even the slightest grasp of English history, but today I'm far from Hastings: the plaque, the pub, the ducks and I are around eight miles east of York. 'The Battle of Stamford Bridge', it says, 'King Harold of England defeated his brother Tostig and King Hardrada of Norway here on 25 September 1066'.

It was one of the greatest victories in English history, yet barely three weeks later it would be almost forgotten as the man behind the victory lay dead in a field some three hundred miles away, his kingdom lost. Harold Godwineson was destined to go down in history as the man who lost the Battle of Hastings, his place in the annals summed up by the opening couplets of a Stanley Holloway monologue:

> I'll tell of the Battle of Hastings,
> As happened in days long gone by,
> When Duke William became King of England,
> And 'Arold got shot in the eye.

There is so much more to Harold than having one of his peepers popped out by a Norman archer and losing England to the French – something I would learn as I followed his journey south from glorious victory to defeat and death. He reigned for barely nine months yet achieved things in that time alone that make him worthy of a greater place in the history books, before even considering the achievements of his entire career. He was a man ahead of his time, a man whose brief life came at one of the great turning points in English history and a man who came within a stroke of fate of becoming possibly one of the greatest and most far-sighted rulers England has ever seen.

The journey I was about to begin would take me from the location of the Battle of Stamford Bridge, at which Harold saw off the Viking threat for ever despite having just marched his army north from London at terrific speed, to Battle, the town outside Hastings where history shuddered and shifted on its axis one autumn day when Harold fought his second epoch-defining encounter, a conflict whose reverberations would continue to be felt nearly a thousand years later.

Harold is inexplicably overlooked in histories of the English monarchy, nearly all of which start with William the Conqueror. It's as if kings before the Normans don't really count (apart from Edward the Confessor, it seems, and sometimes Cnut, because of the misinterpreted story of him commanding the tide to stop and the fact that his name is an anagram of an incredibly rude word). Yet even in the short time that he ruled, Harold steadied and united a turbulent, vulnerable nation, saw off the Vikings once and for all and with just a smidgen more luck would have seen off the Normans too – and how different would history have been if he'd done that? In military terms he pulled off the remarkable feat of marching an army almost the length of the country to decimate one enemy, before immediately marching them back south for a bigger battle with another, and all but pulling it off. In addition he was a wise, educated and, certainly for the time, diplomatic rather than aggressive monarch with a highly developed sense of culture and cosmopolitanism – all facets that make me baffled as to why he's been swept under the Axminster of history. Yes he lost the Battle of Hastings (and yes, history is written by the winners), but don't the English love a gallant loser? Surely he should be up there with the likes of Captain Scott, Gordon of Khartoum and Eddie the Eagle? Add to that the fact that Harold only ascended the throne as a stopgap in the first place – basically he was just minding it for somebody else – and you have the archetypal Englishman. Knighthoods and spreads in colour supplements have been given for much less.

When Edward the Confessor became king in 1042 he was supported by three major earls, Leofric of Mercia, Siward of Northumbria and Godwine of Wessex, this last Harold's father. Edward was married to Eadgyth, Godwine's daughter and Harold's sister, something that gave the family increased power and influence. Harold, then Earl of East Anglia, had plighted his troth to the wealthy local heiress known as Eadgyth Swanneshals ('Swan-neck'), presumably in reference to her beauty rather than a propensity to get tangled up in old fishing twine. Things looked peachy for the Godwine clan. However, four years later Harold's older brother Swegen abducted the Abbess of Leominster and locked her in his castle, apparently because he was smitten with her to the extent of wanting her as his wife. As a method of wooing it left a lot to be desired and after a year Swegen was forced to release the poor woman. He was then exiled and Harold inherited many of his lands, along with the brothers' cousin Beorn. Swegen, encouraged by Godwine, whose major weakness seemed to be an unfailing loyalty to his offspring, soon returned to England covertly, determined to persuade Edward to revoke his exile and return his lands. He arranged to meet Beorn on the south coast when he arrived and travel with him to see the king, a mission that failed and led to Swegen murdering Beorn, thus making his chances of getting back into Edward's good books a little remote.

In the meantime, Edward was persistently failing to produce an heir. Naturally, in the male-dominated mindset of the times this could only be Eadgyth's fault and Edward sought a divorce. The trouble was that Godwine, Edward's father-in-law, was the most powerful nobleman in the land; it could even be argued that in real terms he wielded more power and influence than the king himself. The Swegen situation, however, gave Edward the opportunity to undermine Godwine's influence, and Godwine's persistent loyalty to his errant son led to the earl and his whole family being exiled. Godwine and most of the clan went to

Flanders; Harold sailed for Dublin where he enlisted the help of the local king, Diarmait mac Máel, and set about raising a force of Norse mercenaries to support the aggrieved family's return. While Godwine arrived back in England from the south, Harold came in from the west, masterminding a victorious skirmish at Porlock. The family moved around their old lands in the south and rallied a large body of support, something Edward couldn't ignore. Once Godwine and a significant number of ships had sailed up the Thames to Southwark they negotiated the return of the family lands with the king. One notable upshot of this was that the Archbishop of Canterbury, the Norman Robert of Jumièges – once a favourite of Edward who had lobbied persistently against Godwine for years – was forced to flee to France where, whether truthfully, exaggeratedly or just maliciously, he informed Duke William of Normandy that childless Edward had identified him as his successor.

In the meantime, Swegen, having been sent on pilgrimage to Jerusalem by his father in an attempt to improve his eldest son's appalling PR, died at Constantinople. Then, over Easter 1053 Godwine himself collapsed at a feast and died three days later. Harold thus found himself at the head of the most powerful family in England.

It seems that Edward had great respect and affection for Harold, in marked contrast to how he'd felt about his father. He had no hesitation in appointing Harold Earl of Wessex and probably looked forward to a much more harmonious relationship at a time of great uncertainty in the kingdom. By now it was clear that Edward was not going to produce an heir and discussions began as to who would succeed him. So thorough was the research that one candidate, who would turn out to be the approved one, was sourced to Hungary, where his father had been exiled forty years earlier. Another exiled earl overlooked by the process took rejection badly and Harold was required to lead a force to Wales and put down a mini-rebellion, something he achieved without major bloodshed thanks to his fast-developing astuteness as a tactician. Harold's reliability and favour with the king led to him being involved in the 1057 expedition to bring back Edward Æthling ('man of noble blood'), the winner of this early medieval Monarch Idol, from Hungary, and leading the negotiations with the Hungarian king at Regensburg to bring Edward home. It's also thought that while on this trip Harold, known to be a deeply pious man, escorted the Pope to Rome.

With unfortunate timing Edward Æthling, on his return to England to take up the mantle of the next in line to the throne, died in London before he'd even had the chance to unpack his rucksack and complain about the absence of good goulash, let alone meet the king and start making plans to redecorate the palace. All was not entirely lost to the succession, however, as the late heir had brought his young son Edgar with him.

Harold, meanwhile, was gaining further military experience, leading an expedition to put down the seditious Welsh king Gruffydd ap Llywelyn in 1062. Again showing a strategic brain well ahead of its time, Harold led a lightning-fast raid with just a small cavalry rather than blundering in with a whacking great army, as was the custom. Gruffydd managed to flee just in time, but Harold trashed his palace and lands before, in conjunction with his brother Tostig, leading expeditions to bring Wales firmly under control. The mission was a resounding success.

By 1064 Harold was in a happy position. He was the most influential noble in the land, had no major rivals and had the ear of the king, his own brother-in-law, all the while remaining popular with nobles and commoners alike. During that year, however, came events that would affect the destiny of not just Harold but the country as a whole. We don't know definitely why or even how, but for some reason Harold ended up in Normandy. Norman historians later claimed that it was to confirm Edward's selection of William as his successor, but this is almost certainly untrue. One theory has it that he'd gone to secure the release of two of his relatives, held hostage by William since they accompanied Robert of Jumièges as protection when the disgraced archbishop hot-footed it across the Channel a dozen years earlier. Another possibility is that he was blown there by bad weather, either while out on a fishing trip or on his way somewhere else, while another thought is that he was there to negotiate a politically expedient marriage between a Norman noble and an English bride, possibly even his own sister Aelfgyva. Whatever the provenance of Harold's excursion into the choppy brine of the English Channel, he wound up ashore at Ponthieu, where he was held captive by the delighted local lord probably in the hope of earning a whacking great ransom. When word got back to Duke William as to the identity of the slightly damp and grumpy Englishman languishing in a Ponthieu castle, he pulled rank and had Harold brought to him. Initially William treated him well, even inviting Harold along on a raiding mission against the Bretons. Indeed, Harold, ever the good egg, reportedly saved two men from quicksand single-handedly en route. It was after the raid that William told Harold of his claim to the English throne and insisted that the second most powerful man in England swear an oath to support him. Now, the swearing of oaths in this period of history was deemed binding before God, especially when, as in this case, the oath was sworn on holy relics, but Harold was clearly in a bit of a tight spot.

The Bayeux Tapestry insists that Harold swore support of William's claim in William's presence, and there's little reason to believe that he didn't. He was effectively a captive and must have felt that an oath sworn by force was not a particularly compelling one. In fact, as far as Harold was concerned, the circumstances of the oath rendered it entirely worthless. He also realised that the swearing of the oath was essential if he was ever to get out of Normandy and back to England – his relatives had, after all, been there for a dozen years. Hence Harold placed his hand on the relics, swore his support to William's claim and was then allowed to leave. It would not have been a decision he took lightly: Harold's religious devotion was widely known, and he was himself a vigorous collector of sacred relics (an inventory of Waltham Abbey once noted more than sixty such items donated by Harold). He couldn't pass a shop displaying a withered, wrinkly old saint's finger without dashing inside and buying the thing before the bell over the doorway had stopped tinkling. Given his penchant for long-dead digits and slivers of the true cross, he would have been wholly aware of the implications of the oath and the repercussions of breaking it. But, characteristically, Harold was able to appreciate the wider situation and act accordingly.

William was now certain that the crown would be his: as far as he was concerned, he had Edward's blessing and the support of the most powerful noble in the land, however dubiously that had been attained. The job of King of England was in the bag.

Harold returned to England a worried man. It's unlikely that anyone on the northern side of the Channel had known about William's claim before Harold's apparently chance encounter with the Norman duke, and with no effective heir to Edward's crown Harold wondered with increasing apprehension what might happen if the king died before Edgar was old enough to rule alone. Once news of Edward's death reached Normandy it wouldn't be long before William arrived in town asking about the best place to get some really good cheese and where he should get measured for his crown.

An already eventful year was spiced up again soon afterwards, this time from another direction when the Northumbrians rose up against Harold's brother Tostig, the Earl of Northumbria. As well as levying heavy taxes, Tostig had also had a nobleman named Gamal killed in York, having first granted him safe passage – a huge raspberry to the medieval moral code. Notwithstanding the

Godwineson brothers' knack for clumsily inappropriate murder, Harold went to Northampton to negotiate with the rebel thegns who had declared Tostig an outlaw and replaced him as Earl of Northumbria with Morcar. Harold realised immediately that the strength of feeling against his brother was so great that he could never effectively be returned to power. Also, in the knowledge of William's designs on the throne and the fragile and uncertain nature of what might happen if Edward died at any time in the near future, Harold was determined to avoid any kind of civil conflict. He returned to London and recommended that the rebels' demands be met. Edward, and particularly Tostig, were stunned; it seems that Tostig operated on a very short fuse – to such an extent that he accused Harold of being behind the whole plot against him in order to increase his own influence, something Harold had to swear an oath to deny. However, after his initial surprise Edward came round to Harold's way of thinking and upheld his recommendation. Tostig refused to accept the ruling and was exiled by the king, taking his family to Flanders. It wouldn't be the last they'd hear of him.

It was a brave decision by Harold, not least because of its implications for Northumbria and the country as a whole, but also for his own family. For Godwine, the outlawing and exile of a troublesome son couldn't break the family bond – blood was thicker than politics. For Harold the reverse was true. Once again he had shown that he could see the wider political picture, that bloodshed for the sake of it was pointless and self-defeating. He was prepared to sacrifice even his own flesh and blood, in a powerful family for whom blind loyalty was essential, for the greater good of the nation.

Harold's worries about the immediate succession proved founded. In late 1065 Edward fell rapidly into deteriorating health and Harold began to realise that he was the only effective candidate to succeed him, at least in the short term, should he join the choir invisible. He had shown no previous ambition to rise above his current position but, with a Norman invasion likely and Edward's appointed successor still pushing wooden shapes through holes in the nursery, he was the only logical choice to fill the void that would be left by the death of the old king. He didn't want the throne permanently, it seems, but until Edgar was at least old enough to tie his own shoelaces Harold realised that he was the only one to weather the political typhoon that would inevitably follow Edward's death.

He pressed his case to Edward who, on his deathbed, appointed Harold his successor. Edward the Confessor died on 5 January 1066, less than a week into a year whose events would change England for ever. Harold – however reluctantly, however pragmatically – was now the King of England.

His coronation, the first to take place in a Westminster Abbey not long consecrated by Edward, was on the same day as the old king's funeral. This haste was not unseemly, but practical. Harold was keen to avoid any hiatus of rule that could have allowed unscrupulous folk to pounce on any uncertainty. He also knew that news of Edward's demise would reach Normandy within a couple of days, and it wouldn't be long before William would be setting out to claim what he considered to be rightfully and legally his.

The only dissenting voices within the country came from Northumbria. Perhaps understandably the northern earls feared that Harold would seek to reinstate his brother Tostig, given the Godwinesons' nepotistic background. Another Northampton conference followed, the Northumbrians were assured that they'd seen the last of their erstwhile earl and, without bloodshed again, Harold had the support of the entire nation. He was immediately popular: the historian known as John of Worcester commented that Harold immediately began 'to abolish unjust laws and make good ones and to imprison robbers and disturbers of the kingdom'.

By April 1066 Harold ruled over a largely settled kingdom, albeit one that cast the odd nervous glance in the direction of Normandy, which was ominously quiet. At the end of that month Halley's Comet was visible across much of the country. Such a phenomenon in the heavens was generally regarded as a prophecy of disaster, and with William's designs on the throne now well known there must have been a certain uneasiness throughout the land.

In the short term, though, Harold had to turn his attentions to his errant younger sibling. Tostig was back and raiding the south coast. Harold called out his forces and Tostig retreated almost immediately, having failed to gain the popular support the Godwines had found on their return from exile years earlier. Tostig's actions, however, underlined to Harold the very real threat of cross-Channel invasion, and he set about defending the south coast. The firmness of his rule is demonstrated by the fact that Harold quickly assembled the largest force ever seen in England. He took the threat posed by William so seriously that he moved his administration to the Isle of Wight, while defensive forces were ranged across the entire southern coast, peering nervously into the fog of the Channel for the first signs of Norman ships looming out of the murk.

The early medieval army of this time consisted of two elements. The huscarls were full-time trained soldiers who served their local lords and, by extension, their king. Their numbers were padded out by the fyrd, groups of fighting-age men who received elementary training and who could be called into action at short notice if required. All, or certainly nearly all, of the registered fyrd would have been summoned to Harold's defences along the south coast.

That summer the prevailing winds were almost permanently northerly, a meteorological phenomenon that kept William's ships skulking in Norman harbours. The duke had made preparations to invade as soon as he learned of Harold's succession but the winds kept him at bay and by early September, with no invasion in sight and provisions running low, the men called up to defend the English coast were restless and needed to return to their communities to help bring in the harvest. Harold had little choice but to stand down many of his troops, but he would have done so feeling reasonably confident that the invasion threat had dimmed, albeit temporarily. Now that the summer was nearly over he believed with good reason that the deterioration in the weather towards winter would preclude an invasion until the following spring at the earliest. Having apparently seen off Tostig too, Harold may have allowed himself a period of cautious relaxation.

Tostig had headed north by sea after his hasty backpedal from Sussex. He'd spent the summer in Scotland, nursing his grievances and hardening his resolve to tweak the nose of his treacherous brother. His attention turned across the North Sea to a potential alliance with the King of Norway, Harald Hardråde (or Harold Hardrada), the 'thunderbolt of the north'. A fearsome warrior of terrifying reputation, Harald had spent years gaining control of most of the Scandinavian kingdom, mainly by bashing the hell out of any challengers. He was repeatedly frustrated in his attempts to take Denmark, but may have viewed England as a nifty consolation prize. Harald liked what he heard from Tostig and in the late summer of 1066 put out into the North Sea with a fleet of some three hundred ships, meeting Tostig's considerably smaller force en route and landing at Riccall, some distance inland on the River Ouse. The invaders marched on York and were met by Morcar and Edwin of Northumbria at Fulford on 20 September. Despite a valiant effort by the local forces, after a long, hard (and today almost forgotten) battle the Norsemen emerged victorious and went on to occupy York. By this time word had reached Harold and he quickly assembled a large force, despite the recent disbandment of his army.

Harold arrived in Tadcaster, south-west of York, four days after the Battle of Fulford after a long and rapid route march from London. On setting up camp there he learned that the Norse forces were at Stamford Bridge, to the east of York. The king realised that his best chance of victory, just as he'd realised years earlier when he caught Gruffydd ap Llywelyn largely unawares, lay in the element of surprise. His progress north would have been far quicker than the Vikings expected, and the chances were that they would be completely unprepared for attack. He set off almost immediately for Stamford Bridge.

The Norse army was completely wrong-footed, so much so that most of them had left their chain mail on the ships at Riccall. It's likely that as they lazed around in the autumn sunshine, making squeaking noises by blowing bits of grass and constructing elaborate daisy chains, they wouldn't have even been aware of the English army's impending arrival until they came thundering around the corner. The Scandinavians were ranged across both sides of the river, divided by a wooden bridge. As the English arrived the Vikings stopped holding buttercups under each other's chins and rushed back across the bridge in order to form one hastily unified platoon, pursued by the English army. A later account, possibly apocryphal, tells of one huge lone Norsemen who persistently fought off the English on the bridge, allowing his compatriots time to organise themselves, before being killed by English soldiers who commandeered a coracle and thrust their swords up through the bridge to bring the big man down.

For the English, tired from their lengthy march north, it was a long and hard-fought battle against a fearsome opponent. Medieval battles were usually brief affairs – a couple of hours at most – but it seems this encounter lasted nearly the whole day, until it emerged that Harald and Tostig had been killed and Harold had earned a magnificent victory. The length of the battle belies just how decisive the victory was: of the three hundred-plus ships that arrived at Riccall carrying Norse troops, only twenty-four returned home.

It was Harold's finest achievement. The Vikings never threatened again and would make no further significant incursions into English territory until the advent of flatpack furniture. The events at Hastings just under three weeks later have perhaps unfairly diminished the significance of Stamford Bridge, but it's a battle whose outcome deserves much better recognition than it has today, when the name Stamford Bridge is known only as Chelsea's home ground. Harold had seen off the Viking threat, a threat that had been there for centuries and had cost countless thousands of lives, once and for all. In military terms it was an almost superhuman effort, and was equally a testament to the organisation and efficiency of Harold's administration in this, the fledgling period of his reign.

Today the battlefield is hidden beneath a housing estate on the eastern side of the village of Stamford Bridge. The current bridge stands a few hundred yards upstream of the site of its early medieval counterpart, and there's no direct evidence that a major conflict took place here.

I made my way towards the modern bridge, passing a public toilet block on which three local schoolboys had painted the story of the battle in an impressive pastiche of the Bayeux Tapestry. On a local level at least, the battle has not been forgotten. I continued towards the bridge, passing a community noticeboard strafed with pinholes that advertised a Hallowe'en party and a forthcoming coach trip to Blackpool, crossed the River Derwent and followed the sun's progress west towards York, where Harold had headed after the battle.

Before long the silhouette of York Minster was clearly visible on the horizon, and by the time the sun set fiery orange behind it I was passing through the coolness of its shadow. The next day I set out early and walked the short distance from my guesthouse to the Minster. At that time of the day there were few people around; the silence was respectful and somehow comforting. Two attendants walked past me, their conversation at a volume attainable only by those whose familiarity with the building has long dissipated the need for hushed reverence.

'. . . and there'll be sandwiches and canapés; beer if you don't like gin and tonic.'

I spent a while in the cool silence of the nave thinking about the walk ahead and the man I was following. Having previously associated him, like most people, just with the famous image of a slightly gormless, oddly shaped embroidered image falling backwards with an arrow shaft sticking out of his head, I was seeing a different man emerging from the mists of history, a man of extraordinary gifts and depths. Although most of the current Minster building dates from the thirteenth century, a substantial church has stood here since the middle of the seventh century. It's almost certain that Harold would have prayed here after the Battle of Stamford Bridge. I noticed a black iron rack of tea lights, walked over to it, dropped a coin into the box with a tambourine clatter that echoed around the eaves, picked up a tea light, held it to the flame of one already burning and lit a candle for Harold Godwineson.

That evening I sat in a sixteenth-century pub, a jar of pickled eggs on the bar. As well as praying at the Minster, Harold had come to York to celebrate his victory at Stamford Bridge and rest his weary forces. Within a few days, however, he had received some startling news. On 27 September the winds had shifted northwards. Despite the lateness in the season and the risk of crossing at that time of year, William had still set off across the Channel and landed at Pevensey the following day, before moving on to Hastings and beginning the construction of a castle. William would have known of Harold's absence in the north and would have seen the change in wind direction as a slice of luck, possibly even divinely provided, that couldn't be ignored. It was a terrific opportunity: with Harold otherwise engaged William knew he could land in England unopposed and have time to build defences and raid the surrounding area for supplies. Harold would have choked on his pickled egg. William remained at Hastings for more than two weeks without moving further inland and it seems likely that the news of Harold's startling victory at Stamford Bridge would have reached him and engendered a cautious, nervous defensive strategy.

The news of the Normans' arrival must have been a surprise to the English king, but he seems to have reacted with customary calmness. Almost immediately he gathered up his victorious army and set off south from York, calling up huscarls and fyrd as he went. Again he was able to raise a substantial army at short notice – no small achievement, particularly in a time when communication networks were primitive and the terrain messengers had to cover was pretty rough, even on the roads.

There's no definitive evidence of the exact route Harold took, but as I sat in the pub with a wobbly pink tower of folded Ordnance Survey maps in front of me I thought I'd be able to hazard a pretty decent guess. There is a suggestion that he may have travelled by sea, using the ships left by the defeated Norse at Riccall, but I think this is unlikely for two reasons. First, Harold would have assembled his army as he travelled south. Secondly, the prevailing wind had turned north, enabling William to cross the Channel but making it difficult to navigate long distances south, especially in unfamiliar ships with men who were overwhelmingly soldiers, not sailors.

So it seems likely that he would have travelled by road. Even though they were by then a millennium old, the Roman roads would still have provided the most direct routes. They were hideously dilapidated and would not have made for an easy journey by any means, but Harold needed to travel fast and the old Roman routes were the best option available.

From York there were two choices of road, one leading south-west of the city, one leading south-east, before joining up just north of Lincoln to become what's known as Ermine Street, the main route south. I knew that Harold had stopped at Tadcaster on the way up, which was on the south-westerly branch, and there's every chance that, given the need for speed, Harold would have taken the familiar route and gone back the way he came. Also the south-easterly route would have meant crossing the Humber estuary; it's unlikely Harold would have been game for that. I traced the route on the maps with my finger, drained my drink and headed back through the dark, cobbled streets of York. My journey to Hastings would begin in earnest the following morning, and I needed a good night's sleep before an early start.

As dawn leaked along the horizon I shouldered my rucksack, left the guesthouse and set off into the city, passing through one of the ancient city gates as a gaggle of cyclists in brightly coloured outfits meandered through. I walked up to the Minster, placed the palm of my hand against the stonework for a moment, and set off for Hastings.

I followed the course of the River Ouse for a while, where a stately procession of swans swam languidly alongside me as I passed the sites of the old Terry's chocolate and Rowntree's sweet factories. A barge loomed silently and gracefully out of the morning mist and continued on its way up into the city. I left the suburbs and was soon in the countryside, taking a footpath west at Bishopthorpe and crossing a scarily busy railway line at Copmanthorpe before sitting to rest on a bench by the village's war memorial. It stood on its own little mound where three roads intersect, a simple cross with the dead of the 1914–18 conflict listed on one side of the base, 1939–45 on the other, surrounded by iron railings and with a couple of poppy wreaths from local British Legions propped against the base. As I ran my eye down the list of names it struck me that Harold's army would have been made up of men like this, ordinary lads called up from their communities to serve their country, heading off into the unknown with a sense of duty, excitement and fear, in the knowledge that there was a fair chance they'd never return. History separated the two armies, but the common thread of locality and emotions made them almost inseparable. A millennium may have passed but for the local young men, at times of conflict little had changed other than the style of their uniform and the nature of their weaponry. I felt a small pang of sorrow that Harold's soldiers would never have their names on a memorial like this one. Their names are long forgotten, their lives a mystery, the grief of mothers, wives and sweethearts just as intense no matter how great the distance in years between their losses.

From there I joined the old Roman road known as Ebor Way, the route across the fields laid out by Roman engineers. I walked along the lumpy, uneven track that I'm sure Harold would have thundered along towards Tadcaster, where I arrived in the late afternoon, the smell of mashing, roasting hops from the three breweries that dominate the little town filling the streets.

I headed out of Tadcaster not long after dawn, pausing at the town bridge over the River Wharfe. It's likely that Harold camped here by the river as he had on the way north, and as I looked out at the mist slowly being burned off the water by the strengthening sun I leaned against the bridge and tried to gauge what it must have been like for the English king on the morning he awoke to the same mist on the river, with the same long journey ahead of him.

According to the Bayeux Tapestry and the coins issued during his rule, Harold wore his hair long and sported a fulsome moustache – face furniture that denoted a warrior around the turn of the first millennium. His coinage added a beard, something that may have been associated with a king: Edward the

Confessor, for example, was always portrayed with a beard. The author of the near-contemporary *Vita Eadwardi*, a vital historical document recounting the life of Edward and a valuable record of the times, described Harold as handsome, graceful and strong, also wise, patient, merciful and courageous. Granted, such obsequy in the account doesn't necessarily make it true, but the facts we can glean from Harold's life do seem generally to bear this out. He clearly regarded battle as a last resort, always preferring to find a peaceful path through problems, even, as in the case of the ousting of Tostig from the earldom of Northumbria, at the expense of his own family. He was merciful to the defeated soldiers of Harald Hardråde, allowing them to bury their dead and a safe passage back across the North Sea after Stamford Bridge.

He was a keen sportsman, enjoying hunting and falconry. He is depicted more than once on the Bayeux Tapestry with a bird of prey on his arm, and he is known to have commissioned a hunting lodge in south Wales after ascending to the throne. It was also reported that Harold possessed a number of books about falconry, which suggests that he was educated and literate. He was well travelled, with his excursions to Dublin, Normandy, Germany and probably Rome, and generally seems to have been whatever the early medieval equivalent of a Renaissance man might be. His marriage to Eadgyth Swanneshals appears to have been largely based on love rather than political expediency (he had a second wife Alditha, who had been the wife of Gruffydd ap Llywelyn, whom he married as a political act – apparently Harold's marriage to Eadgyth was never officially recognised by the church, so his political wedding was not seen as bigamous. It seems he remained with Eadgyth, as it was she who identified Harold's mutilated body on the field at Hastings.) I was growing to like Harold a great deal. He may have been a warrior and evidently a brilliant military tactician, but he didn't see war as the only option. He didn't regard diplomacy as a sign of weakness; rather, he saw a more cerebral approach to conflict resolution as the opportunity to avoid unnecessary slaughter.

I tried to imagine how he felt when he awoke at Tadcaster, one day into his journey south. He'd have been confident of defeating William, certainly, but his trip to Normandy would have confirmed that the Normans were a formidable force and Harold would not have been carried away by the victory at Stamford Bridge. He'd have known that he had to keep up the morale of his men. They'd still have been on a high after Stamford Bridge, but another long and gruelling journey with a major conflict at the end lay ahead. Underpinning it all, however, was a king's resolve to protect his throne and his people. He may only have been in the job briefly, but already he was proving to be one of the most successful English monarchs ever, and none of it had been born out of personal ambition. As he lay in his tent while the sun rose behind the Tadcaster trees, Harold was prepared to give his life for his country and for a job for which he had been the only candidate capable of seeing out the coming storms.

I'd not held out much expectation for that day's walk, most of which seemed destined to be spent among the clank and roar of industry. Yet within half a mile of leaving Tadcaster, having watched the yellow disc of the sun rise behind the steaming column above the brewery, I was walking up a hill and into a wooded glade on a gorgeous, hazy, sunny morning with countryside all around me. An elderly man trundled past in an ancient car, waving and smiling at me as he went. As road gave way to track I passed a man with two terriers winding their leads excitedly around his legs as he fed sugar lumps from a paper bag to a horse standing at a gate. A few minutes later, when I'd entered the glade, over the brow of a sharp incline a woman on a beautiful, shiny, steaming, sleek black stallion came towards me. Clouds of breath came snorting from its nostrils and were framed against the hazy golden rays of the sun that filtered through the collage of leaves behind as it made its regal way past me, its rider touching the peak of her hat as we drew level.

The rest of the day was heavy going, mostly alongside the straight Roman length of the A64 in the roadside detritus, among which I found a battered old milestone in the undergrowth. YOR 20 LON 180 it announced with a cold functionality that I found slightly disheartening. When I cut across country towards the end of the afternoon I was startled to look up and see the immense cooling towers – the biggest in Europe, in fact – of the power station at Ferrybridge. Given the flatness of the horizon on my journey thus far, the grey outlines jutting into the sky seemed suddenly disturbing, a man-made middle finger aimed at the natural landscape. Strange as it sounds, I found them quite scary (and if I'd been around in November 1965, when three of them blew over in a gale, my fear would have been justified). They looked unimaginably huge as they thumped into the sky ahead of me. I spent the night in a motel practically in the towers' shadow, their immense and brooding presence penetrating my exhausted dreams.

I was aware of the towers' menace as I headed into the predawn darkness of the following morning. After a mile or so of mashing through the dew-drenched grass of a public footpath I turned to look at them. The first light of the day was almost with us and the towers stood there, red lights marshalling their height, belching steam into the atmosphere. It was a morning heavy with low grey cloud, which merged with the rising mass of steam to give the impression that I was looking at the factory where clouds are made.

The next morning I passed through Doncaster, stopping at a bench close to the racecourse for an egg sandwich and a carton of milk. It was still dark, but the slow procession of horseboxes, and the people crossing the road carrying huge bags of straw, suggested there was a meeting on that day. The lights flickered on in the executive boxes of the grandstand where catering staff stocked fridges and prepared the menu for the day ahead. In front, a weak light spilled over the paddock, where the hopes and fivers of the punters would rest on the silked jockeys urging their snorting steeds around the track, leaving a snowfall of losing betting slips and broken dreams blowing around the concrete steps at the end of the day.

On the other side of the road I passed Belle Vue, the old Doncaster Rovers football ground, apparently in the midst of demolition. I'd been there a decade earlier for the Rovers' last game as a Football League club before relegation. When I arrived from London I'd found the game to be all-ticket and couldn't get in. Now the offices where I'd pleaded unsuccessfully for admission were gone; the old wooden grandstand, the target of a clumsy arson attack by the club's former owner, for which he would be jailed, and where the defeated Rovers players had saluted the fans as they gathered on the pitch in front of them chanting 'Yorkshire', was also gone, now just a pile of rubble and hardcore. I trudged to the top of the heap, roughly where the commissionaire to whom I'd chatted while the game went on inside had stood, immaculate in club tie and blazer, grey hair neatly combed and shoes proudly shiny, and looked out across the overgrown pitch to the cracked old terracing beyond.

I find there's something desperately sad about abandoned football grounds. I don't think there are many places where the dreams and aspirations of so many have been realised or, more usually, dashed. The Saturday afternoon escape from the grind and monotony of the working week, the eleven players in the club's timeless colours playing out the dreams of those watching. I find a definite dignity in football grounds, and when they're abandoned and demolished, like here at Belle Vue, there's a sadness about them. The club itself is thriving now, at a brand new stadium across town, but the sight of the old ground in such a decrepit state was a melancholy one in the milky half-light of the early morning.

I carried on out of Doncaster on to the Great North Road, a once-major artery now replaced by the nearby A1(M) that follows the old Roman route. I stopped at a mobile tea hut in a lay-by and had a welcome cup of hot instant coffee from a polystyrene cup served by Pat, the friendly proprietor, whose immaculately tended moustache betrayed his previous career with the RAF. Standing at the other end of the counter from me was a jowly, white-haired man of a kindly countenance and soft, calm Yorkshire voice that, had I closed my eyes, could have belonged to Foggy from *Last of the Summer Wine*. Both men were well versed in the history of the road and the locality, and Pat was even able to give me pointers on places to stay further on. 'Yes, that's a good, clean place – the owner was in the RAF too,' he'd say from in front of his handwritten notice advertising the range of cheeses available to put into his cheeseburgers: 'Cheddar – Stilton – Red Leicester – Double Gloucester – Wensleydale – Plastic Crap'.

'Have you seen Pat's wall?' asked Foggy while Pat turned to his urn to make a cup of tea for a passing sales rep. He nodded to the rear of the hut, where a dry stone wall about two feet high followed the edge of the gravel of the lay-by, in front of the hedge separating the road from the field behind. 'He's building that all by himself,' said Foggy. 'All from stones he's picked up from the road.'

'Aye,' said Pat, 'and the farmer's pleased because it makes it less likely anyone'll drive into his field.'

I realised that this was the first conversation I'd had in a good long while and so made the most of it, buying another coffee and listening intently to my new friends' tales of the old road. I departed reluctantly, turning down Foggy's kind offer of a lift to Gainsborough, my next destination.

About half a mile further on I found an all-too-common

sight on the roads. Attached to a lamppost on an otherwise unremarkable stretch were some long-dead bunches of flowers, their cellophane flicking in the wind. The ribbons and wrapping were still vibrant, but the flowers had long since withered and drooped brown and dry. A card on one bunch still bore the swirling printed legend 'In Loving Memory of a Dear Son', but the rain had obliterated the handwritten message beneath. On the cellophane of one bunch was a message in marker pen. 'Daniel, miss you, love Benson,' it said, adding, 'Will be very lonely walks now.'

Over the centuries, since before even the Romans came, innumerable journeys of innumerable people had passed this spot. The Great North Road has been both the spine of England and its major artery from deep, deep in the recesses of time. There are Neolithic remains close to the route for most of its length. Roman legions marched up and down it. Within months of Harold's passing along it William's forces did likewise, laying waste to entire towns and communities in the ruthless, murderous 'harrying of the north' that created a divide along the midriff of England that's still evident today. King James travelling south to take up the throne of England; the Duke of Cumberland moving his forces north on a journey that ended with the merciless post-victory murder of Culloden; the mail coaches, the early cars and charabancs. Jes Oakroyd in J. B. Priestley's *The Good Companions* found this stretch particularly thrilling:

At one place they had to slow down a little, and then Mr Oakroyd read the words painted in large black letters on a whitewashed wall. The Great North Road. They were actually going down the Great North Road. He could have shouted. He didn't care what happened after this. He could hear himself telling somebody – Lily it ought to be – all about it. 'Middle o' t'night,' he was saying, 'we got on to t'Great North Road.' Here was another town and the road was cutting through it like a knife through cheese. Doncaster, it was. No trams now; everybody gone to bed, except the lucky ones going down South on the Great North Road.

Journeys of all kinds – domestic, military, political and regal – had passed this spot over the centuries. All but a tiny minority would have noticed nothing more about this stretch than about any other on the long road that forms England's backbone. Yet the flowers were evidence that something awful, something tragic had taken place here, something that would ensure that to a group of family and friends this spot would remain forever tragically significant, written indelibly into their own histories.

I stopped for lunch in a café on an industrial estate at the edge of a small town. In its pomp the place had clearly been a sizeable factory, but today it was home to a range of small businesses, at the heart of which was this tiny café run by two large, jolly women with immaculate matching bouffants and pinnies. I entered the chipboard-panelled room to a scene of pure slapstick. Some plastic cups had fallen behind the chest freezer. A young man in a boiler suit had been press-ganged into retrieving them, a task that was proving surprisingly difficult. The women called out helpful advice laced with innuendo. 'Just grab them and squeeze,' said one, causing the other to collapse in giggles. 'Grab it with both hands,' said the other, prompting a similar response in her colleague. Muffled swearwords emerged from behind the freezer, where the man's top half was entirely hidden, his feet flailing in the air. The innuendoes were relentless, and one of the women laughed so hard she gave herself hiccups. Eventually the cups were retrieved and the man emerged, red-faced and breathless, beneath a chalkboard titled 'Today's Specials'. The board was blank except for the firmly chalked and underlined word 'NOWT'.

I pressed on along a raised dyke next to the appropriately

named River Idle, as it made its glacial, glass-smooth progress beside me. At one point I passed a pair of swans, moving so slowly they barely made a ripple in the water. A few minutes later they suddenly flew past me at head height, their wingtips so close I felt the breeze as they passed. I didn't see another soul for hours, and was surrounded by perfectly flat countryside all the way into Gainsborough. From there I was heading on to Lincoln where, after nearly a hundred miles of walking, I would rest for a day. As I demolished a bowl of pasta in the town-centre pub in which I'd spend the night, half-listening to the conversations around me, I suddenly realised something. The accents. They were totally different from the accents I'd left in Doncaster that morning: they had gravitated from broad Yorkshire to a softer East Midlands sound. Over a distance of twenty miles – during a day's walk – I'd crossed some kind of linguistic boundary. Now that felt like progress.

The route from Gainsborough to Lincoln was a long, flat walk over fairly unspectacular countryside. One footpath did take me right through a chicken coop, but otherwise the terrain was monotonous. It was a murky morning too, and as I walked the back lanes I could hear the distant whine of jet aircraft somewhere in the cloud above. I thought nothing of it until suddenly, as if out of nowhere, five jets flew right over me with an ear-splitting roar and shot up into the clouds. When I'd picked myself and my rucksack out of the hedge into which I had launched myself headlong, I could see the quintet of planes silhouetted against the cloud in the distance, trailing lines of coloured smoke, which was when I realised, as I picked the grass out of my hair, that far from being under a frankly unjustified personal military attack, it was the Red Arrows display team practising. When I checked later to see exactly where they were based I was surprised to learn that the Red Arrows have been going for more than forty years. There have, in fact, been RAF display teams since the 1920s, and I was delighted to learn

that the Red Arrows had succeeded a troupe called the Red
Pelicans. They're based at RAF Scampton, close to where I was
walking, and their training was the reason for their thunderous
parting of my hair.

Scampton has a noble history aside from the Arrows (who
were a hit from the start: a year after their formation they performed in Amman, immediately after which a British company
received an order from Jordan for one million greetings cards
with a picture of the Red Arrows). The Dambusters squadron
was based there and it was from Scampton that they departed
Ruhr-ward on the famous bouncing bomb mission, while during
the Cold War Scampton was home to the Vulcan bomber.

In the afternoon, as the jets continued to muck about in the
clouds above me, I noticed something unfamiliar on the horizon. A hill. It was ages since I'd seen a hill; I almost didn't
recognise it. And on top of the hill was the unmistakable outline
of Lincoln Cathedral. I checked the map – Lincoln was still a
good eight miles away, but the sight of the city on the hill was a
welcome one. I could actually see where I was heading, rather
than facing a persistently flat horizon. The cathedral wouldn't
have been there in Harold's day of course, certainly not in its
present form, but the city would have been a significant point on
his route south and I liked to think he'd have been as pleased to
see it as I was.

Despite the novelty of the hill, as someone used to the skyline
of London the flat, long horizon and big sky of Lincolnshire
came as a welcome contrast. Some regard the fens as dull scenery,
but I'm with Charles Kingsley when he wrote of 'a beauty as of
the sea, of boundless expanse and freedom. Overhead the arch
of heaven spreads more ample than elsewhere, as over the open sea,
and that vastness gave and still gives such cloudbanks, such sun-
rises, such sunsets as can be seen nowhere else within these isles.'
While hill-ranges and mountains tend to present the most popular vistas, for someone like me used to horizons so interrupted

as barely to qualify for the word, the long horizontal between the land and vast skies here was a pleasant sight.

One drawback of the flatness is that distances can be misleading. For a good while Lincoln didn't seem to get any nearer. I checked my pedometer: I was definitely making progress but so, somehow, was the cathedral. They wouldn't be moving Lincoln south today, would they? I was walking along a long, raised, steep-sided dyke and eventually the outskirts of the city became clearly visible. And then I noticed them. The horses. Two of them, in different shades of brown, grazing lazily ahead of me on the path. My approach slowed. The sides of the dyke on which I was now facing this horsey high-noon were too steep to descend without potential injury, so my alternatives were either to retrace my steps a good three miles and find another way, or to try to get past the horses, of which I was inexplicably terrified. I walked forward as nonchalantly as I could, hoping they wouldn't see me and that I could slip by without them noticing, and staring off to the left somewhere in the hope that they'd wonder what I was looking at and I could nip by as they followed my gaze. It would take a bit of nimble dyke-top slaloming, but it might just be possible. Then the light brown horse looked up and saw me. Seconds later, the dark brown one did too. I racked my brains to see if I could recall, while idly surfing the documentary channels, ever noticing any programmes called *Horse Attack!* or *When Gee-Gees Go Nuts*. My experience of horses extended no further than having a prepubescent crush on the Yugoslav girl in the seventies kids' television series *The White Horses* and one ill-advised pony trek in Wales, before which, when the group leader enquired whether anyone had a condition that might prevent them from being able to ride, I'd replied, 'Cowardice' and everyone thought I was joking.

So there I was, facing my equine nemesis on top of a dyke on the outskirts of Lincoln. The two horses, to my cold terror, started plodding towards me. I deduced that the only possible reason they could be heading in my direction was to kill me and eat me, even though deep down I knew horses only ate grass and sugar lumps. Eventually we were just about nose-to-nose. My legs trembled. The light brown one dipped its head and pointedly sniffed my hand. I would later learn that these were clearly calm, domesticated beasts who thought I might have come bearing goodies for them, but to me this action was a decision as to which part of me to eat first. I froze. I didn't move a muscle. This was partly due to sheer paralysing fear, but also because I was sure I'd heard that in the event of being attacked by murderous horses you should make like a statue until they think you're not there and then they'd go away. Or was that bears? Might even have been sharks, come to think of it. In any case, I stayed still for so long I could have painted myself silver and made a fair whack standing on a box in Covent Garden, and it seemed to work. The sniffing ceased, and a couple of clumps of coarse grass seemed a more appetising distraction. Once they'd both looked away I moved gingerly behind them, muttering, 'Hey, yeah, there's a good fella, er, lady, er horse, yeaaaahhhhhh, that's the way, I'll juuuuuuust slip past like thiiiiiiis . . .' in a pathetic tone of voice that I hoped would sound soothing and unthreatening. My impulse was to bolt from the scene as fast as my legs would carry me, but not wanting to antagonise my assailants further I chose instead a steady walk and didn't look back, my ears straining for the sound of impending hoofs that thankfully never came.

My sense of relief was such that the next mile or so just flew by. Eventually my legs stopped trembling, and I celebrated my escape by urinating emphatically into a bush. I walked on along the river-bank towards Lincoln, feeling revitalised and decidedly jolly at my out-thinking of the horses. Half a mile or so later I saw a police-man watching me from the opposite bank. I waved and called a cheery 'Awright, mate?' Instead of responding in kind he looked at me for a moment, before half turning away and whispering something into his radio. That seemed a little odd. A couple of hundred yards further on another policeman looked at me fixedly from the other side of the river before disappearing into the trees. Then it struck me. Although my new outdoors existence (in day-light hours at least) meant that I had little alternative, urinating emphatically into a bush – however remote, however secluded, however far from a fresh water supply – is very likely to be against the law. I was pretty certain I'd made sure I was well out of sight, but maybe the Lincolnshire Constabulary was particularly hot on this topic. Maybe it was Mr Plod's Anti-Wee Weekend. I could see a lock on the river ahead, where the footpath became a towpath, and then my blood ran cold. There, waiting at the end, was a police car, the fluorescent squares on its side panels and lazily rotating blue lights looking even more pronounced after hours of nothing but the green of the landscape and the grey of the sky. Even worse, as I approached I noticed that the end of the path was barred by a line of blue and white tape, bobbing gently in the breeze and bearing the legend POLICE LINE – DO NOT CROSS. Guilty as I felt, I couldn't help wondering if this wasn't a tad over the top for a bit of alfresco widdling. As I approached, a door opened on the far side of the car and a huge policeman unfurled himself from its interior. I'd reached the tape and was obeying its instructions. The policeman gained his full height, placed his cap on his head, made sure it was straight and walked slowly around the car towards me, carrying a clipboard.

'Would you duck under the tape for me, please, sir?' he evenin' all-ed.

I did so, forgetting in my nervous guilt about the massive pack on my back, the top of which completely demolished the tape, sending its ends fluttering to the ground as it looped around my pack.

'Whoops,' I said.

'Can I ask how you got on to the riverbank, sir?'

It was clear that I was bang to rights, and he was saving us all time and trouble by just starting at the beginning rather than detailing my offence first. It was only a matter of time before I'd be cuffed and helped into the back of the car with a firm hand on top of the head.

'I just joined the footpath here,' I said, showing him my route on the map. As he looked at where I pointed I thought I'd better emphasise that I'd had no alternative than to do my business in the open air.

'I had nowhere else to go,' I said in a tone that I thought stayed just the right side of pleadingly whiny.

'I can see that, sir. And there was nobody to stop you walking on to the riverbank at the far end?'

'Er, no,' I said, with the crestfallen realisation that I was destined for a criminal record for the first time in my life. I wasn't sure whether having a wee in the open was a named offence in itself, and a cold creeping sensation went up my spine as the words 'indecent' and 'exposure' floated across my mind somewhere behind the twitching muscle in my temple.

The policeman turned away from me slightly and consulted his clipboard. It may have been just for a couple of seconds, but it seemed like an age as I wondered how I'd explain to people, parents, girlfriend, employers, that I wasn't really a flasher, I'd just needed a wiz in the middle of nowhere. The policeman then murmured something into his radio and straightaway it crackled with a response I couldn't make out. He thought for a moment, nodded to himself and turned back to me. I knew what was coming. I could almost recite it with him. I'd seen enough episodes of *The Bill* to know phrases like 'on suspicion of' and 'may be used in evidence'.

'OK sir,' he began, 'I won't keep you any longer. You won't be able to go back that way I'm afraid.'

I boggled slightly. This wasn't what I'd expected to hear. I'd got away with it? My collar would pass through Lincoln unfelt? My prostate wouldn't be bound over to keep the peace after stern words from the beak? The words came pouring out.

'Oh no that's absolutely fine no problem I wasn't going back that way anyway I'm heading into Lincoln you see I'm walking from York to Hastings just one way no retracing of steps along the riverbank ha ha just following King Harold well he took Ermine Street rather than this riverbank but that's an A road here and too dangerous to walk along mind you it was pretty dangerous back there with those horses I thought they were going to maul me to death and eat my remains I mean should they be loose like that on a public footpath for one thing it could be dangerous you know—'

I drew a great big sucking breath.

'That's . . . fine, sir, have a good day,' he said cautiously, touched the peak of his cap and went back to the car. I carried on along the footpath, the police tape still fluttering around my rucksack, feeling like a condemned man who'd just had his head in the noose only for the trapdoor not to work.

I'd seen from some distance away that Lincoln is on a hill. It's only when you arrive after a twenty-mile walk and have to walk up that hill that you realise just how steep it is. It felt practically vertical. I made the slowest progress of the journey yet, in tiny footsteps as my legs complained bitterly and my nose practically grazed the ground in front of me. Hence by the time I reached the guesthouse I'd booked into I was completely exhausted, not to mention drained by my close encounter of the horse kind and my brush with chokey. I fell on to the bed, groped for the remote control and flicked the television on. The local news was starting with the crashing chords of ominous portent that herald every bulletin in the land.

'Our top story tonight,' said a grey-haired man in suit and tie as the timpani player rose to the occasion. 'Body found in Lincolnshire waterway.' Even in my recumbent state I nearly fell off the bed as the picture cut away to the very police car by which I'd been apprehended and the line of tape that I'd destroyed and dragged all the way here like some crime scene shaman still intact. After the rest of the headlines they handed over to a woman reporter who stood on the spot where I'd bamboozled the policeman with a verbal machine-gunning. The phrases thudded into me, at once blandly familiar from a lifetime of watching news but also given meaning by the fact that I'd been there: '. . . details are sketchy . . . treated as suspicious . . . grim discovery . . . popular beauty spot . . . post-mortem taking place . . .'

It turned out that shortly before I'd arrived on the scene an angler had come across a body floating in the river. The man loomed up on the screen, pale and shaky, saying how he never wanted to see anything like that again as long as he lived. The body hadn't been identified and the circumstances of the man's death weren't clear, but I felt saddened that somewhere in Lincoln that night there was a son, a husband, a brother, a boyfriend who wasn't coming home. Untimely deaths are so common on the news that it's easy, inevitable even, to become immune to their impact. But that night, as I lay in a strange bed in a strange room in a strange city, I couldn't stop thinking about whoever the poor man in the water was. About how there were people somewhere in this town who'd seen the news bulletin and were sitting dry of mouth on the edge of their sofa, kneading their knuckles and wringing their hands, eyes not leaving the clock, waiting and hoping to hear the sound of a key in the door that would never come.

The next morning I headed out to explore the city. In front of the cathedral, on a cobbled square, was what turned out to be the Lincoln Sausage Festival: a range of stalls sending intoxicating smells into the air between the cathedral and the castle – the produce, according to the banners strung over the stalls, of the likes of Peck's Pickles, Lymn Bank Farm, Croft's Apiaries ('Be Healthy, Eat Honey') and John Barclay Rare Breed Meats. It was a scene that struck me as medieval, a scene that dated back hundreds of years on this very spot, with dealers and merchants hauling their wares in from the surrounding areas up the steep slopes to sell to the locals beneath a skyline of cathedral and castle that hadn't changed in more than five hundred years. Lincoln, certainly the centre of Lincoln, is, like York, a town that oozes history from every stone, every brick, every window. There's a real sense of the past without it having become a look-and-point gimmick with touch-screen interactive displays. Lincoln is clearly proud of its heritage and celebrates it with a quiet dignity from which many other places could learn.

Later that day I wandered down the hill and through the main shopping street, commendably kept separate from the beautiful architecture at the top of the hill (John Betjeman, a great fan of Lincolnshire, once described the city as 'ancient on the hill and industrial in the valley'). I lunched in a dark, beamed pub, my fellow patrons being a group of middle-aged men in identical polo shirts that united them as members of an historical transport society. Clearly, by the way one of their number kept calling out things like 'fifteen minutes, boys' and earnestly consulting a piece of printed paper, they were on a pub crawl that had been planned with precision. The oldest member of the group, a thin man with a shaggy grey beard, stood up, picked up his pipe from the table and made his way slowly towards the door.

'Put your coat on, Bob,' said a younger man with a hint of filial concern.

'Why?'

'Cos it's bloody cold out there, Bob, that's why.'

'Oh stop fretting, I won't be out there long.'

The landlord called out from behind the bar: 'There's a garden out the back if you want to smoke. And even if you don't want to smoke, there's still a garden out the back.'

A few minutes later, at a given signal the group drained drinks, pulled on coats, folded up newspapers and made their way out of the door. Just as the door closed behind them Bob came in from the garden, stopped, looked alarmedly at the empty space where his friends had just been and then looked at me with equal alarm. Before I could say anything the door flew open and the man who had advised Bob to wear his coat came dashing back in.

'Bloody hell, Bob, I thought we'd lost you. Come on, hurry up, we're only two pubs down and we're behind already.'

The old boy shuffled towards the door, where his rescuer put an affectionate arm around him, and they disappeared into the Lincoln afternoon, the phrase 'that pipe'll be the bloody death of you' hanging in the air long after the door had banged shut.

Late in the afternoon I headed back up the hill towards the cathedral, passing a newspaper board that yelled 'BODY FOUND IN RIVER' but, to my relief, failed to add 'weak-bladdered horse-botherer sought'. The accumulated fatigue of my walking exertions meant that it was a bit of a struggle and, halfway up, I lumbered into an antique shop for a rest and an aimless poke around. Not being a connoisseur of the antique I didn't expect to find anything much to tickle my fancy among the brass car klaxons and hunting prints, and planned, after getting my breath back, to recommence my ascent. But then, alone in an old umbrella stand between a couple of glass-fronted cabinets of knick-knacks, I saw something that lassoed my attention. It was a walking stick. I'd toyed with the idea of a stick since starting these walks, but didn't much like the glorified ski poles I saw in the outdoors magazines I sometimes bought when I was in the mood for some Gore-Tex porn. If I was going to get a walking pole I wanted it to be a proper one, a wooden one, an old one. I'd tried a shop in York that sold Barbour jackets and flat caps, but when I told the helpful lady inside that I wanted a wooden walking stick but not one with a curved top like, um, ah, Charlie Chaplin's, she told me that it was a thumbstick I was after and I was most likely to find one 'out on the moors somewhere, in one of the villages'.

The stick in front of me now was of a dark wood, almost deep purple in hue. It had a rounded knob on the top and two small sleeves of criss-cross decoration just below. It almost glowered dark in the dimness of the musty old shop. A small tag tied around the top said it was a tribal staff. I pulled it out of the umbrella stand and waggled it about a bit in a manner that I hoped gave the impression of experience in the field of tribal staffage. It was just the right length, just the right weight, and it seemed sturdy enough. The darkness of the wood and the style of the simple carving on the shaft suggested to me that it might be of African origin. I thought back to a highly decorated walking stick my dad owned, all flowery inlaid design. He'd been on a business trip to Zambia in the late sixties and a man at the airport whom he'd never seen before asked him to take it to London, where someone would collect it from him. My dad, the dope, agreed. There was nobody at the other end, and hence in my parents' house for the last forty-odd years has resided a walking stick most likely packed tight with the purest premium-grade heroin.

On my way up the hill, not far from the shop, I'd noticed a plaque on a building that said T. E. Lawrence had stayed there during the war while stationed at a nearby RAF base. The more I regarded the tribal staff, the more convinced I became that its provenance was connected to the travels of the great Lawrence of Arabia. I took it to the counter and unfurled a small roll of notes from my pocket to pay for it. As the shopkeeper took the money I asked if he knew anything about the stick's background. I'd anticipated him gesturing at me to take a seat while he poured us both a whisky, leaned back in his chair and took a deep breath before furnishing me with a tale of heroism and daring, of exploration and triumph, a novella of intrigue that lay behind the staff's crafting somewhere deep in the African continent and its arrival many years later in a dusty Lincoln antiques shop.

'I've no idea, I'm sorry,' he said as he gave me my change.

Someone cleared his throat behind me, a second man whom I'd not noticed before. Maybe he would fill me in on a nightmare sea voyage and a daring escape, all involving my stick and its arrival in the East Midlands.

'Keith brought that in, didn't he?'

Clearly the story behind my new walking accessory was destined to remain a mystery, unless I were to bump into old Tribal Keith at some point in the afternoon. I set off up the hill again, immediately delighted by the assistance the stick gave me. With each passing day I was getting better at this walking lark.

To reach my guesthouse I had to pass through Newport Arch, the only surviving Roman gate in Britain still open to traffic. It straddled the route of Ermine Street too, so it was pretty certain that Harold himself would have passed through, having maybe spent a day in Lincoln assembling huscarls and fyrd from the surrounding countryside. The arch had stood proudly since the third century, unmolested save for an incident in 1964 when a lorry took a big – and expensive – lump out of the ancient masonry.

I set off early the next morning, a Sunday, the day the clocks went back. I walked through the centre of Lincoln again and, as I passed the cathedral in the rinsed light of the early morning, I heard the throwing of bolts and saw the big wooden main door swing open. I couldn't resist a peek inside ahead of the early service. It was a tremendous time to visit. The cathedral was all but deserted; only a few lights were on. It was so quiet that as I looked up into the tower I could hear the wind teasing mysterious creaks and clicks from the ancient stonework and timber. A small central chapel was lit for the early morning service, but I chose instead to sit for a while at the very back of the cathedral. A handful of people passed me, including a woman whose heels made a noisy 'pock-pock-pock' on the flagstones that echoed around the eaves long after she'd taken her seat. Suddenly I was startled from my reverie by a disembodied voice by my left ear telling me that we were all miserable sinners and following this up with messages of a similarly upbeat nature. It seemed that although the service was in central chapel, the priest's sonorous voice was amplified through speakers placed throughout the cathedral. It was an eerie feeling, especially given the content of the message. Within seconds I was out of the door and making for the road to Sleaford, hoping that they wouldn't mind a miserable sinner with a walking stick mooching into their town by the end of the day.

In the square outside the cathedral where the bustle of the sausage festival had been the previous day, my only companion was a man with a Breton fisherman's cap and long grey beard sitting on a bench in the square playing the clarinet. He wasn't busking, just playing gently and quietly to himself on a cool autumn morning before the day had yawned and stretched. I would miss Lincoln.

I spent the morning walking along a ridge south of the city that afforded amazing views across the flat countryside. I could see the dark, churning clouds of a major storm coming from miles away, and donned waterproofs accordingly. About eight miles south of Lincoln the sky went dark enough to unleash a downpour of biblical proportions. Despite this I made good progress, my new walking stick helping me keep up an impressive pace. I'm not sure whether it was affording me extra traction, or whether it was the regular thud against the ground on every fourth step that was providing me with a metronomic pace that wouldn't slow. Either way, it was turning into a successful day's walk. The weather cleared and the sun played splendid optical tricks through breaks in the churning, scudding cloud.

Towards the end of the afternoon I passed a beautiful ochre-stone church close to the wonderfully named Thompson's Bottom, not so much a village as a row of about half a dozen houses, and at the junction of three roads and five tracks. The church really seemed to be in the middle of nowhere: it was a substantial building that looked as though it should belong in a decent-sized village. I poked around in the graveyard for a while, many of whose stones bore the name Griffin. I'd noticed Griffin's Farm on the OS map and guessed that it must have been in the same family for, if the gravestones were anything to go by, at least two hundred years.

It was then I became aware that the sun was setting. It might say a lot for the slower pace of life when you're walking all day that a sunset can take you by surprise, but this was more to do with the change in the clocks that morning. Coming from a permanently lit city I hadn't really realised just how much earlier in the day it would get dark once the clocks went back. I'd been keen to avoid walking in the dark for obvious reasons, but as I sat in the churchyard I became aware that the sun was sinking and I was still a good way short of Sleaford. What made things worse was that the only way to get there was along the A15, which awaited me at the end of the road I was currently on. Already I could see that the cars and lorries racing along it were flicking on their headlights. It followed the Roman road I was sure Harold had taken, and it was sure to be a busy route. I had disturbing flashbacks to my first morning's attempt at following the A-road to Diss. Now I realised that the rest of this day's walking could well be similar, and in the dark. As I reached the junction with the A15 the light was fading quickly. I put my pack down and hooked the rain cover over it. It was bright orange, which would at least make me a little bit more visible. I'd also have to walk with the flow of traffic. The Highway Code recommends that pedestrians face the oncoming traffic, but that side of the road was flanked by a long and deep ditch. The other side had a wider, flatter aspect so although I'd be with the traffic flow I'd at least be a decent distance from the road itself. While the A15 here wasn't a dual carriageway, it was still the main route south from Lincoln and hence very busy, even on a Sunday night.

With at least six miles still to go to Sleaford, my only option as a destination, I was looking at a good three-hour walk, all along a main road with no footpath and in the dark. I don't mind telling you I was scared. Really quite sphincter-constrictingly scared. Yet, with the knowledge that I was in a place where help or relief wouldn't come and that I had no option, it was with a fair sense of determination that I set off as darkness fell in earnest over the unlit road. It was a horrendous journey from the start as the traffic roared past while I picked my way along the bumpy verge. I did have one stroke of luck – on the previous day in Lincoln I had, while browsing in an outdoors shop, bought a small torch on a whim. I held it in my hand, illuminating the patch of ground immediately in front of me; I was careful to keep it pointing downwards so as not to dazzle or distract the passing traffic. The torch meant that I could at least see the holes in the ground and lumps of rock a split-second before falling or smacking into them. My breath came quickly, the fear I was experiencing mining an apparently in-exhaustible supply of adrenalin. I kept going at as fast a pace as possible, grateful for my stick and my torch, both of which had been in my possession for barely twenty-four hours. Even now as I write this, I shudder to think what might have happened if I'd not had them. I'd probably still be out there somewhere. As it was, the terrain of the verge meant that my pace, although steady, wasn't exactly record-breaking. My eyes scanned the horizon for the lights of Sleaford, but I knew it was still hours before they'd appear. The procession of vehicles alongside me was relentless, screaming past me as I struggled on. There was no point in even trying to hitch a lift – the traffic was busy and moving at great speed. They wouldn't even have seen me until they were practically alongside and there were no lay-bys or anywhere to pull in. It was an awful, awful experience and one I never want to repeat. And then something really, really odd happened.

After an hour or so of heart-pumpingly terrifying slog, I suddenly became aware that the traffic had disappeared. There was nothing to be seen in either direction and the sudden silence was as surprising as it was welcome – I could see for a fair distance in both directions and there was no traffic at all. Then, to my amazement, I saw two people in the road. The only light was from my downward-pointing torch and the faint glow of the horizon, so I could only see them in silhouette, but there were definitely two people walking towards me. They were actually in the road on the same side as me, so facing any oncoming traffic that might appear; a man and a woman. I couldn't see their faces, but they looked quite young. He was tall, stocky and appeared to be wearing a T-shirt, she was small, wore her hair in a ponytail and had a jacket folded over her arms. While I was amazed to see anyone out there I was also a little relieved. Seeing other people reassured me a little, just by the fact that I wasn't the only pedestrian on the A15 that night. I'd started to believe that I was the first person ever to walk this stretch, yet here were a couple apparently even worse off than me – at least I was vaguely well equipped. It was a very cold night and I was well wrapped up; my panting, frightened breath came in big clouds. They were just in a T-shirt and a blouse. There must be an explanation for them being out here like this, I thought. Their car must have broken down or something. I expected to see it down the road somewhere, hazard lights winking.

'All right?' I asked as they drew level.

No reaction. Not a flicker. We were a good couple of miles from any kind of house or even turning in either direction; you'd have thought three people in such a similarly tricky predicament would have been pleased to see each other. But they didn't even acknowledge me.

'What are you doing out here?' Again, not a flicker of reaction. They just carried on walking in the road as if I wasn't there, passing within six feet of me.

In the time it took me to walk on a few paces and mutter 'Well, bollocks to you then' to myself, I realised that I had the advantage of a map. I knew that there was nothing in the direction they were going for a good hour's walk at least. If they were going for help they wouldn't find any that way. I turned around to call after them.

Gone. There was no sign of them. It had been barely ten seconds since I'd passed them. The road was completely flat in both directions and there were fields on either side with low hedgerows separating them from the road. There was simply nowhere they could have gone, yet they'd totally vanished. At that point the clouds parted and a big, fat yellow full moon appeared, heaving its way into the sky and illuminating the scene briefly before the clouds joined up again and the traffic resumed with as much ferocity as before. I walked on as the roar of the traffic battered at my eardrums, but the more I thought about it the more confused I became, particularly when I didn't pass any kind of abandoned vehicle all the rest of the way. It just didn't add up. It was a cold night, yet he was in a T-shirt and she had a jacket folded over her arms. It was so cold you could see your breath in clouds. Which is when I realised I hadn't seen theirs. Then there was the fact they didn't acknowledge my presence, even though I'd spoken to them twice. Out there in the dark, on the road with nothing around for miles, they'd not even nodded at me.

Much later, when I got home at the end of the journey, I looked up the A15 on the internet. That part of it on the way to Sleaford turned out to be one of the most haunted stretches of road in Britain. Page after page detailed ghostly experiences precisely where I'd seen those people. In the late 1990s there had even been an entire episode of *This Morning* devoted to it. None of the accounts seemed to tally with what I'd seen (there were frequent tales of motorists seeing a face suddenly looming up in their windscreens out of the darkness and disappearing just before impact, a couple of ghostly horsemen and the usual smattering of Roman soldiers) but it certainly made me wonder. There could well be a perfectly reasonable explanation. I may well have inadvertently embellished the tale in my memory – I was, after all, in a fairly agitated state anyway – but to this day I can't explain what I saw out on the road that night.

It didn't get me any closer to Sleaford either, and I still had a good couple of hours of frightened trudging ahead of me. I was out there for so long that the torch batteries began to fail and the light that saved me from the lumps, clumps and bramble trip-wires began to dim. Eventually, to my immense relief, the lights of a town appeared in the distance, and I can guarantee you right now that nobody, but nobody, has ever been as pleased to see the Sleaford Travelodge as I was.

My route had taken me slightly east of Ermine Street, but I was still following a Roman road south when I left Sleaford the next morning. As far as I could tell it was the most direct route to London so there was still a possibility that Harold passed that way too. By lunchtime I was making good progress towards Bourne and on a pleasant sunny afternoon passed another big church in the middle of nowhere, this time at the convergence of some tracks rather than roads. A man was mowing the church-yard and gave me a friendly wave, and a few hundred yards further along the track I found the most extraordinary thing. There, in the middle of rural Lincolnshire, I found a little piece of Wales. Just off the track, in front of a line of trees was a flat-fronted standing stone, about four feet high. A small border in front of it was crammed with flowers and shrubs, some planted, some laid there by visitors. As I approached I could see there was an oval plaque on it and, to my surprise, most of it was in Welsh. 'GWENLLIAN' it said across the centre, with '*Merch Llywelyn Ein Llew Olaf*' in smaller letters above and the dates 12.6.1282 and 7.6.1337. Beneath the name was an English translation, 'Daughter of Llywelyn, Last Prince of Wales'. In smaller letters around the edge, in English and Welsh, the inscription read, 'Born at Garthcelyn Aber Gwynedd, at 18 months old she was abducted by Edward I and held captive here at Sempringham Abbey for the rest of her life'. Another small plaque nearby said 'In Everlasting Memory – daffodils planted in 1996 by Boston Welsh Society', with another bearing the legend 'Merched Y Wawr', which, I would later learn, is the rough equivalent of a Welsh Women's Institute.

I was intrigued by this small piece of Wales stuck here, far from main roads, in an apparently unremarkable backwater. As for Sempringham Abbey, there appeared to be no sign of it as far as I could see; the OS map gave no clue that there was even a ruin here.

There was a crunching of gravel and a sleek black four-wheel-drive vehicle eased to a halt next to me. A man and a woman got out, stretching and loosening as if they'd reached the end of a long journey. They came and stood next to me at the stone, and for a while none of us said anything.

'Amazing, isn't it?' said the woman eventually. 'Such a tragic story.' Her voice was awed, her accent definitely Welsh.

I had to confess that I had no idea what the stone was for; I'd just been passing. When she told me that she and her husband had driven all the way from Cardiff just to see it I knew that there had to be something special about this place.

'How much do you know about Welsh history?' she asked. Despite having once had a fiercely patriotic Welsh girlfriend, I had to confess that I didn't know much. Patiently she began to explain why there was this little monument to Welshness in the east of England.

'Llywelyn ap Gruffydd had fought hard to become Prince of Wales,' she began. 'He'd had to defeat his own brothers in battle in 1255 and then set about trying to remove the English. Henry III had invaded Gwynedd in 1247, built castles and forced the local lords to kowtow to him. After the battle Llywelyn appointed himself sole ruler of Gwynedd and proclaimed himself Prince in 1258. Henry was fairly amenable to this at first and praised Llywelyn for his restraint, and eventually – in 1267, I think it was – Henry acknowledged him as Prince of Wales. Henry was then succeeded as King of England by Edward I, who wasn't quite as tolerant of Llywelyn's status. But when Llywelyn married Henry's niece Eleanor at Worcester in 1275, Edward gave the bride away and laid on the wedding feast.

'However, it still rankled that Llywelyn had refused to attend his coronation and on five occasions between 1274 and 1279 he had refused to pay homage to the English king when asked. Edward eventually invaded and Llywelyn led a fierce Welsh resistance. Eventually, though, in the winter of 1282 Llywelyn's army suffered a defeat in battle near Builth Wells. Llywelyn was leaving the battle with a handful of followers when they were ambushed and he was killed. When the English realised just who they'd got they cut off Llywelyn's head and sent it to Edward, who had it displayed on a spike at the Tower of London, where it stayed for fifteen years. He's known today as Llywelyn the Last as he was the last Welsh Prince of an independent Wales.'

'But what brings you here?' I asked. 'Why is this place so significant?'

'Well, five months before he died Llywelyn had fathered a daughter, Gwenllian. Eleanor had died in childbirth, so when Llywelyn was killed the baby was orphaned. When she was eighteen months old she was spirited away and brought here, to Sempringham Abbey, as far from Wales and her heritage as possible. The English didn't want her knowing about her background and didn't want the Welsh to have a figurehead to rally behind, so they sent her here to the nuns, where she lived until she was fifty-six. Imagine that: living your whole life not knowing who you are.

'This is such an important place for the Welsh now. She could have been the continuation of our royal bloodline. It's such a terrible thing to do to someone, to take away their birthright, their whole life, yet few people outside Wales know about it. The history books say that the Gwynedd dynasty, the last official independent Welsh royal family, ended with Llywelyn but actually it ended right here, and it's so unfair.'

Her tone was imploring. Her voice was filled with the injustice that echoed down seven hundred years of history. When I explained why I was walking through this part of the Lincolnshire countryside she clutched my forearm, looked pleadlingly into my eyes and said, 'You *have* to write about this. Please write about this. Promise me you'll write about this, that you'll tell her story.'

I promised. She released my arm, wished me luck and they both climbed into the car. Before they pulled away she wound down the window and called out, 'When you walk across that little bridge there, look back at the stone and you'll see,' and with that the car was gone, heading back to Cardiff.

I walked the few yards to the little stone bridge across the stream that ran behind the memorial. When I looked back at the stone I saw what she meant. From that angle it looked exactly like a nun kneeling at prayer.

I spent the rest of the day walking towards Bourne, where I intended to hole up for the night. The walk was uneventful, something for which I was grateful given the tribulations of the previous day, but I was aware that the daylight hours were now short and would only get shorter. I didn't mind leaving in the early morning in darkness, but arriving in darkness and having to find somewhere to stay was a depressing thought. When I arrived in Bourne that night, after an afternoon's walk accompanied by the sound of fighter jets exercising unseen in the clouds above, it had just got dark. It was a decent-sized town and I thought I'd have no problem finding somewhere to stay, yet everywhere I tried was full. Even though I'd been walking for a good while I didn't think my appearance was alarming enough for the curtains to twitch and the 'No Vacancies' signs to go up as I approached the door. After about half a dozen tries, featuring a frosty, indignant response in one pub when my smiley enquiry as to what was going on (meaning what was going on in the town to fill all the beds) was interpreted as the mooting of some Bourne-wide anti-Connelly conspiracy, someone suggested the last place in town, the Angel Hotel, 'although it'll be really pricey'. By this stage it could have required the Koh-i-Noor diamond as a down payment and I would have gone and fetched it, but as it turned out the very swanky Angel did have a room and the extraordinarily helpful receptionist cut me a pretty good rate for the night – unprompted as well, which was even better given that I am such a non-haggler that I'm more likely to ask 'Are you sure that's enough?' when quoted a price than try to beat it down.

I had for once fallen firmly on my aching feet. As I flopped on to the enormous, crisp-sheeted bed while running a bath the size and depth of a small swimming pool, into which I'd emptied every bottle and sachet of shower gel, shampoo and unguent, I reflected on some of the dives and honky-tonks I'd stayed in before this one. It's amazing what you'll put up with when your options are limited and I thought back to some of the stained sheets, lumpy mattresses, freezing rooms (even, in one case, a room whose bed had been left just as the previous occupant had got out of it) and pokey, dribbling showers I'd endured over the lonely weeks so far. That night in Bourne made it all worth it as I slept sounder than on any night of this journey and left in the morning after the fanciest egg on toast I've ever had.

It was another glorious sunny day of unseasonable warmth. So warm was it, in fact, that on one footpath I absent-mindedly looked down at a slight movement that had caught my eye and saw a small green snake at my feet. I reacted with dignity and calm, rocketing up the nearest tree and only staying up there, whimpering, for about three hours. By lunchtime I'd reached the tiny, picture-perfect village of Etton. A series of plaques affixed to a stone plinth commemorated the village's triumphs in the Peterborough and District Best Kept Village competitions of 1974, 1975, 1983 and 1988, and looking around the place I marvelled that there could have been a better-kept village anywhere else over the previous two decades.

A lovely lady greeted me warmly from her front garden and I asked her about the village. She told me that Daniel Defoe's ancestors came from Etton, and that his uncle is buried in the churchyard. It was from Etton that Defoe's father went to London to seek his fortune as a tallow chandler. Even more excitingly, Etton had been home to the UK's longest-living twins, Bob and Mary Bean. Bob lived to be 100 and Mary 105, and there have apparently been Beans in Mary's cottage since Napoleonic times. During the English Civil War Charles I's chaplain, Dr Michael Hudson, was cornered by Cromwellian troops at nearby Woodcroft Castle. He was quite a guy by the sound of things, having already escaped from prison in the Isle of Wight and, most remarkably, from the Tower of London. He was chased on to the roof and over a parapet, only to cling desperately to a gargoyle. Rather uncharitably, the Roundheads loosened his grip by leaning over and chopping off his hands. Even then they had to beat him to death with musket butts as he emerged from the moat with stumps a-spurting. My new friend told me that you can apparently still hear his screams on the anniversary of his gory demise.

This was the kind of place that underlines just what I have in mind when I claim that we are surrounded by history – a passing encounter in a small village and I'd been furnished with a trio of belting local stories. A mile or so further along I was held for a while at a level crossing, where a detailed information board told me that it was along this stretch of track that the *Mallard* set the world speed record for a train – 126mph – in

1938, a record that has never officially been surpassed by a steam locomotive. In 1995 an Intercity 225 hit 154mph on this stretch, a mark that, at the time of writing, still stands. The gates swung open and, believe me, I was looking both ways as I crossed.

Later that day I was heading west, off the Roman road towards the village of Ufford, about six miles outside Peterborough. As I've mentioned before, the custom as set out in the Highway Code is that pedestrians on the roadway should walk facing the oncoming traffic – something I practised even though it's not actually law. However, on occasions road walking with the flow of traffic is the safest option, such as when you're approaching a blind right-hand bend. After several hundred miles of walking, much of it on roads, even a dope like me had developed a pretty good sense of the best place to walk for maximum visibility. Hence, as I approached a right-hand bend where trees were right up against the road, I crossed to the left. Within seconds I sensed a car pulling up alongside me. The passenger window wound down and a female voice said, 'Do you know you're on the wrong side of the road?' I looked across. It was a young woman in a baseball cap, with glasses over a sharp nose and pinched features. 'Eh?' I responded, articulately, given that this was the first human contact I'd had in about eighteen hours. 'You're on the wrong side of the road,' she repeated, her car moving alongside me as I was walking.

'Ah, no, you see—' I began to explain, but she cut me off.

'Don't fucking argue with me, I'm a fucking driving instructor,' she said, jabbing her forefinger at me, her face screwed up in a sudden paroxysm of temper.

'No, listen, there's a right-hand bend . . .'

But she wasn't listening. I was still walking and she was still driving, one hand on the wheel but her other hand and her full attention now on the glove compartment, from which she produced a battered copy of the Highway Code.

'Put that down and watch the road!' I said, aghast, but she was oblivious.

'Put the [I may have used a bad word here, I admit] book down and put your hands back on the wheel!' I yelled with a little more urgency, but she continued to drive while reading out a passage of the Highway Code – presumably the one to do with pedestrians – not even glancing at the road and now beginning to straddle the white line in the middle. If a car shot around the bend now we would both be dead.

I began yelling, pleading with her to put both hands on the wheel and watch the road. Eventually she stopped reading, looked at me for a moment, grimaced and wrenched the wheel to the left, hitting me with the car and almost knocking me on to the verge. With that she went to speed off and I started to run. I can't have exactly looked a threatening sight in her rear mirror, all whiskery, waving my knobbly stick and shouting obscenities. If I'd been wearing a plaid shirt and long johns I'd have looked just like a raging old gold prospector who'd just had his moon-shine stolen again by those darn McGlinchey brothers. To my surprise, she pulled in ahead of me, and in my naivety I thought she might have stopped to see if I was all right. Maybe she'd hit me with the car by accident. I ran up to the still-open passenger window. She looked across at me.

'Do you want to make something of it, you fucking cock?'

'You just hit me with your car!' I replied in what was, I confess, a bit of a high-pitched whine.

'Yeah, and you fucking deserved it too,' came the response from this apparently qualified driving instructor, before she added, bafflingly in the light of recent evidence, 'I'm trying to save your fucking life.'

I repeated the fact that she'd deliberately hit me with her car, which as a method of lifesaving was probably not one recommended by the St John Ambulance, and said I was taking her number and calling the police, only for her to accelerate away with a screech of tyres that would have failed her pupils in a test. I was so busy inventing rude gestures to aim in her wake and

shouting inexcusably uncharitable things about country bump-
kins and the products of cousins marrying that I only got half the
registration number. The wrong half, according to the police
when I reported it the next day. Powerless to wreak legal redress,
I made a mental note that should I ever produce offspring there
is no way they are learning to drive anywhere near Peterborough.

Once I'd parked myself in the frankly wonderful White Hart pub
in Ufford – having first carefully scanned the car park for the
presence of a familiar hatchback, its driver's seat still warmed by
the ire-clenched buttocks of a raging harridan – I related my tale
at the bar to much sympathy from a man whom I chatted to for
a fair while and who turned out to be the son of a man who had
been the rival grocer in nearby Grantham to Alfred Roberts, the
father of Margaret Thatcher.

   In the restaurant I watched my fellow diners in the candlelight: a young couple bringing an ancient relative in for a
birthday meal, with a later whisper to the waitress, 'Can we
have the cake now?' Two women drinking white wine, their frequent glances at the door suggesting they were expecting a third
friend who would never arrive, and a middle-aged couple clink-
ing wine glasses and looking into each other's eyes, oblivious to
everything around them. I had an early night in my four-poster
bed, looking out at the bright starry night and hoping against
hope that somewhere out there, beneath the stars, a rat-faced
psycho with a hatchback in the drive was having a really shitty
night's sleep in a lumpy, cold, lonely bed.

   The next day I headed into Peterborough, a city Harold would
have known well. He was a benefactor of the abbey, and Leofric,
the Abbot of Peterborough, accompanied the king on the Hastings
campaign (only to die, apparently of illness, before reaching the
confrontation). It seems likely, then, that Harold would have at least
spent the night at Peterborough, probably at the abbey itself, and
bolstered his burgeoning forces with local soldiers.

I followed Harold south on another unseasonably warm day, a day rendered even more meteorologically bizarre by the sight of workmen putting up Peterborough's Christmas decorations. I rejoined the route of Ermine Street at Conington, having lain down on the grass using my pack as a pillow and warmed myself in the sunshine near the end of the runway of the local airfield. Several small aircraft took off and landed a matter of feet above me against the background of the deep blue sky before I reluctantly continued on my way. The airfield is now known as Peterborough Airport, but it was the site of a major American airbase during the Second World War. I passed a huge memorial to commemorate the crews that flew from here, an impressive monolith flanked by British and American flags dedicated to the 457th Bomb Group that flew 237 missions from Conington in the later stages of the war, with the loss or imprisonment of 739 men. I sat on a bench for a while and thought about the aerial provenance of the Lincolnshire fens: the OS map littered with the dotted lines of ghost airfields, the constant whine and roar of fighter jets in the sky, and this memorial, with its carpet of acorn husks rummaged by the odd nervous squirrel, a peaceful spot next to the path taken by the English king en route to arguably the most important battle the country had ever seen before the one that was remembered here.

I made good progress along an almost deserted road that ran parallel to the roaring A1(M). As morning became afternoon my rumbling stomach was grateful to follow a sign for a service station that turned out to be one of the more bizarre ones you'll find on British roads. Behind a small petrol garage was a vast, warehouse-sized Indian restaurant, easily the biggest curry house I'd ever seen. I walked in and was led over a little bridge that straddled an indoor pond full of brightly coloured fish, past rows and rows of empty tables until I reached the far end of the building and an area that was absolutely packed with people. At lunchtime. On a weekday. On a near-deserted road. There were whole families seated at tables. On the other side of the apparently endless buffet counter was a long table lined with people, the person at its head being presented with what was presumably some kind of office leaving gift. At the table next to me three salesmen made small talk about mutual acquaintances in the industry, all friendly yet cagey; warily chatty with each other. Where had these people come from? According to the map there wasn't much in the vicinity and the road outside was virtually redundant, yet this cavernous establishment, while not full (the entire population of, say, Switzerland would probably struggle to fill it), was still busy. Fortunately such a mystery didn't affect my appetite, but I left wondering whether it had been some bizarre hallucination. The red stains on my fingertips from a chicken tikka wing, that survived about a week of relentless scrubbing, would remind me it had been very real indeed.

At Huntingdon I booked into an old coaching inn that had once been owned by Oliver Cromwell's grandfather. It was a sprawling Regency-style place where it's rumoured Dick Turpin had stayed on several occasions, and where every year for the last half century they've put on a Shakespeare play in the galleried courtyard. I sat in the bar in the early evening and watched as a group of office workers arrived, their loosened ties and sloped shoulders suggesting it had been a particularly hard day. A portly, awkward-looking man with hair over his collar in a small gesture of mid-life rebellion was clearly the boss, and it had obviously been his idea to take his reluctant underlings out for this, you know, team reward for a bloody good week, yeah?

He arrived, grinning inanely, at the table next to mine where a young, pretty woman from the group had sat down alone. He put her drink in front of her, put his down next to it and in a bizarre attempt to engage with her suddenly shouted 'Booyakasha!' while flicking his fingers in the manner of someone trying to shake a dollop of something unpleasant from their hand. People stopped and looked. 'Aaaaaayyyyy,' he added expansively, and sat down. It was quite the most incredible, ill-advised attempt to be down with the kids that I have ever seen. The girl went the colour of the glass of wine in front of her, at which she now stared intently. From behind the boss, who was beaming at his proof that, boy, did he still have it, one of her male colleagues caught her eye, raised his hand, put the tip of his thumb and forefinger together and moved it slowly up and down.

Cromwell was born in Huntingdon, and the little building where he went to school is now a museum, which I passed in the early morning as I headed out towards Godmanchester. A young Samuel Pepys was also schooled there briefly, and naturally the town has a Samuel Pepys pub complete with a Diary Room, an impressive nod to the town's Pepysian heritage and reference to *Big Brother* all rolled into one.

I left Huntingdon as a market set up in the town square, traders laying out metallic poles with rasping clanks and unloading battered carboard boxes from the backs of vans, their breath clouding in the morning air as they exchanged cheerful banter with each other ahead of a busy day's trading. It was a scene that has been acted out here for centuries. I bought a pork roll from two women high up in a catering trailer that hadn't been there for centuries and became the inadvertent stooge for their affectionate ribbing.

'You'll have to excuse her, she's always miserable first thing.'

'No I'm bloody not, I'm a ray of sunshine compared to you.'

'Take no notice of her, love, she's horrible in the mornings. It's her age.'

'*My* age? You're bloody older than I am.'

'Never mind me, you shouldn't be taking his money before you've given him his roll like that. Do that again and I'm sending you back to the agency.'

Wiping apple sauce from my mouth I crossed the ancient

bridge that connects Huntingdon with the jaw-droppingly gorgeous village of Godmanchester. Well kept and sensitively
restored, it looked at its best here in the early autumn morning,
the frost in the shadows awaiting its turn as the sun eased its way
into every nook. A thin layer of mist hung just above the bluey
grass of shadowed fields and there was barely a ripple on the surface of the Great Ouse as it presented perfect mirror images of
the houses behind. I crossed the river again via the Chinese
bridge, probably Godmanchester's most famous landmark.
Constructed in the then fashionable Chinese style in 1827, it was
believed that the bridge had been built without using a single
nail. Many years ago a local architect apparently sought and
received permission to take the bridge apart to see just how it
had been constructed and, you guessed it, couldn't put it back
together again. Hence a sheepish trip to the ironmonger's was
called for. From the bridge I followed a public footpath over
Portholme, Britain's largest meadow. It had been the original
location of Huntingdon racecourse way back in the eighteenth
century, and once aeroplanes became fashionable Portholme was
a popular spot for early aviators to fire up their machines and
impress the locals. Today, however, there are just a few cows
mooching about the place, none of whom seemed inclined to
race or indulge in any aerobatics. Soon I was joining a golden,
tree-vaulted path along the River Ouse that filtered sunlight
through the branches in dusty rays, the only sounds I heard all
morning being my own breath, the gentle pat of falling leaves
and the mash-mash of my feet through the golden-brown carpet.

I reached Sandy just as it got dark, emerging from the fields
and crossing the railway bridge as an express train shot through
beneath me. I walked towards the town centre along a residen-
tial street, each of whose windows was a snapshot of Saturday
evening domesticity. A man in an armchair cupped a mug of tea
to his chest as the football results filtered through on his television. Two young girls in matching pink pyjamas ran excitedly

out of a room. An elderly woman sat embroidering at the window, paused, put it down on her lap and looked sadly at an empty, threadbare armchair opposite her. A knot of children skipped past me, excitedly discussing whether the fireworks would be before or after the bonfire, while one boy begged an older brother to ring their dad and ask if he could stay out later than usual.

Reaching the main street I fell into a pub in the hope that it did rooms. It didn't, but before long practically the entire staff and clientele had pitched in with advice and suggestions. I sat at the bar phoning various places, the local directory propped up against a beer pump. As I dialled there would be a breathless hush that continued until I'd exchanged pleasantries and enquired after availability. The first few elicited a 'Nothing at all? OK, thanks anyway' from me and a regretful sigh from my audience. Finally I received a positive response and the tension evaporated. I had a long chat with a woman alongside me at the bar. She'd not had a lot of luck. Two hip replacements had left her on crutches, and a string of misfortunes had led to her being made homeless the previous year. After four months – four months! – of living in a cemetery, the local newspaper got hold of the story and within days she'd been provided with a council flat. She was Sandy born and bred, and had married an American serviceman who was now in the States with their daughter. The nods of assent around the place revealed that there were several other wives and ex-wives of US airmen in the place and, reading their expressions, it was fairly easy to deduce who'd picked the good ones and who hadn't.

The woman also told me how Sandy had kept its sense of community, retaining its villagey feel despite the fact that it was, in her words, turning into a bit of a London satellite town. It was then I realised how far south I'd come. On the map, London still seemed a fair way off, but its tentacles were now reaching out to me. I also noticed that the people in the pub spoke with London accents, whereas in Huntingdon that morning the market traders had called out to each other in a distinct East Anglian burr that warmed the morning cold. It wasn't a strong accent by any means, but my walk along the Great Ouse had been enough to see it dissipate and become engulfed in the sound of London.

After a couple of drinks it was with some regret that I left with good wishes and about three different sets of directions ringing in my ears, and my new friend on my arm as I helped her make slow progress across the road to the supermarket – 'Can't be late to get my lottery ticket: I'm due a big slice of luck' – and headed into the Sandy night. I found my bed, apparently the last one in town, in an old coaching inn close to the Great North Road and spent a restful night despite the presence of London looming ahead of me.

I kept heading south, passing through identical towns and villages until I reached Ware, a town I hadn't really expected to be all that interesting but which turned out to be a classic example of how travel and journeys shape a place. Ware sits on one of Britain's oldest roadways, a route that became part of Ermine Street and eventually the Great North Road. It was where Alfred the Great faced down the Vikings nearly two centuries before Harold finally saw them off at Stamford Bridge, and when people began to move around more freely in the late medieval period Ware began to flourish. Nearly every building on the south side of the town was an inn at some point between the fifteenth and eighteenth centuries, and soon Ware developed its own industry as a major centre of malting, to such an extent that the amount of barley coming in and out of the town made the road practically impassable and led to the creation of the world's first turnpike at Wadesmill in 1663 (on the way into Ware I'd found an old milestone reading 'London 21 Wadesmill 2'). The last maltings in the town closed in 1994, bringing to an end six hundred years of continuous business, a trade memorialised in the town by a statue of a defiant-looking malter, one fist against his hip, the other hand resting on the top of his malt shovel.

I left Ware on a cold morning. The heating had broken down in the hotel too, which meant that at breakfast the dining room, most of which was a conservatory, was absolutely freezing. One of the waiting staff pulled back a curtain to reveal a bank of switches that looked like they'd seen service in Dr Frankenstein's laboratory. The waitress cranked down a lever and from just behind me there was a metallic coughing and juddering as an enormous blow heater suspended from the ceiling jolted into life, possibly for the first time since rationing was still in place. It may have been noisy enough to make us feel like we were breakfasting next to an idling motorcycle but it did the trick: if I'd lifted a piece of bread above my head I could have made my own toast, and I finished breakfast just as the hairs on my forearms began to crackle and fizz.

From Ware I followed the course of the River Lea past maltings that were now seeing service as luxury apartments for commuters, and as the distances between towns became notably shorter it was clear that I was almost in London. The Lea towpath provides one of the loveliest approaches into London. Houseboats are moored at the bank and there's little or no traffic noise. The closer you get to the city, the more noise of industry impinges on the rural towpath ambience – mysterious clanking and hammering and the beeping of reversing vehicles from behind stentorian steel fences – but generally it's the only way to arrive in the capital with your hat at a jaunty angle. I would make London by nightfall, but not before calling at the most important location in Harold's life short of the Hastings battlefield.

I reached Waltham Abbey at lunchtime. The town was probably Harold's favourite place, somewhere he could escape the rigours and strains of political life and contemplate his religious devotion in peace. Such was his attachment to Waltham Abbey that it's where he's buried, at least according to legend. He'd been given the Waltham estate as a gift from Edward in the late 1040s. The little church there contained a Holy Cross, a carving of the crucifixion that purportedly had miraculous powers. As we've seen, Harold was a deeply religious man and rebuilt the church on a grander scale in 1064, holding an elaborate consecration ceremony on 3 May of that year, which was conducted by the Archbishop of York and was the focus of eight days of celebration. Edward himself attended, so the new abbey church must have been something quite substantial. Harold spared no expense, filling the building with gold decoration and a sumptuous altar of marble and gold as its centrepiece, and donated a number of items from his prized collection of holy relics.

Harold stopped at Waltham Abbey on his way south to meet William, and it's reported that as he prayed at the altar the canons in the church saw the stone statue of Christ on the cross dip its head towards him. It would be the last time Harold saw his beloved Waltham. After the Battle of Hastings his body would eventually be taken there for burial, with the grave sited in the centre of the nave of the twelfth-century Norman church.

I found the abbey without difficulty in the pleasant centre of the town. It's a small building for an abbey, the size of a substantial but not enormous parish church. I approached the internal door, on which an ancient-looking sign hung. 'Oh God,' it said, 'make the door of this house wide enough to receive all who need human love and heavenly Father's care, and narrow enough to shut out all envy and pride and hate, and its threshold smooth enough to be no stumbling block to children or straying feet, but rugged enough to turn back the tempter's power. Make it thy eternal gateway to the Kingdom of Heaven.'

As someone who'd been thrust into kingship, reluctantly or otherwise, largely as a result of other people's 'envy and pride and hate', Harold was bound to have been attracted by the peace of a church he'd furnished and paid for. If I was ever going to get a tangible feeling for the man I was travelling with, a man I'd already come to admire greatly now I'd been able to put some flesh on the historical bones, it would be here. I took hold of the iron ring, turned it and opened the door. The clack and creak rebounded around the vaulted roof and I walked into the peace of the building itself. There was little of Harold inside the church, but a plaque on the organ revealed that Thomas Tallis, composer of, among other things, *Spem in alium*, probably the closest music has ever come to absolute perfection, had been the organist here. I sat in a pew for a while and until a pair of awed American tourists entered had the place entirely to myself. As there's very little information available about Harold's journey, since lighting the candle for him inside York Minster and imagining him camped at Tadcaster I'd not really felt close to my quarry as I headed south through sun-drenched countryside and a succession of market towns. Here, though, I tried to imagine the king at prayer, placing his considerable and pious faith in his creator, setting his and his nation's destiny firmly in the hands of his God. Harold was an unquestionably brave man and a great leader, with a string of notable military successes behind him, but even he can't have looked ahead to the coming confrontation without butter-flies of apprehension. A few days' travel further south lay the encounter that would define Harold's life and career. Maybe he realised that the battle with William would represent a turning point in English history even without the hindsight we enjoy today. Unlike William, Harold was not after the crown for political gain or personal aggrandisement. He was its custodian, not its owner. Harold had no royal blood in his veins; he was there simply to protect the crown's provenance and heritage. It was probably on that basis that he believed his prayers would be answered.

I walked around the abbey interior to see if I could find his grave. There were some very old tombs, the names of their occupants obscured by the footsteps of hundreds of years, but I felt sure that none of them could be Harold's. The grave of a king, no matter how temporary his reign, would surely have a bit of a song and dance made out of it. Eventually I descended on the gift shop in the crypt and asked the kindly old lady at the till where Harold's grave lay. No wonder I hadn't found it – it was outside. I left the abbey and followed a wooden fingerpost to King Harold's Tomb. It was in the shade of a small tree, paving stones leading to a raised slab with a rough-hewn stone marker at its head. The marker read 'Harold King of England, Obit. 1066'. The slab on the ground in front of it, spotted with tiny, light blue explosions of mildew, confirmed 'this stone marks the position of the high altar, beneath which King Harold is thought to have been buried, 1066'.

On the slab were a spray of winter flowers and an ivy wreath. In front of them lay a small bunch of red carnations, just like at Stamford Bridge, wrapped in muslin. Stones in the ground marked the layout of the church replaced by the current abbey, with Harold's tomb clearly situated just where the high altar, possibly even the gold and marble one Harold had commissioned, had stood. It was a deservedly peaceful spot. I spent a while at the grave, pleased by the presence of the flowers that I wasn't the only one seeking to remember the old king whose bones, sword-chipped by his gruesome end, lay, it seemed, beneath the well-tended turf. I dropped to my haunches, touched the stone and set off again.

I got as far as the Welsh Harp pub adjacent to the abbey grounds, where I called in for lunch. Between its low beams hung pictures of old Tottenham Hotspur players, the Queen and Harold. Two men at a nearby table passed a book between them.

'Is that the new book on the history of Waltham Abbey?' asked a man with a long grey beard at another table, triggering a conversation about the town in times past. They talked of a pub that had recently undergone a major refurbishment.

'I wonder what happened to those lovely old pictures of the town that used to be all over the walls,' said one man.

'Probably went straight in the skip with everything else,' replied the one with the beard. All three fell into a reflective silence.

I began to head away from the abbey and back towards the towpath. I caught sight of Harold's tomb again on the way past and found myself turning back to the town's main square. I passed through the market, with its boxes of batteries on low plastic crates, trays of shrubs and piles of vividly coloured children's clothes, found a florist, bought a bunch of white carnations, took them back to the abbey grounds and laid them on the tomb of one of England's greatest men, whose old bones had lain all but forgotten in the cold Essex ground for a thousand years but whose achievements I was determined to celebrate despite his eventual defeat.

I passed a clutch of superstores that lined the road back to the river, where Harold could have carpeted and furnished the entire abbey on interest-free credit had he waited a millennium, and turned towards London, walking alongside the vast King George's Reservoir that lay behind the steep bank to my left until the London skyline came into view. It wasn't quite as breathtaking as when I'd first seen it on the Boudica walk, but again I realised how far I'd travelled, and also the achievement of Harold marching an entire army from London to York and back again. I'd walked more than 250 miles since leaving an idyllic, sleepy Stamford Bridge, but there was still a fair way to go. Though for one night, at least, I would be able to sleep in my own bed.

Refreshed and laundered I set off, passing through Bloomsbury to Covent Garden and Charing Cross, crossed to the South Bank and followed the Thames past the Royal Festival Hall, the National Theatre and the British Film Institute, the riverside walk at that time of the morning swarming with people on their way to work, the men either immaculately suited or stubbly beneath woolly hats and designer glasses, their takeaway coffees steaming in the chill of the morning. I passed the thumping great presence of the former Bankside power station that houses Tate Modern, directly opposite St Paul's Cathedral on the other side of the river. I passed the historically exact Globe Theatre at Southwark, on the site of an estate once owned by Godwine, and the riverbank where Harold's father had moored his fleet and menaced Edward into rescinding his exile, then HMS *Belfast*, Tower Bridge and, of course, the Tower of London, which was built by William after his victory at Hastings.

Eventually I reached Greenwich, the centre of global time, the regulator of the passing of history. Turning away from the river I headed down through the park to Blackheath and a journey into my own history, for this is the area where I grew up. I passed the old house that served as my local surgery, where the old Irish doctor who'd also been my mother's doctor when she was a child used to ruffle my hair and call me Seamus. I took a detour to the terraced council house where my grandparents lived after they were bombed out of the London docks and placed in prefabricated housing on Blackheath, a quiet corner cul-de-sac where my grandmother had the same neighbours for the forty years she was in that house. It was the house where my mother, aunt and uncle grew up, where enormous family parties took place, and where I used to stay as a small boy, sleeping in the upstairs back bedroom while my grandmother read *Pinocchio* to my sister and me in between yelling downstairs to my grandfather to turn the television down, while he sat in the armchair in which he'd die peacefully in his sleep one night in 1976. I passed the Woolworth's where I'd bought my first-ever record, and the first school I went to, the doors still the same as when I passed through them as a four-year-old. Along a dual carriageway and up a lane, past the house where W. G. Grace spent the final years of his life, and on to the senior school where I'd spent most of my school career successfully underachieving and mooching about with my shirt hanging out and my tie askew. It was maybe even this part of this road – certainly one close to it – on which Geoffrey Chaucer was walking to Eltham with ten pounds to pay the wages of the workmen building Eltham Palace when he was robbed. He returned to London and fetched a replacement tenner, only to be relieved of it by the same rapscallions in exactly the same place.

Before long I was out of suburbia and in the countryside. My boots felt the softer tread of footpaths again rather than the sole-battering relentlessness of the pavement. I stopped for lunch at Pratt's Bottom (stop giggling, they've heard it all before), in a fantastic old pub with board games piled on the window sills and the parish magazine pinned to the noticeboard. A list of landlords dating back to 1575 held my attention. The current landlord came over to join me, telling me that Dick Turpin reputedly used the inn as it was on the main route from London to Hastings. There was no direct Roman road to Hastings from London, so my route-planning had been no more advanced than taking the as-the-crow-flies option as far as possible. The news that this pub in a quiet village in Kent was actually on the erstwhile highway to my destination reassured me that I was in Harold's footsteps.

Eventually I reached Tunbridge Wells, a place about as far removed from the cut, slash and thrust of medieval battle as you could possibly imagine. It's become the last word, or rather two words, in bourgeois tweeness and the home of the fabled letter-writing Disgusted. Certainly the morning I was there it seemed a far cry from the 'rendezvous of fools, buffoons, and praters, cuckolds, whores, citizens, their wives and daughters' that John Wilmot, Earl of Rochester had found there in the seventeenth century. Indeed, so keen is the town to be uncontroversial, they're going to extraordinary lengths. I bought some postcards at the Tourist Information Centre and asked where would be a good place to get a coffee. 'Ooh sorry,' said the woman behind the counter, 'we're not allowed to recommend anywhere.'

Through the window I could see at least three establishments, which I pointed out. The woman nodded encouragingly.

'But you can't recommend any of them?'

'No.'

'Which isn't to say that you wouldn't recommend one or more of them if you had the chance?'

'Oh no, it's not a comment on their suitability or anything, we're just not allowed to recommend one ahead of any other.'

'So if I was to head for, say . . . that one, you wouldn't actively discourage me from going there.'

'Oh no, not at all.'

'So if you're not actively discouraging me from going to that one and I go to that coffee place there, we're agreed that you haven't recommended it and I take full responsibility for the quality of the coffee, the pleasantness or otherwise of the staff, the ambience of the place and the general all-round quality of the coffee purchase and consumption experience in the establishment that I have just identified by a gesture of the hand?'

'Yes. Um, I think so.'

'Great, thanks.'

It turned out to be a particularly good cup of coffee in a particularly pleasant establishment, but I won't say which one it was in case word gets back and my friend at the tourist information place gets put in the stocks for indirectly hinting that she may possibly have recommended it, despite my firm disclaimer to the contrary.

The rest of the day was a wonderful walk through the Kent countryside and into East Sussex until I arrived at Wadhurst. I booked into a magnificent old pub called the Greyhound which I would recommend with some vigour without implying that similar Wadhurst establishments are in any way inferior. It's an ancient place dating back to the turn of the sixteenth century when its first landlord was the magnificently named Ebenezer Cucknow. His wasn't the best name on the roster of former hosts, however. Oh no. Step forward the guv'nor from the 1670s who went by the euphonious appellation of Redfuss Pring.

History adorned the walls of the place. The notorious smugglers the Hawkhurst Gang used the pub as a base in the eighteenth century, while some framed yellowing newspaper cuttings told of a tragedy of more recent times. In January 1956 a Meteor fighter plane crashed in the heart of the village, destroying several buildings in the resulting fireball and killing four people, including the pilot and the navigator. It turned out that the pilot was a young local man who'd only just received his wings. A man in the pub who'd been a boy in the village at the time sighed as he recalled how the theory was that, as the plane was based far from Wadhurst, the youngster had flown low over the village to impress his parents and lost control of it. The dark photographs gave a vivid sense of the destruction that fell upon the village from the sky that day, the jagged walls of buildings and the concerned faces of policemen and rescuers still as pained and poignant half a century on as they were on the day of the tragedy itself.

I woke early the next morning with the slightly melancholy realisation that I was nearly at the end of my journey with Harold. That night I would reach Battle, the end of my walk and the end of Harold's story. It was a long day's walk, that final one into Battle, and I eventually emerged out of the Sussex Weald and walked up a steep hill as the sun set an appropriately sanguine shade of red. I imagined that Harold's journey had by this stage attained an apprehensive air, the hubbub and noise of the soldiers diminishing the nearer the army got to their final destination. I booked into a pub and looked out of the window of my room across the main square to the huge brick gatehouse of Battle Abbey and the battlefield beyond, darkly foreboding in the orange street lights, entirely dominating the small town that had sprung up on its perimeter.

I was woken early the next morning by the sound of a

mournful wind at the window, a low moaning that rose and fell with each lazy gust. Pulling back the curtain revealed a grey forbidding sky over the gatehouse. After breakfast I crossed the square, passing a small farmers' market and men with ladders against lampposts hanging Christmas lights, bought a ticket, passed through the gate and walked out on to the battlefield to the end of my journey.

If you stand with your back to Battle Abbey, the well-maintained ruins of the church commissioned by William on the spot where Harold fell, and look out across the grassy undulations, trees and ponds spread below you, it's impossible to tell that here, on this spot, on this hill, English history changed for ever.

According to the accounts, Harold went into battle hastily, before all his forces had assembled. Some have viewed this as recklessness on his part, but the evidence suggests otherwise. On his enforced stay in Normandy two years earlier Harold would have seen the Normans' military tactics at close hand: how their cavalry would move at speed over a wide area, ravaging and plundering. The land on which the Normans now lay in wait was Harold's land, and he had already received reports of Norman raids on the locality and would have wished to engage William as soon as possible to prevent further incursions. In addition, the Normans' location was advantageous to Harold. They had their backs to the sea, an English fleet was on its way, and with the Saxon army ranged in front of them the Normans were effectively cut off. In numbers the armies were roughly matched, with an estimated seven thousand soldiers on each side, but Harold had reinforcements on the way, by land and sea. William had no such luxury. Hence Harold's haste would have been inspired by a desire to keep the Normans pinned back as close to the coast as possible, containing them until the reinforcements arrived.

When the Normans began to move inland from Hastings,

Harold moved quickly to assemble his men in formation at the top of Senlac Hill, where I stood on that cold, blustery morning. It was a terrific position for the Saxons. Their lofty perch meant that the Norman archers would be rendered nearly impotent – from such a low position their arrows would fall harmlessly short. Also the Norman cavalry and infantry would have to attack up the steep hill, making momentum difficult to gain. Harold had neither reason nor desire to attack; he just needed to hold his position and hence would have had no qualms about going into battle before his full force had assembled.

By around nine o'clock the two armies faced each other across the grassy expanse, the Saxons banging their shields and screaming their warcry of 'Ut! Ut! Ut!' It would have presented an unnerving sight to the Normans at the bottom of the hill. I followed the footpath around the edge of the field to the Norman positions below. The hill looked daunting enough from there, and when you consider that the top of the hill would have been even higher in 1066, its summit having been levelled to construct the enormous abbey, it must have been a dispiriting prospect for the Norman infantrymen. According to legend, William's minstrel, Taillefer, noting the apprehension in the Norman ranks, galloped out into the no man's land between the armies and performed an inspiring ballad that was popular at the time before plunging into the Saxon shield wall and immediately being hacked to death. At this the battle began, with the Normans launching missiles at the English followed by a charge up the hill. The Saxons responded with missiles of their own and the charge faltered. Next, William's knights attacked the English shield wall and their opponents responded by hitting out with their axes. The wall stood firm. The English were comfortably holding out against everything the Normans threw at them, which meant they were winning. Then, around lunchtime, there was a crucial development. A rumour passed along the French lines that William had been killed – the Bayeux Tapestry reports that he removed his helmet in the midst of battle to prove other-wise – causing a phalanx of Breton soldiers on the Norman left wing to break ranks and run back down the hill.

Harold's orders would have been firm. Maintain the shield wall at all times, no matter what. However, the troops at his disposal would not all have been experienced campaigners. Harold would have lost a number of specialist huscarls at Stamford Bridge, and the haste with which he'd assembled his troops at Hastings meant that his trained, full-time soldiers may not have been as well spread among the willing but amateur fyrd as he would have liked. Whatever the reasons, the right flank of the English shield wall broke and set off down the hill in pursuit of their fleeing opponents.

I tried to put myself in the place of an English soldier at that point of the battle. A poorly trained but loyal and enthusiastic member of the fyrd, collected by Harold on his way south from Huntingdon, say, taken out of the monotony of subsistence farming and embraced by the biggest army the nation had ever seen. I've travelled south, listening agape to the vivid, gory tales of the defeat of the Vikings, my anxiety and excitement increasing with each mile travelled. Then, finally, the arrival at Senlac Hill and the end of a nervous, sleepless night before the battle as I watch the sky begin to brighten towards dawn. The dryness of my mouth as I'm given my position in the shield wall, the churning of my stomach as I line up between two of the lads I met on the way south. I look between my shield and my neighbour's to the Normans ranged at the bottom of the hill, this strange, alien force with their odd-looking helmets and their curious language. I see the minstrel disappear into our ranks never to return and feel the first rocks and stones thudding against my shield and dropping to the ground in front of me. As the Normans commence their charge up the hill I'm gripped by fear, a cold nausea in my stomach and bile rising in the back of my throat. Suddenly the monotony of rural life seems appealing again. I think of my wife, the concern and love in her eyes as I left, and for a moment I wish more than anything that I was back there with her. But it soon passes as the adrenalin takes over from the fear and I realise that the feral voice I can hear shrieking 'Ut! Ut! Ut!' is actually mine. I'm now able to see the faces beneath the helmets that race towards me, contorted with rage and passion and howling oaths that I will never understand, as the anxious cries and entreaties of my fellow soldiers to hold firm lads, to trust in God, to repel these invaders fill my ears. It's then I realise that I feel alive like never before. I am part of something, a defender of my land, my king, my God, my way of life. Oh, the stories I'll be able to take back with me once victory is ours. And then the Normans fall upon us, axes are thudding into my shield, and before I know what's happening I'm hitting out with my axe, my new battleaxe that I spent the last week flexing and swinging, buffing and sharpening, getting used to its weight in my hand, and for the first time feeling it hit chain mail and flesh; the cries, the screams, the shouts and the smells, new smells in my nostrils, the smell of fear, of war, of the rancid breath of the man trying to kill me, and I'm swinging my axe and bellowing and striking and slashing, and the lads with me are doing the same, and we're holding firm, we're together, we're fighting as one and God is on our side, and I belong here, I'm a soldier, I'm a real soldier now.

And suddenly, after two or three hours – time that has gone by in a flash; it seems like it can only have been minutes – all of a sudden I notice a change in the timbre of the Norman voices, a weakening of their resolve. The attack is losing its momentum. I can see the Normans glancing at each other and suddenly the thumps against my shield stop. My axe, my blood- and gore-smeared axe, is no longer hitting anything. It's swinging free in the Sussex air and the Normans are running. They've turned their backs and they're running down the hill.

I look at my friend next to me and we laugh, we splutter and shriek with laughter. His eyes are sparkling now while minutes earlier they'd been dark with determination. They're retreating, we've won: we held out just as Harold told us and we won. The adrenalin kicks in again. My friend makes a move forward and it's the only trigger I need. We're away, I'm running down the hill and I'm screaming and I'm hurdling bodies and feeling the snapping of fallen arrows underfoot. Harold told us to keep in formation until victory was ours. And now it is ours, and I'm running with my comrades and my friends and you can hear the laughter and excitement in our cries, the sheer beautiful release as we pursue the vanquished Normans. I swoop low and pick up a discarded battleaxe and now I've got one in each hand and we've nearly caught them and I look back at the hill expecting to see the whole of our army rampaging down with us . . .

But the rest of the ranks were still massed at the top. The Normans hadn't been defeated: a moment of panic among one flank, maybe even a feigned retreat, meant that an inexperienced group of Harold's force broke and charged down the hill towards the very spot where I stood looking upward. The Norman cavalry, seeing what had happened, quickly cut off the rampaging Saxons and hacked every last one of them to pieces. It was a crucial point in the battle, but the majority of Harold's army still stood firm at the top of the hill. It was a blow, and the urge to run to the aid of the stricken men must have been strong in the remaining forces as they saw the carnage below, but all Harold had to do was hold out for the rest of the day. There were further feigned retreats from the Normans, but they had nothing like the impact of the first, and as the long, exhausting battle went into the late afternoon things looked grim for William. Once darkness fell and fighting was no longer possible all would be lost and his claim to the throne would be doomed. Harold's reinforcements would arrive by the following morning and the exhausted Norman soldiers would be routed. William decided to put everything into a desperate, frantic assault.

He marshalled his remaining archers, cavalry and infantry and ordered them into one last push: they were literally fighting for their lives. The cavalry rounded and charged, the infantry gathered for the heave and the archers collected every fallen arrow they could find and launched them at the English forces.

One arrow shot from its bow and whooshed and arced in a parabola into the fading light of the Sussex sky, crossing the setting sun before dipping and falling towards the English ranks where it embedded itself in the eye of the English king as he raced up and down his lines, encouraging, roaring and cajoling. Word soon spread through the English ranks that Harold was dead. Their spirit was broken and so were their lines; the majority fled, pursued through the deepening gloom of the early evening by the invaders. In a stroke of the illest fortune, the battle and the kingdom were lost.

I walked up the battlefield to the ruined abbey, a journey that took me ten minutes. I passed the remaining part of the abbey, the dormitory and latrine, whose size gave an impression of the immensity of the original structure, and crunched across the gravel to a stone slab on the ground, a square of granite that represented the end of my journey. The end of my three hundred-plus miles alongside the man who, in my opinion, deserves to be right up there in the pantheon of great men, a man overlooked by history but whose amazing abilities and far-sighted outlook led him to within a whisker of seeing off the challenge that changed the country for ever.

Nobody knows who shot the fatal arrow – maybe it was even one of the men Harold had hauled out of the quicksand en route to Brittany with William – but whoever it was, as he picked up the missile from the grass, pulled back his bowstring and fired, he could claim to be one of very few individuals who definitively changed history. There have been arguments that the man on the Bayeux Tapestry with the arrow in his eye isn't

Harold, but certainly the king's name is written above him, as it is throughout Harold's representation on the historic artwork, and his battle standard is beside him. The best accounts of the battle tell of Harold being 'laid low by a chance blow'.

While the slab in front of me wouldn't be the exact spot where Harold fell, thanks to the levelling of the hill to construct the abbey, it was still the end of my journey. I approached it slowly, cautiously, reluctantly, as if by avoiding it the outcome of the battle might become different somehow, and dropped to my haunches to read the mildew-flowered inscription. 'The traditional site of the high altar of Battle Abbey founded to commemorate the victory of Duke William on 14 October 1066. The high altar was placed on the spot where King Harold died.'

A gust blew up and made the trees rustle. A wind-borne oak leaf danced into view, hung there for a moment, and dropped gently on to the slab with barely a sound.

Chapter Three

c. 1150: On the trail of Olaf the Dwarf, King of Man

I really should have known, of course. I'd been to the Isle of Man once before, where on a foolish whim I'd thought it would be a really good idea to travel the fabled TT course on a push-bike. It was an occasion when I was not only suffering the after effects of my first and so far only encounter with Cointreau, but was also soon discovering the hard way that the circular course was somehow uphill all the way round. Even I, the least scientifically aware sentient being since we emerged from the primordial stew, knew this defied physics. I also realised the hard way that I was attempting this feat, one that takes you to the most remote and exposed parts of the island, in some of the worst weather Man had seen in years, and that really was saying something. It didn't go well.

I survived – largely by cheating – and my short time on the island made me yearn to come back and explore more of this remarkable place that drips with history and mythology, a place that is frequently and unfairly overlooked outside its own shore-line. It's a quirky, idiosyncratic lump of rock in the Irish Sea, an island community at the very centre of Britain and Ireland yet one that retains a fiercely proud identity, independence and national pride. I mean to say, anywhere Norman Wisdom decides to call home has to be pretty special, doesn't it?

The threads of history weave through everything. Sometimes they get so tangled up you can trip over them. Actually no, you probably can't, but you know what I mean. There are the famous, thumping great A-list aspects of history of course (the causes of the First World War, the French Revolution, Columbus discovering [*sic*] America and so on), but the darker recesses of history, its meandering tributaries, can be equally fascinating, if not more so. Take the history of everyday people, for example. One of the most awe-inspiring places I've ever visited is Ellis Island in New York, in particular the galleried hall where desperate immigrants exhausted and traumatised by a harrowing sea voyage were processed once they'd disembarked. It's immaculate now, the tiled floor polished, the sun streaming through the high windows through which you can see the Statue of Liberty, but it's not hard to imagine it packed with desperate humanity and their battered cardboard suitcases, men in fraying suits and flat caps, women in stained shawls, grubby-cheeked children with bright eyes. Even in its modern, sanitised condition you can feel the apprehension in the air, the hope, the desperation, the fear, all bottled up in an attempt to be polite and deferential to the brusque man with the roster book sitting at the tall desk at the end, this person you'd never seen before and would never see again, who in the space of a few seconds in a noisy, packed, fetid room had the power to decide your future and that of your descendants.

The walls of the Ellis Island complex are covered with pictures of emigrants, none of whose faces we recognise or names we know. I wondered what happened to them, and marvelled at the individual histories caught in the fleeting instant of a camera shutter. They weren't historically famous – there's no Marco Polo of emigration – but each of their stories is worth just as much as that of a monarch; each individual experience has helped shape lives ever since. Every one of those faces had a story to tell.

Similarly, the dark corners of historical geography fascinate me. The places overlooked by the big sweeping themes: communities who could have asked, 'Romans? What Romans?' Such remoteness from the giant traction pull of mega-history does not make their stories any less interesting or worth any less because the Normans didn't conquer them or the Reformation passed them by. Theirs is a different history, a separate thread from the blockbusters, but one that frequently entwines with them, often in a surprising manner. In the case of Britain and Ireland, the Isle of Man seemed to fit this bill perfectly.

But, as I said, I should have known better. It was winter when I arrived on a Euromanx propliner at Ronaldsway airport, and a two-day hike across the island lay ahead of me. Yes it was winter, but two days, how hard could that be? I'd just walked from York to Hastings for heaven's sake, this would be a stroll. And anyway, heh, the weather couldn't be any worse than last time.

From the airport I arrived in the island's main town of Douglas in the chilly dark of the blustery evening to see a newspaper headline board swaying in the breeze and announcing 'GALES LASH ISLAND'.

Bugger.

I'd been extraordinarily lucky with the weather on my journeys so far. I'd wandered through the English countryside for hundreds of miles perspiring and squinting beneath autumnal sunshine, but now, it seemed, my meteorological luck had mooched off somewhere else. Gales. Not just blowing across the island, but *lashing* it. It all sounded so merciless. I tried to look on the bright side, but the only positive I could come up with was that at least I had a woolly hat in my pack. I had to ask myself, what would Olaf have done?

I'd come to the island to follow in the footsteps of a man whom history has to a large extent passed by. A man who didn't have a huge impact on the world or even on the Isle of Man. He was a king all right, but a king whose realm and reign have been parked under a tarpaulin in a historical cul-de-sac for centuries, for it has been decided by others that, in the greater scheme of things, Olaf Godredson, a twelfth-century king of an ancient, forgotten nation, didn't really matter. He didn't win any major battles, execute anyone of note, invade anywhere, define an epoch or even particularly stand out in the roster of Manx monarchs. We don't know much about him at all. Indeed, we don't know much about the Norse kings of Man in general. But I'd come to Man to follow a journey Olaf made, a route that gives a rare tangible link to an obscure and mysterious period of history when this small, oft-ignored island was at the centre of an empire. I'd also come because I quite fancied following in the footsteps of a man who is known, quite brilliantly, to what posterity he's afforded as Olaf the Dwarf.

In its early years the Isle of Man was punted around like an historical football. Everyone had a crack at it: the English, the Scots, the Irish and, most successfully it seems, the Norwegians, all of whom spotted Man's handy position at the exact centre of our islands. As a base for trading and raiding it was ideal, but somehow most people passed the place by: it was unaffected by the rise and fall of both the Romans and the Anglo-Saxons – the only incident of real note was the conversion to Christianity of the bemused locals some time during the fifth or sixth century. By the early ninth century, however, the Norsemen had arrived, bringing with them a new language, interesting ways with seafood, water-based corn milling and some truly brilliant names for kings. The first recorded Norse king of Man, for example, ruling during the 830s, is Kjetil Flat-Nose. If that's not terrific enough, he was a grandson of Grim the Ram. Kjetil's daughter became known as Aud the Extremely Wealthy, who married a Dubliner called Olaf the White, presumably named for the colour he went when he first caught sight of one of Aud's bank statements.

Why didn't we have such tremendous names for our monarchs? After all, Harold's illegitimate nemesis was always known (although probably not to his face) as William the Bastard until we started calling him the more obsequious William the Conqueror. Edward the Confessor was about as controversial as we got, and it's just not good enough. How much more fun would history have been at school if we'd learned about when Charles the Shagger was restored to the English throne after two grim decades under Oliver Miserybollocks? I'd have paid more attention in class if we'd learned about George the Bonkers or Elizabeth the Ginger. Even the most cursory perusal of Norse monarchs throws up some belters. Most people have heard of Erik Bloodaxe, but how about Harald the Ruthless? Or his more sartorially minded descendant, Harald Greycloak? Or another Harald, he of the Broad Shoulders? One can imagine what a meeting between Olaf the Quiet and Sigurd the Talkative might have been like, while the derivation of Gluniarvin of the Iron Knee's name can only be wondered at. Maybe he specialised in irony, and was wrongly transcribed. My favourite Norse monarch has to be Ivar the Boneless, who was apparently so floppy he had to be carried around on a shield. This is possibly a reason why some people think our history is dull: while the Norse were sitting around discussing people's physical quirks or character traits and coming up with thigh-slappers like Sigurd the Fat, we were just sticking Roman numerals on the end of our kings. For goodness' sake, where's the fun in that?

Anyway, the territory Kjetil (pronounced 'Shay-til') Flat-Nose inherited did not just consist of the Isle of Man, it also included most of the Inner and Outer Hebrides, an archipelago nation known as the Kingdom of Sudrey that, although largely forgotten today, boasts the fact that its Tynwald parliament, still meeting on the Isle of Man as it has since the 970s, is the oldest continuous national parliament in the world.

Kjetil of the two-dimensional conk had a nephew Ørlig, who

comes close to peeping over the mainstream historical parapet in that he was educated on the Isle of Man by none other than St Patrick, towards the end of the ninth century. Indeed, when Ørlig decided he wanted to emigrate to Iceland, St Patrick gave him a few things necessary for the starting of a new life abroad, such as the foundations, timber, bell and consecrated earth necessary to build a church when he got there. Ørlig probably thought just some sandwiches and a couple of Björk albums might have been more practical given the long sea journey he was about to make, but he can't have been too ungrateful as when he arrived in Iceland he named the spot where he put ashore Patreksfjørdur in honour of his old teacher (whom the Norse kingmakers might have named Patrick Excess Baggage).

The succession of Norse kings of Sudrey continued relatively uneventfully for the next century and a half or so, the throne rotating between various Olafs and Sigurds of a range of physical aspects, until 1066 when the slender thread of Manx history became entwined with one of the thicker ones. Godred Crovan was one of the few Norsemen to survive the Battle of Stamford Bridge, Harold's finest hour and the departure point of my previous walk. It seems that Godred chose not to return to Norway with his fellow Vikings but instead journeyed to the Isle of Man to visit his cousin Godred Sitryggson. Crovan must have liked what he saw because he returned in 1075 and again shortly afterwards to attack the island with a view to acquiring it for himself. His first two incursions failed, but in 1079 he made a third attempt – an account of which we have, thanks to the document that would be my travelling companion on the Isle of Man and my main link to Olaf the Dwarf.

The *Cronica Regum Mannie et Insularum*, the *Chronicles of the Kings of Man and the Isles*, is a wonderful resource. Written in an ecclesiastical community probably in the mid-thirteenth century, the *Chronicles* detail the history of the Isle of Man for the couple of hundred years after the coming of Godred Crovan. It's no

Book of Kells and it contains much that is inaccurate (some of the dates are askew by as much as twenty years) and much that is probably hearsay bordering on wild speculation, but it's an invaluable chink of light in a period of historical gloom. Without it we might never have known about Godred Crovan and the Battle of Sky Hill in 1079, arguably the biggest and most significant set-to in the history of the island.

Godred, it seems, arrived on the Isle of Man with a substantial force, three hundred of whom he hid 'in a wood which was on the sloping brow of the mountain called Sky Hill', near modern Ramsey in the north of the island. There was no way he was getting caught out unprepared and picking buttercups as he had been at Stamford Bridge. Battle began the next day, and to the locals' dismay the three hundred men suddenly came charging out of the trees. It was the decisive moment, and 'those who were then left begged Godred with pitiful cries to spare them their lives. Moved with compassion and taking pity on their plight . . . he called off his army and forbade them to pursue the enemy further.'

It was a victory that would shape the future of the island and its empire, certainly for the next few hundred years. Godred was the first to set down laws in writing and truly established Sudrey as an independent nation in its own right. It's even likely that he briefly conquered Ireland during his reign. Either way, for all that he bullied his way to the throne Godred Crovan was a visionary king who greatly improved the lot of the island and its people before handing in his pail in 1095.

Three years after that the throne of Sudrey passed to – you'll love this – Magnus Barelegs, named for his favouring of the long kilt, which had to be tucked up in battle to avoid his tripping over its hem at an inopportune moment. One can only sympathise with the poor soldiers whose last sight before shuffling off their mortal coils was of a great big bearded Norseman bearing down on them with a bloodcurdling roar while wearing what appeared to be an enormous nappy. Barelegs, it seems, considered Man to be the best of the Sudrey islands as he became the first king to have his main place of residence there, probably somewhere near Ramsey – the best landing place on the northern side of the island that the Norse ships would approach on arrival.

Barelegs seems to have been a bit of a wag if his treatment of Muircheartach O Briain, King of Ireland, is anything to go by. In the winter of 1100 he was back in Scandinavia helping his compatriots to see off the Swedes when, in the midst of all the fighting, he decided to send his shoes over to Ireland with the order that on Christmas Day the Irish king should demonstrate his subjugation by walking around the royal court with the shoes affixed to his shoulders. What a gas. Naturally the Irish nobles didn't think much of this, but Muircheartach recognised the might of the Norseman and complied with the order, commenting 'if it means King Magnus not destroying a single province of Ireland, I wouldn't just carry his shoes, I'd eat them'.

Clearly to Muircheartach a pair of cheesy plimsolls on the shoulders was preferable to a posse of nappy-wearing Norsemen coming ashore waving axes and shouting angrily about shoes. It appears he did the right thing as historians have speculated since that such was Magnus's prowess as a warrior king – and certainly Muircheartach's gastronomic suggestion seems to indicate he regarded him as pretty fearsome – that had he not been killed fighting in Ulster he might have seen off the Normans altogether, and then how different history might have been.

It was on Magnus's death that the chieftains of the isles sent over to England for the man I was here to follow, Olaf, son of Godred Crovan, better known as Olaf the Dwarf. When you're reading ancient primary texts you have to look between the lines a little to try to gain a more rounded idea of the people and events in question, not least, as in this case, when the writers are describing events that took place more than one hundred years before. And, going beyond the factual but occasionally perky style of the thirteenth-century monk who inscribed this part of the *Chronicles*, I found myself liking Olaf a lot. Maybe it was because he, like me, had been raised in London (in Olaf's case the court of Henry I, son of William the Conqueror, *né* Bastard), and maybe because, also like me, he clearly wasn't blessed vertically. Nobody knows quite how ickle he actually was, but as someone whose inside leg measurement was outstripped by his age earlier than most I was already rooting for the little guy.

Olaf seemed a pleasant contrast to both his father and his predecessor. Not for him the wearing of battle kilts, secreting troops in trees or posting his footwear to all parts of the kingdom. The *Chronicles* describe him as a 'peaceable man' who 'had all the kings of Ireland and Scotland as confederates in such a way that nobody dared disturb the Kingdom of the Isles during his lifetime', as if the Scots said, 'Naebody bothers the wee man, ken?' and the Irish replied, 'Sure, he's a grand little fella all right,' like protective older brothers.

Although he was a religious man, it seems Olaf wasn't a complete drink of water. 'He took a wife called Affrica,' says the *Chronicles*, 'by whom he had Godred and he had many extra wives from whom he begat three sons, namely Reginald, Lagman and Harald, and many daughters, one of whom married Somerled, ruler of Argyll; she was the cause of the collapse of the entire Kingdom of the Isles.'

Dirty dog he may have been – what Manx maiden could resist a chirpy little guy full of tales of London courtly life? – but Olaf founded the abbey of Rushen, close to modern Castletown on the south of the island, the very abbey where years later an ecclesiastical scribe reported sniffily, 'he also granted land and privileges to the churches of the isles and he was devout and enthusiastic in matters of religion and was welcome both to God and men, except that he over-indulged in the domestic vice of kings'.

Other than the odd bit of extra-marital swordsmanship, it

seems Olaf's rule of what appears to be around fifty years didn't trouble the historians further until the account of the king's rather nasty death, more of which later.

I read up on Olaf propping my copy of the *Chronicles* against a ketchup bottle in the incongruous surroundings of an American-style diner close to the seafront in Douglas as the wind rattled the door and sent the dustbins tumbling outside. Each booth was named after a state of the union. I was in Missouri and I looked across at Illinois, reading the basics of the twelfth-century Norse succession beneath framed reproductions of 1950s car adverts while getting to grips with a steak the size of Idaho.

Before heading to Ramsey, where I'd start my walk the next day, I called in to the impressive Manx Museum. Just inside the entrance the Connelly misfortune sirens began to wail – there was a large three-dimensional relief map of the island, and boy, did it make full use of that third dimension. My plan was to follow what's known as the Millennium Way, a trail that leads from Ramsey in the north right down the centre of the island to Castletown in the south. It's a route based upon that taken by the Norse kings of Man when they arrived from their travels at the port at Ramsey and headed down to the royal residence at Rushen. My new friend Olaf the Dwarf was the first of the kings to establish his residence at Rushen, and moved the bishopric from Ramsey down to the new abbey, so he would have been the first to make the trip. I circled the map slowly, lips pursed, the hills and mountains looking challenging even on this scale.

The Manx Museum is a terrific introduction to the history and culture of the island. As well as the usual cases full of coins and arrowheads there are displays about all aspects of Manx life, from the steam packets that brought trippers over from the main-land, to the wartime internment camps – to me, a hitherto unknown facet of Britain at war. German, Austro-Hungarian and Turkish men in Britain were placed in camps on Man during the First World War, while some eight thousand people passed through the Isle of Man's camps during the Second. These included not only German and Italian citizens living in the UK, but also Jewish refugees who had fled the rise of Fascism, and British-based Nazis.

There was a collection of photographs of life in some of the Manx fishing communities around the turn of the twentieth century, which reminded me of one of the reasons why I was making my journeys. A young girl stood outside a cottage. She looked around thirty or so, but given the toughness of island fishing life back then it's likely she was younger. She looked shyly at the camera, but despite her apprehension at this odd box being pointed at her by a complete stranger there was a definite suggestion of a smile tugging at the corners of her mouth and a slightly cheeky, flirtatious look in her dark eyes. The caption described her as 'an unknown woman'. Yes, she may be unknown now to people looking at this picture, but she deserved more than that as an epitaph. Here was a woman who lived a life, who laughed, who cried, who fell in love, had hopes and dreams, some fulfilled, doubtless many not. I could detect a real personality in that photograph as I thought about the people who knew her, friends, lovers, relatives who had memories of her, three-dimensional ones in colour, who knew her laugh, the sound of her voice; yet here she was, summed up as an 'unknown woman'. Like the faces I'd seen in the pictures at Ellis Island, she was someone captured by posterity just for an instant yet discarded by history. For all her achievements, for all the people who might have loved her, for all her descendants whom I might even have passed in the street outside, she was just an unknown woman.

I still had a little time to kill before my bus to Ramsey so popped into a pub close to the bus station, all dark oak and cig-arette smoke (the smoking ban had yet to arrive on the island). Noting my boots, rucksack and waterproofs, a man at the bar asked, 'You been trekking?' Nope, I replied, but I was about to walk the Millennium Way. I noticed a slight widening of his eyes, barely perceptible except to someone as paranoid as me.

'Not a good idea, that,' he said. 'I'd wait until the snow goes.'

I let out a nervous laugh.

'No,' he said, 'seriously, wrong time of year.'

On the other side of me a man turned from the bar with his drinks, having just heard our exchange. He caught my eye, nodded slightly and said, 'Fair play to you, son,' just as members of Scott's Antarctic expedition might have done to Captain Oates when he announced he was going outside for a bit.

It was early evening by the time I got to Ramsey, a quiet harbour town on the northern tip of the island. I stayed in a magnificent guesthouse at the end of a secluded lane, with gold taps on the bath, and spent a cosy night in a comfortable bed beneath reassuringly heavy and crisp bedclothes while the wind rattled the windows and sprayed bullets of rain against the panes.

It was still dark when I left in the morning, splashing through puddles up the lane and back into Ramsey with a steady pat-pat of rain on the hood of my waterproof jacket. Having popped into a supermarket for the water and bananas that I trusted would get me through the day, I walked out of Ramsey as the rain stopped and the sun reluctantly thought about coming up. I passed an old milestone that told me Castletown was twenty-five miles away. I'd toyed with the idea of making the journey in a single day – after all, I'd regularly topped twenty miles on my previous jaunts. But with the shorter daylight hours of winter now upon me I thought I'd take it a bit easier and split the journey over two days. I'd make it as far as Crosby, a little over halfway, by nightfall and finish the walk the next day. I didn't expect it to be too taxing; after all, Olaf did it and he was only little.

Once I'd left the road I commenced a steep, tacking climb, on which I came to a sign commemorating the Battle of Sky Hill.

The trees I was walking through, and that filtered the watery morning sunlight, were descendants of the same trees that concealed Godred's secret three hundred, the winning hand in the battle that shaped the future of the island. As he passed through at the start of his journey south I'm sure Olaf must have known that this was where his father had secured control of the island. Who knows, he may even have deflowered a local maiden to mark the occasion.

I soon left the sea behind and walked across the beautifully bleak, craggy top of the island. Yellow-tinged clouds let through smudges of blue, and the fierce wind blew shimmering ridges of beige across the dry grassland. Ahead of me rose Snaefell, the island's highest peak, but to my relief the route took me around it rather than over it. Thanks, Olaf. I descended to a gorgeous stream, passing a long-abandoned ruined farmhouse, and crossed a small wooden bridge before a near-vertical ascent up a grassy incline brought Snaefell sharply into view; its peak now entirely hidden among low cloud, its flanks sugared with the snow I'd heard about in Douglas the day before. Dark, round circles in the grass betrayed the former locations of shielings, the shepherds' summer shelters, long gone but indelibly marked in the landscape, possibly for ever. It must have been a fairly bleak existence out here all right, with the wind relentless and civilisation far off and only sheep for company.

I crossed a road and descended towards a small river, the infant Sulby that runs out to the sea at Ramsey and which hemmed in the local forces as Godred's army threatened to overwhelm them. I stopped on a packhorse bridge and looked back to the south-western slope of Snaefell. There on the hillside was the strangest thing. A huge circular brick structure, from the edge of which protruded four single walls apparently corresponding to the points of the compass, dominated the hillside. It must have taken some amount of work to put together – it was absolutely massive – but I just couldn't see what it could be. With Man such a centre for mythology and superstition, I wondered whether it could possibly be some kind of landing guide for alien spacecraft. Later, however, I discovered it to be nothing more mysterious than a sheepfold. Or so they say. I'm not convinced.

I spent about an hour travelling the next half mile or so having, for the first time on my travels, come truly unstuck. The route seemed to follow the river, which now babbled and gurgled over a rocky bed between two frighteningly steep coarse grass and rock walls. Even with a map I couldn't tell which side of the river I was supposed to be on. What would have been a helpful waymarker at the bridge lay on the ground. The high sides of the cleft in the rock around me made my map useless, so I took out my compass which all but said, 'Yeah, and what do you expect me to do?' I made a slow, awkward climb up one side and convinced myself that I needed to be on the other. I descended again, my boots slipping on the wet grass and almost sending me tumbling into the river below. Naturally when I reached the other side I was convinced I'd been better off where I started. I descended again, and as I leapt across the river with all the grace and agility of Tommy Cooper attempting a pas de deux I landed awkwardly and sent a searing pain through the knee that had been grumbling at me persistently, that caused me to emit a noise not unlike the one a little terrier makes when you inadvertently step on its paw. Not only that, but my right foot squished up against the end of my boot causing, I would later discover, some grisly damage to the nail of my big toe. I flopped by the riverside and considered my options, the first of which seemed to be that flopping by the riverside might not be such a great idea. My grumbling knee could stiffen up and, given that I was in the middle of precisely nowhere and there was a freezing cold wind throwing its weight around the place, I needed it to be at least pliable in order to get me anywhere. I gingerly stood up on about a square foot of flat ground between the river and the sheer wall next to it. I flexed the knee. It hurt. Luckily the pain in my toe took my mind off it. Then the pain in my knee took my mind off that too, so effectively I was now in no pain at all. Except I was. Oh, I really was.

I waddled around for a bit waiting for the pain to die down and wondered again, what would Olaf have done? Made sure he knew where he was going for a start, and no doubt arranged for a fruity young lady to be there when he arrived. This was no good to me. After a while I crossed the river with a squawk of pain and started picking my way along the bank about halfway up. The grass was wet. The rocks were sharp and often hidden. I had a whacking great rucksack on my back, a sore knee that was seriously threatening to give way altogether, and there was the knowledge that an ill-timed slip would send me tumbling down ten feet of craggy rocks and into the river to the sound-track of a very loud, long and rude word. Add strong, roaring, blustery winds bouncing in all directions and it didn't look good for our hero. Granted, I wasn't in as much of a pickle as, say, Ernest Shackleton had been, but I was certainly failing to see the existence of a funny side. Somehow I made it out, up and over but it was slow, awkward, wincing progress involving a lot of pausing, some heavy breathing and a fair selection of vigorous and imaginative profanities which, given the strength of the wind, might well have offended people as far away as County Antrim. I reached the top, saw a road that I knew crossed the route and started to limp towards it across boggy, tufty ground. I could go no further than about twenty yards without stopping – as well as the pain in my knee and toe I was absolutely knackered, having come up against hills for the first time on my travels. The wind was a relentless roar in my ears as well as another impediment to my already barely perceptible progress, and I was so exhausted I was feeling physically sick. After an age I reached the road and my speed picked up, but only inasmuch as I'd have been neck and neck with a slug rather than dropping behind it. The firmer, flatter ground seemed to appease my knee a little and before long my limp had decreased from that of a pantomime ham to being just mightily pronounced.

I left the road to head across some incredibly muddy fields and away to my left could see Douglas, its lights winking as the day-light began to fade. Darkness fell just as I hobbled into Crosby, cold, sore and deafened by gales. I took the bus along to St John's, as I was staying off route, and hobbled into a pub oppo-site the site of the Manx parliament, the Tynwald, to sit by the fire and warm myself up a bit before taking a taxi up to a warm room, a warm bath and a warm bed at the Glen Helen Inn.

I woke the next morning and was reassured to discover that the sharp pain in my knee had remained at a dull ache all night. I swung my legs out of bed, put my feet on the floor and stood up. The pain barometer stayed at dull ache, which was fine. Had I been at home I would have been falling into a dead swoon and seeking a comely maiden to sit at my bedside and pat the back of my hand while cooing 'there there', but out here, in the wild wilderness of, er, a well-appointed and comfortable inn where within minutes I'd be getting outside a handsome breakfast, things were different. It was a bit of an achy knee. It's not like I'd have to saw my own leg off and dip the stump in a barrel of tar or anything. I'd survive.

After breakfast I took a taxi back to Crosby to the point at which I'd left the route the previous evening. I chatted to the taxi driver about the island and asked what the population was. 'Seventy-five thousand alcoholics clinging to a rock,' he replied in the faintly Scouse accent that prevails on the island. He gave me a sorrowful look as we pulled in at Crosby, because at the precise moment he indicated to pull in the heavens opened, great swathes of rain sweeping down from the hills in translucent grey curtains and battering against the windscreen. I gave him a sorrowful look back, paid up, pushed the door open, grabbed my pack from the back seat and dived into a bus shelter to dig out the waterproofs. It was an unforgiving uphill road to start with, a river of rain streaming down and washing up against the toes of my boots. The rain was falling so hard that the landscape ahead was entirely invisible. I saw a sign loom up out of the deluge, pointing across a field to St Patrick's Chair, a small group of standing stones, two of which are engraved with crosses.

The story goes that St Patrick, between sourcing ecclesiastical building materials for itinerant royal nephews, once preached here. According to local legend, anyone who sits against one of the stones will never suffer fatigue again. Given my exertions of the previous day, not to mention the slow, heavy plodding progress I was currently making, that was a prospect more welcome to me than an invitation to judge the Miss Isle of Man contest would have been to Olaf. I turned off the road and sloshed up a muddy track, sending fantails of yellow sludge up the legs of my waterproof trousers. I passed through several gates, carefully untying and re-tying the coarse wet string holding each one in place, but when I came to the field containing the miraculous stones I found the entrance entirely blocked by sorry-looking, shiny wet cows. I waited for a moment to see if they'd move, but no luck. Then they started to move towards me, which I took as my cue to resign myself to a life of exhaustion and splash back to the road as fast as I could. I trudged on uphill, the rain stinging my face and starting to penetrate even my top-of-the-range waterproofs. Then I finally reached the high point of the climb and there, in the distance, through the rain, I could see Castletown bathed in a pool of watery sunlight. It was still a way off, but having trudged for nearly two days across remote, rocky grassland and a featureless horizon, it was a welcome sight all right. It was probably from this very spot, in fact, that Olaf first saw the place that would become his royal residence and the site of his abbey.

I descended through the small village of St Mark's and into a boggy field, after which I got lost again, traversing the sloping, muddy expanse several times, leaping from muddy clump to muddy clump above the collected brown water. Eventually, inevitably, I found myself straddling two clumps, my momentum going awry. My arms were whirling as I first leaned perilously backwards and then bent forward almost double. Finally I gave in to the pincer movement of gravity and ill fortune and splashed into the muddy lake. The filthy water cascaded over the top of my boots and found its way into every available space. I was freezing, I was lost, I was soaked and I was really dreadfully pissed off. But worse was to come when I found the right path. It ran between a coarse, prickly hedge and a stream, a stream that had burst its banks and flooded the path right up to the hedge for its fifty-yard length. It was the only way through. There was no other option. It crossed my mind to say bollocks to it and just plunge in thigh-deep and wade to the other end, but I still had a good five or six miles to go. I wanted my boots to be given every possible chance to dry, especially now the rain was easing off. Hence I spent the next hour inching along the hedge, spearing the fleshy parts of my fingers on gorse and thorns, snagging my waterproofs with every movement. At one point I noticed the water was shallow enough to see the bottom and it looked firm, like the ribbed sand of a beach at the sea's edge. I put my foot down. It sank into the mud with little resistance. I lunged for a branch and just managed to grab it before I overbalanced. If I hadn't succeeded in catching hold of that branch there's every chance there'd have been just a stream of bubbles and a woolly hat floating on the surface to show I'd ever been there.

I made it eventually. I won't bore you with the details but it involved barbed wire, thorns and yet more loud and inventive swearing. Thoroughly fed up and way behind schedule I made my sorry way across the last couple of fields to the road. Bedraggled, shuffling, muddy up to the thighs and with a gaping tear in my waterproofs just below the heart I must have looked to passing cars like a vagrant. My socks squelched and my clothes were soaked through to the base layer. My mood improved as I

passed along Silver Burn, through a wooded glade in the nervously emerging sunshine, charming little bridges crisscrossing the
stream, and again saw Castletown ahead of me. I followed the
river over the fields and came across a lone derelict house, one
that had clearly been quite something in its day but that now lay
ruined, its roof and windows gone, with just the shell left standing. I peered through the windows and tried to imagine what
life had been like here, picturing who might have lived here,
waking in the morning and seeing the sun rise over the fields
out of the window. Children running in and out of the rooms,
a fire roaring in the grate, a tree in the corner at Christmas. I
walked into Castletown, seeing human beings for the first time
in what felt like a lifetime, beyond caring about my sodden, mud-
splattered, torn-open appearance, and walked right up to the castle
gate, just as Olaf would have done eight hundred and fifty years
earlier. The castle was closed and shuttered for the winter, but I
placed my rain-wrinkled hand against the door and marked the
end of another journey into the past.

I found a room at the George, an old pub that looks out on the
castle. Darkness was beginning to fall and the streetlights were
firing up and flickering on. It was a grey twilight, the only splash
of colour being the floodlit inflatable Santa anchored to the top
of a twenty-foot plinth in the square, his happy grin not even
flickering as the wind battered and pulled him in every direction,
guy ropes singing in the gale.

    As the light faded, gradually removing the definition of the
castle towards silhouette, I hoped that Olaf's stay there had been
a happy and peaceful one. Alas his demise in 1152, within sight
of his father's epic victory at Sky Hill, was far from either. When
I'd peeled off my sodden clothes and distributed them around
every radiator in the place I pulled out my battered, soggy paper-
back copy of the *Chronicles* and found the passage I was looking
for.

The three sons of Harald, Olaf's brother, who had been reared at Dublin, collected together a large throng of men and all the exiles of the king and came to Man demanding that half the entire Kingdom of the Isles be given to them. Now when the king heard that, he replied in his wish to placate them that he would take advice on the matter. And when they had arranged the day and place where council should be held, those most wicked men were talking among themselves of the death of the king. On the appointed day both parties convened at the port called Ramsey. They sat in rows, the king with his men, the conspirators with their men.

Reginald, the middle brother, who was to strike him, was standing apart talking with one of the chieftains. When he was summoned he came to the king, and turning himself as if to salute him he raised his axe into the air and with one blow cut off the king's head.

I felt sad for Olaf. Even when faced with such a serious threat to his rule he chose diplomacy over battle, a course of action that ended up killing him. His horrendous nephews didn't last long, though. Olaf's son Godred sailed from Norway as soon as he heard what had happened to his father, and that spelled the end for Huey, Dewey and Louie.

'Godred therefore came to Man and seized Harald's three sons and in revenge for his father's death he punished them with the death they deserved,' said the *Chronicles*. Godred took over and was to rule for thirty-three years but in that time would lose half the kingdom to his brother-in-law Somerled, leading to a split in Sudrey that fractured the country and would lead, a century hence, to the islands being claimed by Scotland and Man itself being governed by Scottish bailiffs. Bloodshed was minimal – Magnus III, the last Norse king of Man, negotiated a settlement at Dumfries with Alexander III of Scotland that prevented a Scottish fleet ravaging the island – but the Norse era on the island came to an end.

The castle loomed up out of the gloom. It was founded by Somerled, Olaf's son-in-law, but it had been Olaf, the little guy with the pious heart and perky libido, who had established what's now Castletown as the seat of Manx rule. The moon appeared from behind a cloud and lit up the Manx flag strung out straight in the wind, the three-legged symbol on a red background that embodies the spirit and independence of this extraordinary nation.

When I'd returned from the island I realised that the original *Chronicles of the Kings of Man* was in the British Library at St Pancras. It seems that it had been kept at Rushen Abbey until it was closed as part of the dissolution of the monasteries in 1540, whereupon the *Chronicles* came into the hands of George Stanley, the governor of the island at the time. It next turned up in the collection of Roger Dodsworth, an antiquarian married to one of Stanley's descendants – indeed, the only surviving bound copy apparently contains a label stating 'Chronicles of Man from the home of Roger Dodsworth of York, a keen student of antiquity, 1620'. It then passed into the library of the famous antiquarian Sir Robert Cotton and, although his collection was damaged by fire in 1731, survived intact enough to be acquired by the British Museum in 1753, from where it was moved to the new British Library.

I had to see it. Yes, I had my modern copy, now frayed and curly from the soaking on the island and with a brown blob on the cover that, inexplicably, appeared to be curry sauce, but the chance to see the original thirteenth-century document was too good to pass up. Hence one appropriately rainy day I ascended the stairs to the manuscript room of the British Library and asked if it was possible to see the *Chronicles of the Kings of Man*. An elderly librarian with unruly grey hair trailing over his collar advised me that many of the very old and delicate manuscripts were only available to view on microfilm, then disappeared for a moment and came back with a massive ring binder that he placed on the counter between us. He flipped over a series of pages, alighted on one and ran his finger down it.

'Ah,' he said. 'The original is available to view, but you need a letter of introduction to see it.'

Oh.

'But it's not all bad,' he continued, tapping his forefinger on the page. 'There's a note here to say that it's actually being exhibited at the moment, downstairs in the Treasures Gallery. It was only taken down there a fortnight ago, in fact.'

I was a little disappointed that I wouldn't get to turn the pages myself but at least I'd see the original, even if it would be through glass. I knew that the *Chronicles* had been bound together in a volume with a bunch of ecclesiastical records of properties and rents so the chances of it being displayed open at a relevant page were slim, but I descended the stairs and entered the dimly lit Treasures Gallery anyway. It's a room I know well, as I can often be found loitering in there when poring over books in the reading rooms becomes too much. They have some extraordinary things on display: a priceless Shakespeare First Folio; the handwritten manuscript of Hardy's *Tess of the D'Urbervilles*, open at the front page where you can see that the author had originally intended to call it *The Daughter of the D'Urbervilles* but changed his mind, put a line through the first two words and wrote *Tess* over the top. There's Captain Scott's journal, open at the final page where he writes 'I'm sorry I don't think I can write any more. Robert.' Beneath which, in spidery scrawl, are the words 'for God's sake look after our people'.

I walked among the cases until I found the display of illuminated medieval manuscripts. And there, in a case next to the enormous *Anglo-Saxon Chronicle*, was a small leather-bound book, rubbed furry at the corners and blackened at the edges, presumably as a result of the 1731 fire. I'd found it. I peered closely through the glass, misting it with my nostrils. The opened pages were brown and contained closely written lines of Latin in a strong black ink. The first letter of each new paragraph was larger than the rest and, almost eight hundred years after it had been written, still in a vibrant red ink. At the edge of the page was a simple faint outline drawing of a twin-steepled church – the cleric, taking a break from the painstaking close work of his calligraphy or waiting for some more ink, had clearly had a quick doodle in the margin. As I looked closer I noticed that the book had been placed open at the *Chronicles* itself. I had my copy with me, rolled up in my hand, and I leafed through the pages with bramble-scarred fingers, trying to match the eight-centuries-old handwritten Latin in the case with the modern typesetting in front of me. I found the right passage and had to stifle a yelp of disbelief.

The page at which the book lay open began with the sentence *anno m.c.ii olauus filius godredi crouan cepit regnare super omnes insulas*. Which translates as 'in the year 1102 Olaf, son of Godred Crovan, began to rule over all the islands'. Not only had I found the original *Chronicles* on display, not only had a thick book of precious manuscripts been open at the relevant section, but here, displayed in a room full to the eaves with priceless documents, was my guy; the meek yet priapic little fellow whom history had passed by and in whose obscure honour I had schlepped across mountains and been soaked to the skin.

Here was his story. Here, in this most tremendous of rooms in the company of some of the greats of world history and literature in the British nation's most precious trove of knowledge, was little Olaf the Dwarf, King of Man and the Isles. As historical culs-de-sac go, this one had ended at the big mansion on the hill. Nice one, Olaf.

Chapter Four

1403: Owain Glyndwr rises up against the English

I like to think of myself as someone who does his bit for the environment. I put out my recycling every Sunday night. I buy recycled stationery. I got rid of my car. I even started using a brown, woven Budgen's shopping bag despite the fact it flies in the face of the hip young gunslinger image I like to project (daddio) in an effort to cut my plastic bag use. I've tried to make myself as carbon neutral as possible, especially after realising that the amount of air travel I was undertaking meant that I hadn't just popped my own hole in the ozone layer, I'd practically carved my initials into it. Until I started walking everywhere, my carbon footprint was that of a great big clown's shoe. Chinese coal-fired power plants were working around the clock just to keep up with the trail of environmental carnage I was leaving in my wake. I may not yet be a shining light of ecology (with an energy-saving bulb, of course), but even the most well-intentioned amateur environmentalist would leave Machynlleth's Centre for Alternative Technology feeling a little ashamed. Nothing goes to waste there. Just about everything is self-sufficient, from the chickens mooching about and pecking in the dirt to the bio-house made entirely from sustainable or recycled materials.

It's a place that humbles you. An introductory video narrated by Michael Palin, for which you sit on plush seats rescued from an old cinema, compares the history of the earth to a hundred-storey building. If the building from the ground up is the chronology of the history of the earth, says Michael, the industrial revolution is the coat of paint on the ceiling of the one hundredth floor, and in that microscopic amount of time we've given the future of the planet a thorough rogering. As I walked back to the town I felt like flagging down every car on the road and lecturing the driver on the environmental havoc that he or she personally was causing to . . . those lambs, those fluffy lambs over there.

I wasn't in Machynlleth to ease my liberal environmental conscience, however. No, I was there in preparation for my next journey through history, in search of a man who in his native land has reached almost mythical proportions; a man apparently bestowed with magical powers and who fulfilled the prophecies of the ancients, a man who is today at the forefront of the proud resurgence of national pride in a small, fascinating and oft forgotten nation. Machynlleth was the seat of the parliament of Owain Glyndwr, the last Welsh-born Prince of Wales, a man who came closer than anyone to shaking off the yoke of English rule and establishing an independent, free Wales.

I have a real soft spot for Wales and the Welsh. For a tiny country of barely four million souls, assailed for centuries by wave upon wave of cultural and military Anglification, Wales has kept a fierce sense of patriotism and independence. Yet in three-quarters of a millennium the Welsh have never truly been subjugated and for a nation that has been prodded and poked by its neighbours for so long its patriotism is surprisingly non-confrontational. Unlike most national anthems, the Welsh 'Mae Hen Wlad Fy Nhadau' is not all about vanquishing foes and taking up arms against invaders. No, the gist of the Welsh national anthem is a burning desire to preserve Welsh culture, particularly the language. It's quite possibly the most environmentally friendly national anthem there is.

I love the comfort that the Welsh have with their nationality. They're in a curious position – a nation but not a state, with a parliament but somebody else's monarchy yet, as Owain Glyndwr showed, Welshness is more about consciousness than the trappings of state. There's a dignity about the Welsh, with few wilfully ostentatious displays of Welshness, no showboating or posturing, except when the Welsh rugby team beats the English and even then it's about celebration rather than taunting. I love the passion of the Welsh, and there's no greater barometer for that than the fortunes of the national rugby team. When they're winning, the whole country is on cloud nine; when they're losing, the place goes into a collective funk. There's no middle ground with Welsh passion, but at the same time their sense of national pride is always in equilibrium. A map was recently produced by the European Union that somehow completely omitted Wales; there was practically a straight line running from Liverpool to Bristol. Newspaper journalists and camera crews flooded the streets of Cardiff, expecting frothy-mouthed outrage and red-faced, finger-poking indignation. They got nothing of the sort. There was a collective shrug. No one was really bothered. This was not through any forelock-tugging self-effacement, more a comfortable knowledge that Wales is superior to everyone else anyway, so why get exercised because a European bureaucrat has wiped the country from a map?

I was looking forward to my walk among the Welsh on the trail of Owain Glyndwr, and as I sat by the enormous roaring fire in the sprawling old Wynnstay Arms in the centre of Machynlleth I read up on the man who is a national hero in Wales, someone said to be the embodiment of the spirit of Welshness, but who is largely overlooked in the Anglo-biased, written-by-the-victors histories that dominate these islands. Mind you, if it hadn't been for a bit of litigious argy-bargy with a neighbour over a patch of land, Owain may have just remained a run-of-the-mill local noble forgotten by history altogether.

Yet even from the bare facts of his life it's clear that Owain Glyndwr (pronounced Owayn Glun-door, incidentally) was a special guy by anyone's standards. He claimed descent from the last of the Welsh princes, Llywelyn ap Gruffydd, who was defeated by Edward I in 1282 (and the father of Gwenllian whose memorial I had stumbled across while on the trail of Harold). The name by which we know him comes from his vowel-free home estate of Glyndyfrdwy; Owain's real name was Owain ap Gruffydd and as a youngster he became a page at Chirk Castle under the Earl of Arundel. While there he became proficient in English, Latin, French and Welsh and eventually studied at London's Inns of Court before being called to the Bar. In 1385 Owain served in the French wars under Richard II and in the campaign against the Scots under John of Gaunt: a knighthood was bestowed on him, a style he never used. In 1399 England was thrown into turmoil when Henry Bolingbroke overthrew his cousin Richard II and became Henry IV, a move that would indirectly trigger the biggest rising of the Welsh nation in history.

Owain's lands lay close to those of Reynold de Grey, Lord Grey of Ruthin. A strip of land between their estates had long been the source of an ownership dispute and when de Grey took the land by force and evicted the tenants in 1399 Owain appealed to parliament. De Grey, however, was a close confidant of Henry IV and as Owain was so strongly associated with Richard II, de Grey was awarded the disputed lands. Not only that, but Owain was forced to make a number of humiliating concessions to the English lord. The Bishop of St Asaph tried to intervene on the Welshman's behalf, pointing out with great prescience that the affair could spark a revolt by the Welsh, but he was dismissed by parliament who said – with a startling lack of, well, basic common sense – that they couldn't have cared less about such 'bare-footed clowns'.

Later that year Henry began to prepare an invasion of Scotland and sent out word that his nobles, including Owain, should assemble for the coming conflict. As Chief Marcher for the region it was de Grey's job to call up the nobility and gentry in the area, but it seems he deliberately delayed summoning Owain until it was too late. De Grey immediately told Henry that the Welsh noble hadn't shown up, Owain was declared a traitor and his lands were forfeited on the grounds of high treason.

Reynold de Grey was, it seems, an arse of the highest order. Not only that, he was a blindly vindictive arse and he wasn't finished yet. Not content with merely framing Richard's former confidant, he invited Owain to dine with him at Ruthin to discuss the situation. Owain agreed but was, being in possession of more brains than a hollyhock, suspicious and insisted that no more than thirty unarmed men should accompany his host. De Grey agreed, but naturally had no intention of keeping his part of the bargain. As they sat down to dine a substantial military force began to gather outside the castle ready to clatter through the gates and do whatever it was to Owain that de Grey had had in mind. Having expected such underhand jiggery, not to mention a fair bit of pokery, Owain had stationed Iolo Goch, his bard, outside to look out for precisely this kind of thing. On seeing the soldiers emerging from the trees, creeping forward all giggly and shushing each other in the dark, Iolo hurried to the dining room, strummed his harp and sang a warning to Owain in Welsh. De Grey and his cohorts didn't understand the lyrics, allowing Owain to excuse himself from the table and make his escape.

As he and Iolo crashed through the bracken and away into

the night it was clear that some kind of uprising was now inevitable. As an outlaw charged with treason, the only way to reclaim his property was by armed insurrection and, early on 21 September 1400, he led two hundred and fifty men dressed as peasants through the gates of the town surrounding de Grey's castle. On a given signal they threw off their disguises and wrecked the place to such an extent that only three buildings were left intact. They failed to take the castle, but then Owain probably never expected to with such a small and hastily assembled force. He'd certainly given de Grey a bloody nose, with a couple of good digs in the ribs and a sly knee to the goolies for good measure.

The moment his men had thrown off their peasant garb and set about Ruthin there was no going back for Owain, and a rebellious momentum immediately began to build. He moved on to sack the nearby towns of Denbigh, Rhuddlan, Flint and Harwarden but came unstuck when he faced a strong band of English soldiers at Welshpool. His ragged army scattered into the hills and a minor disturbance over a land dispute appeared to be over. In truth, the seeds of a national uprising had begun to sprout.

As far as the English were concerned, Owain had disappeared. Given his status and military record, silence was a bad sign, prompting the English king to lead a substantial army deep into Wales. He encountered barely a whimper of resistance, but the army's subsequent withdrawal caused the first whispers about Owain's magic powers, for on Henry's return to Shrewsbury the heavens opened over his forces and unleashed some of the worst weather in living memory. The army's supplies were either ruined or washed away in swollen rivers, the weather probably causing more damage and destruction than a Welsh army might have done. When a soggy and grumpy Henry finally squelched into the sanctuary of Shrewsbury he immediately confirmed Owain's outlaw status and, in the aftermath of a good, hard Welsh downpour, the rebellion was truly underway.

While Henry and his troops were being washed through the valleys back to England, Owain had made a base in the mountains at Plynlimon, which was central enough to stay within striking distance of most of Wales. At the end of September 1400 Owain fought his first serious battle against a hastily assembled yet numerically superior force close to his mountain base. Despite being outnumbered three to one, the five hundred Welsh troops comfortably saw off the army of English soldiers and Flemish mercenaries. The news of the rising spread throughout Wales and far beyond, and people flocked to the cause from all over. The Welsh nation, subjugated for more than a century since the demise of Llywelyn ap Gruffydd, the last Prince of Wales as an independent country, was rising again: Welsh students at Oxford University left their studies and headed for home where they were joined on the road by Welsh farm labourers filtering from English fields, all fired by resurgent patriotism. Owain capitalised on this latent pride by adopting the standard of Llywelyn alongside his own. He even had spiritual backing: at the end of the thirteenth century, a prophet had foretold that Wales would be a nation once again thanks to a saviour called Owain. Within days of the victory at Plynlimon, Owain was crowned Prince of Wales at Glyndyfrdwy. What had begun as a dispute about land that could have been resolved by bureaucrats had become a widespread national revolt around a charismatic, inspiring leader.

In April of the following year, on All Fools' Day as it happens, Owain's forces captured the important military stronghold of Conwy Castle, using the startlingly advanced guerrilla tactics for which the rebellion was becoming renowned. Owain's cousins Rhys ap Tudur and his brother Gwilym – ancestors of the Tudor family that would eventually accede to the English throne – commanded a daring and brilliantly successful hit squad. On Sunday mornings most of the Conwy garrison would leave the castle to attend church in the town, with just two sentries guarding the castle in their absence. One of the Tudurs' men posed as a carpenter arriving to do some maintenance – a kind of Trojan sawhorse, if you like – and once inside overpowered the sentries. Owain's men poured in to take over the castle, an occupation that would last well into the summer.

By the autumn of 1401 Cardigan, Powys and the whole of north Wales was under Welsh control. Owain had spent the summer mounting lightning attacks on English strongholds, which were remarkable in both their thoroughness and their ruthlessness. At New Radnor the English troops were beheaded and their bodies hung from the ramparts as a statement of the rebellion's intent. When Montgomery Castle held out against attack Owain's forces laid waste to the surrounding town with such ferocity that it wouldn't be rebuilt for two hundred years.

Henry realised he needed to act. For the second time he marched an army into Wales looking for the Welsh leader, or at least to engage an army in battle, and for the second time he was unsuccessful. When he reached Llandovery, a local landowner named Llywelyn ap Gruffydd Fychan said he knew the cave where Owain was hiding and offered to show Henry where it was. The king readily agreed, and they set out into the hills. After five long, weary and entirely unproductive days of wandering the mountains, Llywelyn finally admitted that his two sons were fighting with Owain and Henry realised that he'd been hornswoggled. Henry had him hanged, drawn and quartered in the town square at Llandovery and the Glyndwr cause had a martyr. Remarkably, Henry's withdrawal from Wales was again beset by appalling weather, even snow. Indeed, Henry was lucky to escape with his life when his tent blew down one night; only the fact that he was sleeping in his armour prevented the heavy central pole crushing him to death.

Despite these successes the rebellion stalled slightly at the turn of the year. In November Owain suffered a heavy defeat in an attempt to take Caernarfon Castle, and the following month saw a similarly unsuccessful attack on Harlech. February 1402 brought Halley's Comet back to the skies above Britain and, just as in 1066, it was seen as an omen – a favourable one in Owain's case thanks to the vigorous spin-doctoring of sympathetic fortune tellers. Their soothsaying seemed to be borne out when just weeks later the Welsh forces managed to capture their leader's nemesis, Reynold de Grey, for whom they would secure a massive ransom; they also made him swear an oath never to cross Owain again. By now, however, the insurrection had gone way beyond a bit of personal score-settling. In June the Battle of Bryn Glas saw another heavy defeat for the English, whom some chroniclers claim lost eight thousand men during the fearsome, bloody battle on a Welsh hillside. By the end of the summer Owain had taken the castles at Usk, Caerleon and Newport as well as sacking Cardiff Castle: now the whole of Glamorgan was his and Owain could finally come down from the hills and be a visible leader.

In the summer of 1403 he did just that, leading a triumphal progress down the valley of the River Tywi surfing on a wave of national fervour. It must really have seemed as if Wales had found its saviour and was about to throw off the oppression of English rule once and for all. That summer saw a remarkable flowering of the Welsh nation, with Owain's journey along the Tywi providing its impetus. Hope and expectation blossomed as the Welsh fell into step behind their leader. It was this journey that I was about to follow.

Machynlleth is some distance from the Tywi Valley but it was unquestionably the place to start. It was here that Owain Glyndwr called a Welsh parliament in 1404. Six centuries after Offa's Dyke gave Wales a physical boundary from England, Owain was harnessing every aspect of Welshness he could gather, pulling the myths from the mists in the valleys and turning them into a political and cultural consciousness that had been dormant for generations. Even today Machynlleth feels 'Welsh' in a way that many other towns don't. It's almost as if it's the unofficial capital of the country thanks to its connection to Glyndwr. The Welsh language is spoken here more than in most towns and cities in Wales – in 1888 Beatrix Potter wrote in her diary: 'Machynlleth: wretched town, hardly a person could speak English.' The parliament building is there in the high street, although it dates from after the time of the rebellion, and the Welsh Museum of Modern Art can also be found in an old Wesleyan chapel in Machynlleth. It's this mixture of the ancient, the mythical and the modern that gives the town its noticeable air of confidence and pride. Barely two thousand people live here, but you get the sense that Machynlleth is bigger and more important than the sum of its parts. Darkness shrouded the town by the time I'd returned from the Centre for Alternative Technology and the giant standing stone memorial to Owain Glyndwr glowed with an almost eerie candescence as I passed it on the way to the Wynnstay Arms.

I'd picked up a copy of the Welsh national newspaper, the *Western Mail*, to check the weather forecast. It listed the immediate meteorological prospects for places around the UK. In Belfast it would be cloudy, in Aberdeen fair, but running down the long list of Welsh place names, all the way from Aberdaron to Trawscoed, there was just one word, listed vertically and repeatedly like a naughty schoolboy's lines: showers. An old man with kind eyes slid off a stool at the bar and went over to the huge hearth, in which the fire was slowly dying. A few expert pokes and a couple of sturdy logs had it roaring again, and he walked with a stoop back to his stool. I folded away the newspaper and took out my pile of maps.

My plan was to walk from Machynlleth to Llandovery, where

I'd pick up the River Tywi and follow it south to the coast, just as Owain Glyndwr and his army had done six hundred years before me. There might be a few hills, but even my poor grasp of physical geography (I never passed a geography exam in my life until O level when, the night before the exam, I split my head open: with a bald patch shaved into the top of my head and a bunch of stitches sticking up like the laces of an old football, I sat my geography O level and sailed through with flying colours) told me that rivers don't go over hills, and I'd be following a river.

I folded away the map and pulled out an old book I'd been saving for this evening. I'd stayed at the Wynnstay Arms because a century and a half earlier one of my walking heroes had done likewise in the course of producing *Wild Wales*, one of my favourite travel books of all time.

George Borrow was an author and astonishingly gifted linguist. He also had more opinions than you could shake a stick at, and even then he'd have given you a fulsome appraisal of the stick too. For example, in his first published work, a translation of von Klinger's *Faustus*, he managed to insult the city of Norwich so badly that copies of the book were burned in the streets. Among the many things he disliked intensely were sherry, Catholics, railways, cavaliers, Sir Walter Scott and the Scottish people as a whole, and these prejudices, coupled with his high opinion of himself, ensure that his travel writing is never dull. In the book I was carrying he postulates that 'the inhabitants call their country Cymru. Wales or Walia, however, is the true, proper and without doubt original name.' So that's sorted then.

He travelled widely in Europe in his work for the British and Foreign Bible Society (a job he had secured after walking the 112 miles from his Norfolk home to the interview in London in a little over twenty-four hours), but Wales held a deep fascination for him and in 1854, aged fifty-one, he embarked on a walking tour, the journal of which I was reading in the Wynnstay firelight.

On his way into Machynlleth, Borrow had asked a man in the street his name. When the man answered, Borrow said, 'Why, you are a Frenchman.'

'"Dearie me, sir," said the man, looking pleased. "Am I indeed?"

'"Yes, you are," said I, and giving him sixpence, I left him.'

I was going to enjoy walking with George, and realised with a slight frisson of historical delight that when he wrote of staying at the Wynnstay and 'going down to the parlour which I found unoccupied' and 'sitting some time in front of the fire' he was in the exact spot that I was occupying, reading his words a century and a half later.

I set off in darkness, leaving Machynlleth and rising quickly uphill in a downpour. For a while I'd be following the Glyndwr's Way national trail, a 135-mile route around central Wales that takes in many of the places associated with Owain's life and times. As dawn broke I negotiated puddled footpaths and steep climbs, distant villages betrayed by pinprick orange lights. That morning afforded terrific walking through chilled, vaulted cathedrals of conifers, but at lunchtime I faced a heartbreakingly steep climb up a hill called Foel Fadian, the highest peak in the area at 1530 feet.

In summer, Glyndwr's Way must be spectacular. In the dark depths of December, however, it's windy, wet and dangerous. I climbed slowly, my boots slipping on soaking slate and my rucksack being blown from side to side by the strongest winds I'd yet encountered. The climb seemed to take for ever, the force of the elements no better illustrated than near the top when I noticed that a waterfall was anything but: such was the strength of the wind being forced up the hillside that the waterfall was going upwards, flinging stinging pellets of water at me like grapeshot. Once up on top and crossing a large, flat expanse of heathery bog, the wind could really concentrate on giving me a thorough pummelling unobstructed by the mountain. It flung itself headlong at me, buffeted all around me, snuck up behind me and nearly pitched me face-first into the bog. It whipped the rain cover from my rucksack and every time I caught up with it as it snagged on the flora the wind would whip it away again as I reached out for it. You know it's going to be a hard day when the weather is actually taking the piss out of you. I started descending at the far side of the bog, passing a deserted lead mine that, given the remoteness of the location and the hardships of the employment once you actually got up there, must have been some place to work in its day. It was just after the lead mine that I slipped and fell for the first time on my travels, pitching forward with arms outstretched, the momentum of the pack sliding up my spine causing it to thud into the back of my head and mash my miserable face into the mud.

As time passed and my progress slowed I was aware that it was getting late and I was some way away from where I needed and wanted to be: an agreeable inn in Llanidloes. It will be dark soon, I thought, and I'm up here on this big plateau whose lofty position makes it clear that there's not much for miles around. After what seemed a windswept, chilly age I finally arrived on the outskirts of a village. I'd got myself lost and had little idea of where I'd ended up. I guessed that I was about seven miles behind schedule and hence around three hilly hours away from my destination. There was a growling rumble from behind me and an ancient, wheezing coach pulled up, a school bus that dispensed a small dark-haired boy with a wide face and a little rucksack on his back before pulling away up the hill with a grinding of protesting gears and a hiss of complaining hydraulics. The boy ran into a house nearby, rucksack bouncing on his back, as I trudged towards the centre of the village hoping to find a pub where I could warm up, dry out and summon a taxi to take me the rest of the way. I was exhausted and it was, of course, uphill. A man emerged from the house the boy had just disappeared into, huge, fair-haired, in blue overalls and with the biggest bandage I've ever seen wrapped around his right thumb.

'Hello mate,' I said, mustering as much cheery bonhomie as I could. 'Is there a pub up there?' I nodded in the direction of the village.

'There is, yes,' he replied, 'about four miles.'

Bugger. Bug. Ger.

'Is there a bus I can get to Llanidloes?' I asked hopefully.

'There is, yes. But you've missed it today.'

This really wasn't going well. Further questioning revealed that there was nowhere to stay in the village and there were no local taxi firms; at least, none that wouldn't take less than about an hour to find me.

'Just a minute,' he said. 'The school bus might be coming back this way: maybe you could flag it down and see if he'll take you. Depends who's driving. Hang on, I'll ask my son.'

He disappeared back into the house, calling 'Geraint!' as he went.

'You're in luck,' he said, grinning as he emerged from the house again, 'today's driver lives in Llanidloes and he'll be taking the bus back there. He should be passing through again any minute.'

We both stood at the roadside for a few minutes, scanning the horizon for the bus. I asked what he'd done to his thumb.

'Ach, I cut it wide open with a grinder,' he said, in the manner of someone who thought they might have given themselves a paper cut but hadn't. 'I drove to Aberystwyth, but by the time I got there they said they didn't have anyone to stitch me so I had to drive down to Morriston and get patched up there.'

Now, Aberystwyth was a good twenty-five miles away as the crow flies, let alone around the winding lanes of rural west Wales. Morriston hospital is in Swansea, way down on the south coast: the equivalent of driving from Manchester to Birmingham with your thumb sliced down to the bone. I think I was in the presence of the hardest man in Wales. After about five minutes the bus appeared out of the gloom and my new friend stepped out into the road and held up his good hand. The door of the coach groaned open, he stepped aboard, there was a brief conversation and the biggest bandage in the world gave me a hearty thumbs up through the windscreen.

I felt a bit of a cheat accepting the lift, but I considered it a stroke of good fortune it would have been foolish to turn down. I was exhausted after my hardest day's walk yet, I was miles from anywhere and if I'd been just ten minutes later I'd have missed the bus altogether and who knows what I would have done then. The walking gods had taken pity on me and proffered a slice of good fortune. American hikers have a name for this serendipity; they call it Trail Magic. Given how my predicament had been triggered by incompetence and bad preparation, I preferred to call it Fuckwit's Luck. I gushed my thanks to my overalled saviour, climbed aboard and sped through the darkening hills until the lights of Llanidloes appeared on the horizon.

I fell into a pub and booked a room and got chatting to the landlord. When I told him why I was there he said to me, 'You should have been here yesterday – we have a Welsh history class every week. We have an academic come down and we talk about the history of Wales over a glass of wine. Well, he has a bottle, like. Last night we did Welsh courtly poets of the twelfth and thirteenth centuries. It was absolutely fascinating.'

Every local pub of my acquaintance has put on nothing more taxing than a quiz hosted by the resident drunk who becomes less and less coherent with every pint and every round, contested by teams whose names are largely derived from bodily functions, sexual organs or a less than politically correct reference to a topical news story. Yet here the regulars gather weekly and discuss aspects of their nation's history prompted by a bibulous academic. I really can't see the regulars at my local uncorking a bottle of the good stuff and getting to grips with the crisis of the post-Elizabethan succession somehow.

My host had assured me that my planned route for the following day wouldn't take me as long as I thought, so rather than depart at dawn as I usually did I had breakfast in the pub. The news was on the television in the corner and the weather forecast was about to begin. The forecaster looked concerned. Next to him on the screen was a huge exclamation mark inside a red triangle. 'Wales – Severe Weather Warning' it said as he described how the principality would be lashed by blustery gales and heavy rain. Oh whoop-de-doo. I finished my breakfast, zipped up my waterproofs, heaved the pack on to my back and set out to reach Rhayader by the end of the day.

The previous evening I'd asked the barmaid for the best route. 'Where are you parked?' she asked. 'I'm walking,' I replied, an answer that appeared to be the funniest thing she'd ever heard in her life. When she'd stopped holding her stomach with one arm and propping herself against the bar with the other she told me the route she thought was best then decided to solicit a second opinion from her colleague. She also found the fact that anyone would walk from Llanidloes to Rhayader hilarious, and between guffaws and wiping her smudged mascara from her eyes she told me a totally different route. On my way out of town I stopped for supplies at a corner shop and a greengrocer; both proprietors asked where I was walking to, and both of them laughed like I'd just told the greatest gag in the world. Obviously this wasn't the case as I know the greatest gag in the world and it involves a crocodile and I hadn't mentioned a crocodile; but coupled with the gale warnings the trail of hilarity I was tossing out in my wake didn't bode well for a day's walking.

It threw it down all day. I mean really chucked it down with a vengeance. It was all road walking alongside the River Wye, and the water gushed from the sky and ran along the road in torrents, slopping over my boots. It was one road all the way to Rhayader, and the rain was constant. The only piece of good fortune I had was that the road passed along a river valley and was largely protected from the gale force winds up on top. On a clear day it would have been a lovely walk; on that day it was anything but. I was grateful to reach Rhayader as darkness fell, booking into a bed and breakfast swathed in scaffolding.

Once inside I peeled off my layers and arranged them around the room to dry. I opened the rucksack and found that despite the raincover wrapped around it, everything inside was soaking wet. A puddle of water had collected at the bottom of the raincover in which the bottom of the rucksack had sat for most of the day. A banana had split open and spread like porridge over my clothes which, any sensible walker will tell you, should have been in plastic bags anyway, even inside the rucksack. I found my least wet clothes, wrung out a pair of socks over the sink and spludged out into the night to find something to eat.

I holed up in a pub for a pie and a pint, and while at the bar saw a man looking at me. 'Did I see you out walking earlier?' he asked. I don't know how he'd recognised me from the three square inches around my eyes that weren't swathed in waterproofing – maybe it was because I was still squelching as I walked up to the bar. It turned out he'd passed me in his car in the mid-afternoon. He came over and sat down for a while, nodding towards a big family group at a large table at the other end of the pub. 'They're family, over from Australia,' he said. His face was lined and weathered beneath spiky, sun-bleached hair, and he couldn't have been much older than his mid-thirties.

'I'm a sheep farmer, right up in the hills. I'm a bit unusual, old-fashioned I suppose, as I do it on horseback.'

A young girl in a bright red velvet dress came over, held out a five pence piece and blurted out something that neither of us understood before running off again.

'She's my niece,' he said, 'although I've never seen her before. I've never seen three of these kids before, in fact. That's the only reason I'm down in the town, because they're over. I don't normally come down here, it's a bit too busy for me. I much prefer being up in the hills on the farm.'

He was a terrific bloke, quite possibly the happiest man I've ever met. His life is out there in the mountains: it's where he lives and works, it's where he's most content and it's beautiful. He's practically self-sufficient, to the extent that he rarely comes into the town. So remote is his existence that even Rhayader, little more than two streets on a crossroads, is too racy and metropolitan for him. He oozed a rare calmness, an air of total contentment. It's unusual these days to meet somebody so open, so unsullied by agenda, so untainted by the modern world. In addition, he really was one of the nicest people I have ever come across. By the time he went to rejoin his family, having left people he'd not seen for years in order to talk to a lonely stranger he'd never met before in the corner of a pub, I was chastising myself for my weather-induced grumpiness, my self-pity about the dampness of my clothes and the prospect of another long, rainy day tomorrow.

I woke the next morning to more Welsh weather chaos. Across the country railway tracks and roads had flooded and were out of action. Bedraggled breakfast television reporters gamely grappled with umbrellas and held down errant raincoat lapels as they related the sorry tale playing out behind them, raindrops lit by arc lights bulleting past the camera like fireflies on amphetamines. I peeped out of the curtains. It was still dark but the orange glow around the streetlight was strafed with rain.

Big dark puddles spread across the street, filling and spilling over the kerbs.

I headed out into the elements for a thoroughly miserable, soggy, slippery, flooded and muddy morning. Progress was slow, much slower than I'd hoped, but in the circumstances not surprising. The fields I had to cross were often ankle-deep in mud. Steep descents to cross racing streams had to be negotiated carefully and very, very slowly to avoid a comprehensive defeat by gravity and sudden Connelly-immersion. By the early afternoon I'd only got as far as Newbridge-on-Wye, barely ten miles from where I'd set out. I was wet and miserable, so much so that I even checked the bus timetable to what should have been my destination at Llanwrtyd Wells, still more than a dozen miles distant. The bus had left an hour earlier. Squelchily dejected, I made for a large, sprawling pub at the edge of town. By all that's holy and much that isn't I needed a pint and a sit down in the warm. I approached the doorway and stood out of the rain for the first time in about six hours. I unshouldered the rucksack, loosened my hood and unzipped my waterproof jacket in the porch. I bent down and awkwardly pulled up the zips on the legs of my waterproof trousers so they flapped around like the flares on the suits of a mid-seventies football team on Cup Final day. They were disgusting, with splashes of mud and God knows what else in a range of colours from dark brown to yellow right up to thigh level. After a short and inelegant hopping manoeuvre that might have looked to a passer-by like some kind of ancient folk dance, I managed to get the trousers over my boots and stuff them into the top of the rucksack. My cotton walking trousers had curiously placed wet patches all over them, while my fleece had two dark, wet stripes corresponding to where the rucksack straps had been. After a good ten minutes of wiping my boots on the mat I was ready to enter the pub. I mustered what dignity I could and walked through the door. I found an elderly couple looking at me in the same curious manner as the woman behind the bar.

'We wondered where you'd got to,' said the male half of the couple. 'We saw you walk up to the door but that was ages ago.'

'Ah, yes, well, I had to . . .' I indicated my bedraggled appearance.

'Where have you walked from?'

'Rhayader.'

'Jesus,' said the barmaid, 'I think you need a pint.'

By crikey, she was a woman of both perception and understatement. I perched on a stool at the end of the bar and within half a pint of Brain's Bitter had decided to stay the night. The rain continued to lash down outside, the pub was warm, the people were lovely and I needed a rest and the opportunity for at least some of my clothes to dry out. The barmaid gave me a room key.

'I've given you room eight,' she said. 'The key ring says six, but it's actually eight. We use six for room eight as we don't have a room six.' I knew I was going to like it here.

I slipped off the stool and took my rucksack up to room eight, opening it with the room six key. Room eight was next to room one. The barmaid had told me that, as there was no number on the door of room eight, which opened with the key for room six, which didn't exist.

I hung my wet clothes out all over the room and returned to my perch at the end of the bar. For a while my only companions were the wine-sipping couple who'd greeted my arrival. Then the door opened and a dark-haired man in a suit and tie who bore more than a passing resemblance to John Nettles blew in, followed by his wife. He marched straight over to the jukebox and called out, 'What was that song again, Henry?'

'My Ding-a-Ling,' replied my new friend.

'Who sang it?' asked John Nettles, jabbing at the buttons.

'I don't know.'

'Well a fat lot of good you are.'

'It was Chuck Berry,' I ventured.

'See, Henry? You'd be bloody useless in a quiz team.'

He jabbed at a few more buttons and the sound of Chuck Berry's double entendre-laden live offering filled the room.

John Nettles stepped away from the jukebox and turned to look at me as if noticing me for the first time. 'Are you a grockle, sir?' he asked.

Fortunately I was well armed with an answer. With parents who left London for the countryside a few years ago, I knew that a grockle was rural parlance for a tourist. 'I'm afraid so,' I replied with an apologetic look.

He looked at the ceiling and spread his arms wide. 'Oh, not just a grockle, but a *saesneg* grockle at that,' he roared. *Saesneg*, I knew, was a less than complimentary term for an English person.

'Oh David,' said his wife, 'do stop showing off.'

So began a terrific afternoon. David had worked in the brewing trade and seemed familiar with every pub in every town I mentioned on my itinerary. Later in the afternoon a family group from the Black Country came in, and when he discovered where they were from David, to their astonishment, rattled off a list of pubs in their immediate vicinity.

David was also well versed in Welsh history and culture. When I told him of my Owain Glyndwr quest he warmed to me considerably, after first correcting my anglicised pronunciation, and told me stories and legends from the life and legacy of the man himself. I might be a *saesneg* grockle, but I was clearly all right and David kept me spellbound until well after dark as the rain still fell outside.

As more people joined us more pints appeared. I remember a man called Andrew whose son was judo champion of Wales, and I think I even agreed to join him and David in going to watch Cardiff City play Spurs the following week, but it's all a bit of a blur. The next thing I knew I was waking up flat out on my bed and fully clothed at four o'clock in the morning, with a raging thirst and a head thumping so hard it was as if Thor himself was using it for a bit of target practice.

Later I struggled down to breakfast and got talking to the landlord. When they'd taken the pub over a couple of years previously it was in a terrible state. Bailiffs had taken away everything and they'd had to start from scratch, and by crikey they'd done a good job. Like most rural pubs nowadays they'd had to diversify and had converted a part of the place into a butcher's shop, selling locally produced meat. The restaurant was also proving to be a roaring success.

'We only use local produce,' he told me. 'Last night a woman asked me where her lamb was from. I said to her, hang on, I'll go and get the farmer from the other bar.'

It was with some reluctance that I left Newbridge; I could have stayed for days, but I was already behind schedule and so had to brave the elements once again. This time with a hangover. At least my socks were dry.

Hungover or not, it was still a depressing day to be out walking. The rain fell with relentless determination from a featureless sky the colour of the slate in the surrounding hills. I'd set off with the notion of heading for Llanwrtyd Wells, my final stopover before finally reaching Owain Glyndwr's triumphant Tywi procession, but as the most direct route was a full day of road walking I decided to take the less direct but easier-on-the-feet option of heading south along the river towards Builth Wells and then west from there. Again my progress was slow, muddy, slippery and drenched. I was by now absolutely and thoroughly pissed off with being rained on constantly. My feet were sore, everything was wet and I was thoroughly sick of the sound of my own breathing and the spatter of rain on my waterproofs. After filling my boots with muddy water crossing a submerged field, I was sick of walking, sick of rain, sick of wet socks, sick of being cold, sick of the permanent definition-free grey of the misty horizon, sick of mud, sick of opening gates, sick of closing gates, sick of being looked at quizzically by cows, sick of being barked at by chained-up sheepdogs, sick of rounding a bend to see my way blocked by a breeze-ribbed expanse of brown water, sick of how my allegedly waterproof pockets kept filling up with rain and sick of seeing the swollen, speeding torrent of the River Wye on my left.

I plonked myself on a tree stump, pulled out the map and tried to work out what to do – and soon became sick of that as well. I did notice that there was a railway line crossing the river a bit further along. I traced its route west and saw that it went right through Llanwrtyd Wells. A little red dot told me that there was a railway station about an hour's walk away, at a little village called Cilmeri. I'd head there and catch a train the rest of the way. It was cheating, but I'd not actually reached Owain's route yet and I deserved a break. I persuaded myself that this was allowed.

I left the Wye behind, crossed through a farm, frightened the life out of a moustachioed farmer tinkering with the engine of a mechanical digger in a lane, who hadn't heard me approach in the teeming rain, crossed a stream that had burst its banks into a farmhouse garden right up to the French windows and trudged into Cilmeri.

I turned left at the Prince Llywelyn pub and followed the sign for the station. It was a muddy dirt track at the end of which was a single line, a single platform and what appeared to be a garden shed with one side cut out. This was the only station building and there was a timetable in a frame inside it, which told me that there was a train to Llanwrtyd Wells but it was two-and-a-half hours away. I sat on the bench inside the shelter, the rain drumming on its roof and pinging off the shingle bed of the track in front of me. As soon as I sat down I started to feel the cold, the damp combination of rain and sweat in my clothing now being probed by chilly gusts of wind. Two-and-a-half hours. Oh well, at least there's a pub in the village – I'll kill a bit of time there. Just as I was about to depart a thin, grey-haired man appeared, nodded at me, sat down on the bench, opened a small rucksack and poured a cup of steaming soup from a flask. He took a sip and turned to me.

'You waiting for a train?'

I was on a station platform at the end of a long track that led nowhere but here. What else would I be doing?

'Um, yes,' I answered, before adding, 'You?'

'Nope,' he said, looking ahead and taking down a long draught of soup.

He saw me looking at him a little bit askance.

'I'm here for the commemoration.'

'Commemoration? At the station?' I asked, sounding like a really bad rapper.

He looked at me as if I'd just said something startling about molluscs.

'No,' he replied, 'up at the memorial.'

My face still registered blankness.

'For the anniversary?'

I shook my head faintly.

'Llywelyn the Last?'

I had, it turned out, struck historical gold. My new friend Jim told me between gulps of soup that Cilmeri had been the site of the demise of the last of the Welsh princes, killed at the end of the village on a spot now marked by a stone memorial. The pub up the lane was packed with people who'd come from all over Wales for the ceremony – Jim himself had come in a minibus from Pontypridd – held annually to commemorate the end of the Welsh succession, the last Welsh Prince of Wales save for Owain Glyndwr.

It was a coincidence of startling proportions. I'd not even intended to come to Cilmeri. I knew nothing of its historical significance. Yet of all the days I could roll up here by chance on an historical quest of my own, it was the anniversary of one of Welsh history's defining moments. Not only that, but the two-and-a-half-hour window before my train was exactly the right amount of time to allow me to see the ceremony. Jim told me that he'd come down to the shelter because all his friends were having lunch in the pub. He'd brought his own lunch so set out to find somewhere to eat it. If Jim hadn't brought his soup there's a chance that I'd have missed the ceremony.

Perhaps most remarkable of all was the fact that Llywelyn was the father of Gwenllian, the cloistered princess whose memorial I had stumbled upon, also by chance, in a remote corner of Lincolnshire just weeks earlier. I still had the photos on my camera, much to Jim's delight when I showed him.

'Shall we go up to the pub then?' said Jim after he'd finished his soup and shared his cheese sandwich with me. We trudged up the muddy lane in the rain, pushed open the door of the Prince Llywelyn and were immediately engulfed in a cloud of warmth, bonhomie and all-encompassing national pride. On the way up I'd asked Jim if I'd be all right in there, what with being a *saesneg* and everything, and he'd just smiled and thumped me on the back. 'You'll be fine,' he said.

Jim went off to find his friends and I went to the bar to get us a drink. Everyone seemed to be dressed in some kind of patriotic clothing, whether the noble scarlet of the Welsh national rugby jersey or, as in one case, a shirt that appeared to be made from the Welsh flag itself. A range of souvenirs had been laid out for sale on a table, little Welsh flags and badges and pennants of the red and yellow arms of Llywelyn, cannily adopted by Owain Glyndwr more than a century later. As I trousered my change a man next to me suddenly called for silence and addressed the room. A huge framed collage detailing the life of Llywelyn appeared on the bar next to me. The man said that it had been prepared as a gift for the pub in thanks for their hospitality. A woman behind the bar hissed at me to hold the edge of the frame to keep it upright. A newspaper photographer snapped away, taking pictures of the landlord, the man who'd made the thing and, er, me. It's quite likely that somewhere out there there's a Welsh newspaper containing a photograph of two men proudly shaking hands while a bedraggled, unshaven, awkward-looking bloke in torn waterproofs smiles idiotically next to them.

Before long there was a scraping of chairs and a donning of coats as people began to prepare to leave for the procession. I drained my pint and shouldered my rucksack as Jim straightened his flat cap and zipped up his anorak. We moved out into the car park where a marching band was gathering, about a dozen young musicians in military-style dark trousers, pullovers and berets, each wearing a red and yellow sash and squinting against the driving rain. People rummaged in the boots of cars and produced enormous Welsh flags while a piper in green kilt and jacket inflated the bright red bellow sack of his instrument in the scant shelter provided by the leeward side of a parked van. A man in a padded green anorak, sporting a long grey beard that wouldn't have looked out of place on a member of the Dubliners, marshalled us into the road and formed the procession, the marching band at the front then about a hundred or so of us, turning our faces away from the rain. The flags stood rigid to attention, only their fringes whipping in the wind; umbrellas were buffeted relentlessly. Jim pointed me out to his friends – 'that's the chap with the pictures of Gwenllian's monument' – and my camera was passed around gloved hands, which wiped the moisture from the little screen to appreciative 'oohs'. Soon the drums struck up and we were on our way, this hardy collection of Welsh patriots, the ringing sound of the glockenspiel and the thump of the bass drum leading us the five hundred yards or so from the pub to the memorial. It's a sharp, roughly hewn menhir of granite about twenty feet high situated on a little mound, purportedly the very spot where Welsh independence was finally ended. The plaque in English describes him as 'our prince'. The Welsh plaque reads *Llywelyn ein Llew Olaf* which, Jim told me, is the more poignant 'our last leader'.

The band became a colour party, ranging themselves around the memorial with Welsh flags and Llywelyn standards alternating, and there they'd stand for the next three-quarters of an hour, motionless and proud, while the weather did its worst. At least we spectators could turn away from the wind and shelter ourselves from the rain as best we could.

The man with the druidic beard walked up the mound to the foot of the monument and addressed us in English and Welsh about the significance of this date and this spot for the Welsh nation. Llywelyn's story was related before various dignitaries gave short bilingual tributes. A small choir sang beautifully in a cappella Welsh, huddled beneath a clutch of umbrellas. The piper played a gorgeous lament that echoed around the hills and among the dark skeletons of the trees, and heralded a minute's silence for the recently departed Welsh patriot and former rugby international Ray Gravell, for whom the flags were lowered in unison. Finally there was an emotional rendition of the Welsh national anthem, during which I looked around me at these proud people from all over the country who'd gathered here among the hills in the foulest of weather to remember a time when their nation was a nation in every sense, eyes closed, singing the anthem that represents them and the landscape around us, in a language that has survived concerted attempts by the English to wipe it out, only to go on and thrive.

As the last note died, stolen by the wind and taken far away, there was a moment's reflective silence before the hubbub of conversation started and the crowd began to disperse. I sought out Jim, shook his hand and said goodbye. Thanks to him I'd been privileged to witness a major event in the Welsh patriotic calendar, an event that served to make me even more in awe of the Welsh and their national consciousness. I made my way back to the station where, before long, a single-carriage train appeared around the bend. This being a request station, I flagged it down, boarded and looked through the rain-bleary window towards the grey memorial as we pulled away, a solitary Welsh flag now the only splash of colour among the dark greens and greys.

Before long I was walking into the Neuadd Arms in the centre of Llanwrtyd Wells, a vast, shambling old coaching inn of undulating floors and labyrinthine corridors. Despite its size I managed to secure what was the last room in the place; a curious thing for a wet weekend in December. As the woman who ran the place showed me to my room – there was one particular floorboard in the corridor leading to it that made a pot plant on a little table six feet away actually jump into the air every time you trod on it – she suggested I might want to book a table in the restaurant as it was likely to be busy. 'We've got a big party in this weekend,' she said, 'but I'm sure we could squeeze you in.' I said that, as a lone diner among couples and groups, I'd probably look like a bit of a gooseberry.

'Not tonight you won't: everyone else is single and on a speed-dating weekend.'

It was a relatively short hop to Llandovery – 'about the pleasantest little town in which I have halted in the course of my wanderings', according to Borrow – the next day and, remarkably, the sun shone from a deep blue sky flecked only by the odd tufty cloud. It had been so long since the sun had appeared in the skies over Wales that people barely recognised it. Locals tried to rake its reflection out of the river.

Llandovery is a beautiful little town hunched around a square, the spot where Henry IV had Llewelyn ap Gruffydd Fychan executed in grisly fashion after he'd led the English king on a mazy and pointless meander through the surrounding countryside in order to throw him off the scent of Owain Glyndwr. I booked into a bed and breakfast that overlooked the square, called the Drover's Arms, where I was the only guest. The owner made me a cup of tea and brought me a slice of home-made cake, leaving me to look out on the square and to try to imagine the barbarity that had occurred there six hundred years earlier.

Presumably a crowd had gathered, possibly by order so that the locals could see an example being made of the man who had dared pull a fast one on the King of England. Some kind of scaffold would have been set up and a noose placed over the head of the doomed Llywelyn. There would have been none of the pomp and ceremony of a royal execution, no last words, no roll of drums; this would have been swift, summary and without fuss. At a given signal from the king, Llywelyn would have been hanged from the hastily erected gallows, kicking and twitching and twisting and choking as women gasped and children wailed. While there was still life and breath within him, he would have been cut down and revived with cold water and slaps, reluctantly brought back from the hazy world of semiconsciousness to witness the next atrocity to be committed on his person. Llywelyn would have been laid on his back, his limbs held fast and his head raised by soldiers, his eyes forced open by grubby thumbs as his abdomen was cut open before him, blood, guts and gore spilling out on to the cobbles and the screams and cries of the onlookers joining his own as he succumbed to his horrendous end.

From the cool of the darkened wood lounge, through the leaded windows, the sunny square seemed entirely out of keeping with such brutality. A small plaque commemorating the execution is affixed to the wall next to the cashpoint of the HSBC bank, but a much more substantial memorial stands close to the castle, to which I headed in the afternoon sun.

Little remains of Llandovery Castle now, just a few lumps of stone and part of a wall two storeys high, but this was where the Glyndwr rebellion really began to take hold. It was here that

Owain emerged from the hills and met his supporters. They would have seen the man himself for the first time, the man who already was being imbued with magical powers and becoming wreathed in myth. It was midsummer when he arrived here, and the castle seems to have fallen to him with the minimum of fuss. I climbed the small hillock on which it stands and stood among the ruins. There may not be much of it left, but the castle retains a noble dignity, 'majestic though in ruins' as Borrow had it. For the first time in days I could see the horizon, looking out across the town whose hotchpotch of roofs followed a street plan that hadn't changed in centuries to the green hills beyond. Owain himself may have stood here and surveyed what was rapidly becoming his domain, the craggy hills and valleys of Wales that, it seemed, would soon be rid of the oppression of the English. It's likely he would have stepped down from the castle and visited the square where Llywelyn was killed – a martyr to the Welsh cause, to him personally – perhaps even accompanied by the man's sons, who fought in his army. No doubt standing on the exact spot where such an atrocity took place would have further hardened the resolve of the Prince of Wales as he looked down at the ground where Llywelyn's blood had congealed.

I walked a few yards from the castle, along the top of the hillock, and stood close to the life-size memorial that commemorates Llywelyn ap Gruffydd Fychan. It's a fantastic structure of stainless steel that glinted in the winter sunshine and reflected the blue sky in every fold and expanse. A silver cloak fell from invisible shoulders, puddling on the sculpture's rocky base. A battle helmet hung suspended above it as if in mid air. A shield engraved with Glyndwr's coat of arms clung to the right of the cloak while a lance pointed at the sky; a sword hung unsheathed on the left. The sculpture leaned forward slightly, overlooking the site of the execution, its battle garb and patriotic shield showing how even six hundred years on Llywelyn ap

Gruffydd Fychan was still watching protectively over the people of Llandovery. As statues and memorials go, it is one of the best I've ever seen – it's moving, it's inspiring and it's an entirely fitting way to commemorate a man who gave his life for Wales, and the greatest leader that nation has ever seen.

It was a perfect day to be there, knowing that for the first time on this journey I was standing exactly where the man I was following had also stood. Owain may have addressed his supporters from this lofty position, overlooking as it did the marketplace (it's a car park now). He may even have spoken from the very spot where Llywelyn's statue now stands, citing him as an example of why this rebellion was necessary, calling his supporters to arms and urging them to join him on his march through the Tywi valley and on to the greater glory of Wales.

I headed back towards the town centre and called in at the Llandovery Heritage Centre. As well as a tourist information office staffed by a lovely, helpful old lady, upstairs there is a small museum, which I asked if I could see. 'Of course,' said the lady behind the till excitedly. 'Go straight up.'

As I climbed the stairs she called out from the bottom, 'Dilys, can you switch everything on, there's a gentleman coming up.'

'Switch what on?' came the reply.

'Everything.'

'Which?'

'Everything, switch everything on.'

When I arrived at the top of the stairs Dilys was standing behind a counter at a bank of switches, clicking each one in turn and bathing different parts of the room in light. It was quite a display: as well as glass cases packed with snippets from Llandovery history there were four mannequins with blank faces and costumes of various vintage.

'Now,' explained Dilys, 'each of these talks in turn. I don't think there's any particular order, they just start. Would you like a chair to sit on while you watch them?' I declined with thanks and Dilys left me to it. Within a few seconds the face of a local Lady in the Lake lit up and a woman's features appeared on it. It was a great idea – they'd employed actors to tell the story of each character in the first person, filmed it and projected their faces on to the mannequins. Alas, the Lady in the Lake's projector had slipped a little and her nose was on her chin and her mouth spoke from her throat. They were great presentations, but normally I wouldn't have chosen to sit through all of them; given the trouble that Dilys had gone to in switching everything on, however, and the encouraging looks she gave me every time I turned around, I made sure I watched each one right to the end.

The display cases were troves of remarkable popular culture treasure, largely donated by townsfolk. A 1956 cinema playbill advertised *Carry On Sergeant* supported by *The Tommy Steele Story*, while a pair of child's Victorian hobnail boots had been found in an attic, as had several packets of post-Second World War tea and a battered top hat. I dallied a long time up there, marvelling at how such seemingly inconsequential objects could all be pieced together to bring Llandovery's past to life.

Later I had a walk around the town, picking up a local paper as I went. There were some terrific stories. An eighty-two-year-old man had just been banned from driving for three years. A local thirteen-year-old girl was breaking all sorts of Welsh archery records despite having picked up her first bow barely four months earlier. An unknown driver was roundly condemned for speeding up to avoid stopping for the imminent departure from the kerb of a lollipop lady. But my favourite story contained this quote from a local policeman, and I promise you it's true: 'A sexual assault has been reported,' he said, 'but there's nothing to worry about, it's all in hand.'

I took a slow walk back towards the Drover's Arms, over-hearing snatches of local life. Two men in woolly hats passed me as one said, 'What the team needs is someone who can just plonk the ball over the line.' Two women were chatting on a bench, with one saying, 'I'm hoping to combine traditional Welsh dance with traditional Indian dance,' while an older woman harrumphed as she told a friend, 'Well, the bookshop has a book of Bible *stories* in Welsh, but not the actual *Bible* in Welsh.'

I set off in darkness the next morning following the lazy mean-der of the Tywi towards Llandeilo. The clear night skies had left a frost that crunched underfoot, and as I left the outskirts of Llandovery there was the most glorious sunrise. Thin bars of high cloud warmed through pinks, purples and oranges as the frosty hills gleamed with the expectation of the coming day. Once at Llandeilo I left the valley for a detour that if Owain himself hadn't made his forces certainly had, south-east for a few miles towards Carreg Cennen Castle. It became another sunny day, with the hills picked out in vivid greens, and eventually I caught my first glimpse of the ruins of Carreg Cennen. It sat on a ridge, its jagged remains looking like a vast human jawbone scattered with broken teeth.

Word had spread throughout the south that Owain was on his way. Whether or not the garrison at Carreg Cennen would have known he'd taken Llandovery is just speculation, but certainly the constable of the castle, John Scudamore, went to see Owain when he reached Dryslwyn to ask for safe passage from the castle for his wife and mother. Owain, perhaps inured against mercy by having stood the day before on the spot where Henry had had Llywelyn ap Gruffydd Fychan put to death, refused. His forces would never actually take the castle, but they laid siege to it for an entire year. As I approached I could see why it had proved difficult to conquer. It perches on the edge of a sheer limestone crag, with a steep climb on the other side in full view of the castle's occupants. For Owain's men, even though buoyed by the momentum of the rebellion, it must have presented a daunting sight as they approached from the same direction as me. What would it have been like to be inside the castle as the rebels approached? Would I have felt unnerved by the arrival of hordes of hairy, aggrieved Welshmen with the intention of removing my head and hanging my body from the castle ramparts? Or would I have felt secure in the impregnability of my stronghold?

I explored the remains of the castle. Despite its ruined state it retains an impressive charisma, a glowering presence both outside and within the walls. I spent a while up there, the only brief company I had being the fighter jet that suddenly came roaring through the clear sky and flew low over the ruins.

I reached Carmarthen and early impressions weren't good. I gained an immediate feeling that the town reluctantly tolerates its heritage rather than celebrates it – a dual carriageway bisects the town, separating the centre from the river that established it and turned it into the prosperous place it became. Soulless modern buildings characterise the centre of the town, while the local newspaper headline hoarding that read 'CARMARTHEN GRANDMOTHER ANGRY AT CRAMPED TRAIN SERVICE' didn't suggest the place would be a festival of fun. It's the local focus for the region – I heard more Welsh spoken here than anywhere else on this journey – but there seemed little to detain me. Owain had reached here on 5 July 1403, setting fire to the town and killing fifty men in the process of taking the castle the following day, but it seems he didn't tarry long and headed south after having his ranks swelled further by supporters coming in from the surrounding countryside.

Having passed through so many small towns and villages I'd expected a little more from Carmarthen than I found. It's well served with pubs – more than sixty, in fact – so, with an entire afternoon to kill, I decided that once I'd visited the few ruined remains of the castle I'd try to get a sense of the place in local hostelries.

I booked into another Drover's Arms on Lammas Street, a wide boulevard of many inns that was presumably the main thoroughfare used by the drovers themselves. It was an old and deceptively large building, and when I arrived at the bar it was still early enough in the day for the barmaid to plonk her paper-back book face down on the bar and bid me a good morning. A small group of grey-haired men were already seated around a table by the door, pint pots of dark beer in front of them, attempting conversation with the barmaid.

'What's that ring on your wedding finger?'

'It's the only finger it fits.'

'You'll be getting engaged to your young man though?'

'Oh goodness, no, not me.'

'Ah yes, you're travelling around the world first, aren't you?'

'Yep, not long now.'

'You might finish that book before then.'

'Well I might if you lot weren't so thirsty all the time.'

In a pub further down the road I overheard an exchange that could have been scripted by Alan Bennett himself. Three middle-aged women came in, plonked themselves at the table next to me and began speaking in broad Yorkshire accents – 'Eee, it's nice to sit on a comfy seat, in't it?' I worked out that they must have come by coach on a shopping trip, although why the merchants of Carmarthen were worthy of an excursion from Yorkshire I couldn't work out. They all had bouffant hair and large-framed plastic glasses; shopping bags gathered around their feet. I over-heard a number of references to the imminent arrival of the bus and eventually, after a few minutes of small talk over their halves of lager shandy, one of the women stood up and said she was going outside to wait for it. Once she'd gone one woman said to the other, ''Ere, Edna, we like the same things, don't we?' It was immediately clear that this was a verbal nod and wink to commence discussion about their recently departed friend who, it seems, liked to keep her money firmly in her purse.

'You won't get a drink back out of her, you know.'

'Ooh, I know, I think she only brought a fiver with her.'

'I saw her counting out her change when she bought them chocolate brazils. I said to her, you'll have to break into a note.'

'No chance, the only thing she's changed today is her drawers.'

At breakfast the next morning I was given a clear indication of how I was falling for Wales in a big way. My only fellow diners were two businessmen from the English Midlands, a paunchy man with back-combed grey hair and a younger, skinny colleague with gel in his hair and boils on his neck. I'd taken against them when I spotted that they'd swiped the communal orange juice jug and placed it on their own table. Their conversation consisted largely of disparaging comments about Wales and the Welsh, something that caused me to spear my sausage hard with indignation.

There was the usual nonsense about walking into a pub and everyone deliberately starting to speak Welsh, when the fact is that they'd have been speaking Welsh before they arrived and would be after they left. Customary nudge-nudge references to the Welsh enjoying carnal relations with sheep peppered the conversation too. At one point the lights in the room went out and immediately came back on again. The older man rolled his eyes. 'Well, we are in Wales,' he said with an exasperated look, as if the Welsh deliberately go around flicking light switches on and off thanks to some kind of flaw in their national character.

He picked up the breakfast menu. 'Full Welsh breakfast,' he sneered, as if this was another deliberate attempt at subversion by those crafty Cymry. 'Imagine what would have happened if I'd asked for an English breakfast,' he said, the answer of course being absolutely nothing, even if the image that popped into my head of Owain Glyndwr himself materialising in the corner of the room with sword raised and rushing over and slicing his head clean off his shoulders did seem highly appealing. His colleague, clearly his junior and clearly away on a business trip for the first time, just chuckled and agreed on cue, dabbing at the egg yolk on his tie with a tissue.

I've never been able to understand the not uncommon antipathy towards the Welsh that I hear frequently among the English. From rugby supporters to the likes of A. A. Gill and Anne Robinson, the Welsh are often vilified for no other reason than their Welshness. Is this seen as the last acceptable form of racism? If A. A. Gill had called any other race 'pugnacious trolls' would it have engendered the same sniggering and tacit agreement? Can it really go back to the ancient border raids on English farms ('Taffy was a Welshman, Taffy was a thief . . .')? Or is it a deep-rooted indignation that the Welsh have never truly been subjugated and suppressed by their neighbours, that their language and culture remains strong and is if anything getting stronger? Or is it the sense that the Welsh are entirely comfortable with their nationality? While I was in Wales there was a television news story about an advert for Welsh vodka that pitted a team of Welsh students against a posh college on *University Challenge*, in which the Welsh team displayed amiable stupidity and naive charm. Did it pander to negative stereotypes, the columnists and pundits wondered. A series of vox pops was broadcast, nearly all of whom said that they weren't bothered, really. I think that's the thing I like about the Welsh: they're just not exercised by posturing from the likes of A. A. Gill. There are more important things to worry about. The national rugby team, for example.

This didn't stop me from wanting to empty the orange juice jug over the heads of the pair next to me, however, or at least to nip out and let their tyres down, but instead I contented myself with the knowledge that, given they were clearly salesmen of some kind, they were about to spend the whole day having to be really, really nice to Welsh people.

From Carmarthen I left the River Tywi and headed west across country, reaching first St Clears, where Owain and his forces camped, and then making the descent to the mouth of the River Taf and the extraordinary town of Laugharne, a pleasant jumble of houses and buildings that seems to have been washed down the hillside to the edge of the estuary. I'd booked in to the Boat House Inn, a wonderful bed and breakfast close to the water and the castle that used to be the Corporation Arms pub, whose bar was a regular haunt of the man most closely associated with Laugharne and its pubs in particular, Dylan Thomas.

They made a great combination, the town and the man who is arguably the finest wordsmith this loquacious country has ever produced. Quirky and remote, Laugharne was a perfect place for Thomas to settle and work. And drink. For if Dylan Thomas was famous for his poetry, he was equally renowned for his consumption of booze. Not for nothing were his last words were long thought to be, 'I've just had eighteen straight whiskies; I think that's the record,' before slipping into a coma and succumbing to what his death certificate recorded as an 'insult to the brain'. Just about every pub in the town has its Dylan Thomas connections, but I was still awed by the thought that I'd be getting my head down in a building that had been associated with him. I'd arrived as the sun was setting and a pinky-purple light was reclining over the estuary. The castle gradually darkened to silhouette as I looked out of the window and the sleepy town began to doze.

I spent the next day wandering about the town. Leaving the Boat House Inn I crossed the road and headed across the car park to the castle. It was here that Owain Glyndwr's triumphant Tywi odyssey came to an end and the momentum of the insurgency slowed slightly. His men had taken the nearby castles of Newcastle Emlyn and Llanstephan with ease, and the same minuscule resistance was probably expected here. So successful had the Tywi

progress been that it's possible a little complacency might have set
in among the burgeoning rebel force. On arrival at Laugharne
on 10 July, Owain proposed terms of surrender to the Lord of
Carew and probably expected them to be accepted without fuss.
After all, Carew's men were hemmed in by the estuary on one
side and the rebels on the other with all the nearby strongholds
now under Owain's control. That night, however, a large chunk
of the rebel army reconnoitred the hills that overlook the town,
a move that Carew had expected. He'd hidden a large number of
troops on the hill and they set upon the rebels, killing seven
hundred of them. It was a major blow, but not a grievous one.
It meant that Owain would not capture the castle and, on the
advice of a local soothsayer, he retreated back to Carmarthen. A
superstitious man as well as a warrior, Owain had been to consult
the local bard Hopcyn ap Tomos, who said that he could see a
vision of Owain being dragged away from the area under a black
banner. Taking no chances, and in the light of the nocturnal
rout by Carew's men, Owain decided upon a hasty retreat from
the area and one of the great journeys of Welsh history came to
an end.

Much of the shell of Laugharne Castle still stands, the guts of it
having been destroyed during the English Civil War, and its
imposing presence dominates the bottom of the town. Such is
the gradient on which Laugharne lies, however, that you don't
have to walk too far uphill before you're barely aware there's a
castle in the town at all.

I crossed the little hump-backed bridge over the stream to the
car park on the apron of the castle, which is possibly where
Owain and his troops settled in expectation of its imminent surrender. I sat on a bench close to a bust of Dylan Thomas and
tried to imagine how it would have felt to be here in July 1403
when rebellious morale was at its peak. It's possible that this was
the site of one of the great flowerings of Welsh pride. Most of

Wales was behind Owain, and in reaching the coast he'd reached the limits of his land at a time when the limits of his revolt must have seemed endless. Finally it seemed as though the English oppressors would be driven out. There was still a long way to go, but such was the confidence and support of the nation that Owain had felt able to progress his cause by shifting from targeted guerrilla attacks to a very public display of Welsh pride and military prowess. Henry seemed to be reeling – three excursions into Wales had been fruitless, beaten back as much by the weather as the opposition, and in Owain Glyndwr the Welsh had a strong, charismatic leader with blood ties to the ancient Welsh princes, a brilliant strategic mind and, as far as many were concerned, magical powers that could summon inclement conditions to disperse enemies at will.

Laugharne in the sunshine of a July day in 1403 must have been a pretty pleasing prospect. Merlin's prediction that 'Kidwelly was; Carmarthen is; but Laugharne shall be the greatest of the three' must have seemed apposite that day, as Owain prepared his terms of surrender and his troops took in the sunshine.

From the car park I wandered away from the centre of the town to follow a more recent Welsh folk hero. Dylan Thomas had first come to Laugharne to visit friends in 1934, describing it as 'the strangest town in Wales'. Four years later he and his wife Caitlin returned to live until 1940, when they were largely driven out by creditors. But in 1949 the Thomases returned and Laugharne would be the poet's home until his death in New York in 1953.

A couple of minutes' walk out of town is their first home in the town, a house overlooking the sea. Back then it was pretty basic – they had to get their water from a pump in the town square – but it was from here that Dylan would have taken the short jaunt to the Corporation Arms, holing up in the corner and producing epithets on demand in return for drink. Before long they had moved to Sea View, just the other side of the castle.

For such a small place tucked away from the rest of the world, Laugharne has a remarkable literary pedigree. Coleridge visited in 1802, recording some of the gravestone inscriptions in the churchyard at the top of the hill. Mary Wollstonecraft's family had a farm there, while her daughter Mary Shelley also stayed in the town. The poet Edward Thomas spent several weeks in Laugharne in 1911, completing his biography of my companion George Borrow, and returned for a holiday with his daughters just before leaving for the service in the First World War from which he would never return. Kingsley Amis wrote *The Old Devils* in Laugharne, and it is the setting for Margaret Atwood's short story, 'The Grave of the Famous Poet'. Richard Hughes, the author of *A High Wind in Jamaica*, lived for twelve years in the imposing Castle House and frequently entertained the Thomases. Indeed, Dylan wrote *Portrait of the Artist as a Young Dog* in the castle gazebo that overlooks the sea. Add to that the fact that Turner once painted the castle, and it's clear to see that Laugharne has long punched above its cultural weight. Dylan Thomas dominates the place above all else, however, and I headed out past the castle and along the seafront to the house most associated with him, a precarious-looking whitewashed building that seems to jut straight out of the cliff face and over the water.

Before you reach the Boat House you come upon the converted garage that the poet used as his writing shed. Built to house Laugharne's first-ever car by a previous owner of the house, the shed, which Thomas referred to as his 'bard's bothy', his 'wordsplashed hut', has been recreated to resemble as closely as possible how it would have been in Thomas's day. For me the best kind of history, one of the main reasons I was undertaking these journeys, is when it demonstrates the humanity of its protagonists. The mundane can often be the best way of gaining an insight into a person and, peering through the glass into Dylan Thomas's writing shed, here was a classic example of the mundanity of genius. At the far end of the room, overlooking the sea, was a table, with a chair pushed back as if the poet had just popped out for a minute. There were pieces of paper strewn over the table, a newspaper, screwed up balls on the floor and clustered next to the wastepaper basket where they'd been inaccurately lobbed in frustration at a stanza that wasn't going to plan. There were two heavy glass bottles on the table, postcards and pictures pinned to the wall. An oil lamp rose above the chaos of paperwork and books lay higgledy-piggledy on a bookshelf along one wall.

When reading the works of Dylan Thomas the neatly typeset verses and stanzas are ordered and tidy. One glance through the window of the shed is enough to prove that their creation was anything but. Worried by poverty and with one eye on the clock, waiting for opening time, Thomas would have scribbled away here. Some days the words would have flowed easily, on others they'd have stuttered, hastening departure to the saloon bar of Brown's Hotel. He'd have been cold here in the winter, too hot in the summer, shambolically dressed, on occasion just in a dressing gown, unshaven, hung over, smoking too much, scribbling away enthusiastically, stopping, reading back over the words and resignedly screwing up the page and lobbing it at the bin. The clean, printed pages of the poetry collection give no hint as to the frustrations of the creative process, the poems needing to be completed so that payment can be secured and another debt settled.

But when you read the works of Dylan Thomas the fruits of those hours in the shed ring with a sonorous magic, with rhythms that are a product of his Welshness. For all the chaos on the outside, those words came from somewhere inside that was essentially calm and organised, and there, in the writing shed, was exactly where it happened.

The Boat House is another example of how mundanity and greatness make strange bedfellows. Although more than thirty thousand visitors a year pass through it, and although there's very little in the house remaining from Thomas's time (Caitlin frequently had to sell furniture and personal effects to raise cash), you still feel as though you're walking into someone's home rather than into a museum. The parlour is set out much as it would have been in the early fifties, but it's upstairs that the place has most effect. Display cabinets combine the everyday with the extraordinary. A photograph of the poet that went into space on the space shuttle Columbia in 1998 is in a cabinet close to a tiny yellow plastic toy house with a red roof that was found in the garden. A model of an outrigger canoe that Dylan brought back from one of his American lecture tours for his young son sits downstairs, while above is a letter from the former US president Jimmy Carter addressed to 'the citizens of Laugharne' detailing how he fell in love with Thomas's work after finding one of his poems in an anthology, and how, on a presidential visit to Westminster Abbey, he tried to take the curates to task for omitting Thomas from Poets' Corner; they replied with embarrassed shuffles and murmurs about 'dissolute lifestyles'.

On the wall there are framed front pages of the *Carmarthen Journal* noting Dylan's death and funeral. The poet's death is not the lead story – the search for a missing local couple dominates the page – and it notes only that 'Mr Dylan Thomas, a poet of international fame' had died of 'a brain disease of unknown origin'.

From the house I walked back along the path, with the sea lapping gently against the rocks below and to my left, past the castle and up the main street, just as Dylan would have done on his way to the pub. I passed Brown's, his favourite haunt, and kept going up the hill until the church came into view at the very top of the town. I passed through the gate and up the path to the graveyard and saw the grave immediately, a simple white cross among the rows of grey and black marble. For a man who did so much with the very sound of the English language, who immortalised Laugharne as Llareggub in *Under Milk Wood*, his epitaph is a simple 'In Memory Of' in black Gothic script with his name and his dates.

Owain Glyndwr has no grave, at least not one we know about. The setback at Laugharne was a minor one and the rebellion gathered strength well into 1404. Wales, while nominally independent with the crowning of Owain as prince, was becoming physically so, with the last pockets of English presence restricted to a few castles. A treaty with France brought Wales much more tangible support and a Franco-Welsh force marched into England and got within striking distance of Worcester before a stand-off with Henry IV ended with a Welsh retreat without conflict. Eventually the rebellion began to lose momentum as the greater numbers and resources of the English began to tell. The French support wavered and evaporated. What would now be called economic sanctions meant that by the end of the decade the Welsh were surrendering castles to England across the country. Nothing was heard of Owain himself after 1412, but his death was never confirmed. By 1415 Wales, physically and emotionally wrecked by the revolt that, among other things, left the country mired more deeply in poverty than ever before, was back under full English control. Nobody heard from Owain again, but despite the devastation and destitution, the grisly deaths and draining battles, he had given the Welsh something priceless; something that resonated more than six hundred years later: a sense of themselves. A unity, an appreciation that being Welsh was a consciousness as well as a home on a piece of ground called Wales.

There couldn't be more differing characters than Owain Glyndwr, the semi-mythical warrior prince, and Dylan Thomas, the chubby, booze-addled genius of verse, but both endure deep in the consciousness of the Welsh people. As Owain Glyndwr occupies a central role in the marvellous recent resurgence of Welshness that drives the nation on through devolution, it really does seem that, in the words of the poet, 'death shall have no dominion'.

Chapter Five

1568: Mary, Queen of Scots escapes from Loch Leven

It was a blustery day in Kinross as I walked up to the low building by the side of the loch, its summer tables and parasols piled
against the wall and the ice cream sign jutting out from the wall
swinging in the wind. It would be a few weeks before any ice
creams were sold from here, and as I rounded the corner of the
building a strong gust tried to push me back by the shoulders and
a solitary raindrop smacked against my forehead.

A small cruiser with a tarpaulin lashed across its open rear
bobbed and bonked against the jetty and I looked out across the
choppy surface of Loch Leven to see if I could see the bleak little
island that would be the departure point for my next journey
through history. At that moment, two large, friendly Labradors
came bounding around the far corner of the deserted, shuttered
building ahead of a colossus of a man with a big, friendly smile
creasing from beneath a Historic Scotland woolly hat.

'Duncan?' I asked.

'Charlie – nice to meet you. Welcome to Loch Leven. Right,
let's get the boat started up and we'll get you over to poor Mary's
prison.'

Given that the tourist season was in remission it was hugely kind of Duncan to accede to my pleading e-mails and take me over to Loch Leven Castle. 'We're putting one of the boats back in the water today,' he told me, 'so I had to come up here anyway.' He unhitched the tarpaulin, the dogs bounded into the boat, Duncan and I joined them, he started the engine and we puttered over to the little lake-bound fortress from where in 1568 Mary, Queen of Scots escaped from captivity and made a journey that, thanks to a bit of ill judgement, would represent the last days of freedom in her extraordinary life. Like many of the journeys I was making, it was one whose consequences still reverberate down the centuries.

It was a ten-minute crossing to the island. Duncan brought the boat around past a line of trees, in front of which a regimental row of curious herons regarded us quizzically, and secured the boat to the jetty.

'I've got a few things to do here so I'll leave you to it. Give me a shout when you're done and I'll run you back ashore,' he said. I walked up to the castle entrance, just as Mary herself had done over four hundred years earlier, and reflected on the chain of events that brought a woman who had been queen of an entire nation, and who had enjoyed all the ostentatious trappings and ceremony of a sixteenth-century monarch, here to this tiny island and its austere castle as a prisoner.

Mary Stuart was an extraordinary woman. Nearly six feet tall and arrestingly beautiful, she was warm, vivacious, witty and generous. From the accounts we have of her life she sounded quite a gal; certainly one who didn't deserve the cruel fate that befell her, even if that fate was to some extent exacerbated by some particularly dozy decisions on her part. If Mary was a great queen she was also a lousy politician. Born in December 1542 at Linlithgow Palace, she was the daughter of James V of Scotland and his wife Mary of Guise. A fortnight earlier her father had been defeated at the Battle of Solway Moss, the latest in a long line of scraps in the endless local derby between the English and the Scots since Edward I first tried to conquer Scotland, in 1290. Within a week of Mary's birth her father was dead, possibly the victim of dysentery and possibly of the combination of any number of icky sexually transmitted diseases contracted during the perpetual sowing of his wild oats. Strange as it may sound, it's also possible his end had been hastened by the gender of his new child. Two sons had already died in infancy, and when his wife then produced a daughter it seemed the Stewart (as it was spelled at the time) line that had begun with Marjorie, Robert I's daughter, in 1296 would now end. 'It came wi' a lass, it will pass wi' a lass,' was James's reaction to the news before his painful death at Falkland House.

Hence Mary became Queen of the Scots at just six days old and would know no life other than one blighted by religious disputes, political intrigue and fevered debates about succession. Given that both England and France were eyeing Scotland with a view to possession, plots and plans were already being made to either marry Mary (usually to someone wholly unsuitable, but that became something she'd specialise in herself before too long), murder her or abscond with her. These were threats and possibilities that would hang over her for the rest of her life: not so much a sword of Damocles as an entire armoury.

Immediately the news of her birth had reached London, Henry VIII, one of the most vehemently expansionist monarchs ever to park a pampered posterior on the throne of England, set about ensuring that Scotland would come under his control by requesting that the infant Mary be raised in London and betrothed to his son Edward. The Earl of Arran – appointed by Mary of Guise as the infant's governor, and an English sympathiser – headed south to negotiate the Treaty of Greenwich, which would keep Mary in Scotland until she was ten years old before bringing her to London and her pre-ordained nuptials with Edward. Despite this, Mary of Guise, fiercely protective of her daughter's birthright, had no intention of ever releasing Mary into the clutches of Henry and removed her daughter to the better-fortified Stirling Castle where, on 9 September 1546, Mary was crowned Queen of Scots. A strong French presence at the coronation made it clear to Henry that the Treaty of Greenwich was now barely worth the parchment it was written on and he'd be better served in using it to sketch out a follow-up to his early hit 'Greensleeves'. Henry, about as likely to back down from a confrontation as he was to say 'no more pudding for me, thanks', embarked on some fearsome military hassling of the southern Scots lands. Edinburgh was almost completely flattened and further incursions (which destroyed 124 villages in little more than two months) were only ended when his troops were called back south for battle with France, bringing a hiatus to what became known in one of history's classic understatements as the 'Rough Wooing'. Mary, just out of nappies, was already the focus of strife and political machinations way beyond her control; people were dead because of her very existence.

In January 1547 Henry died, followed three months later by Francis I of France. Henry's son, Edward VI, was still only nine years old so the Earl of Hertford, who'd been the brains behind the Rough Wooing, acted as regent. Meanwhile the new French king, Henry II, appointed himself Protector of Scotland and sent troops to support the Scots on Hertford's resumption of wooing hostilities. Mary's guardian, the Earl of Arran, meanwhile recognised that the Catholic French might be the best way forward for Scotland against the English threat and set about arranging Mary's betrothal to the dauphin. She was moved to Dumbarton Castle, then collected by French ships and taken by sea to France with her attendants.

Life in the French court was happy for Mary. She quickly became fluent in French and learned Latin, Spanish and Italian. There was no 'w' in the French alphabet so when Mary spelled her name she used 'Stuart' instead of 'Stewart', a change that would remain for the rest of the dynasty. In 1558, at the age of fifteen, she married Dauphin Francis and cemented a Catholic alliance between France and Scotland.

In England, things were much more turbulent. Edward VI had outlived his father by only six years. He was succeeded for nine days in 1553 by the unfortunate Lady Jane Grey, before Mary Tudor was crowned and Catholicism returned. Barely five years later, however, Mary died and Henry's Protestant daughter Elizabeth ascended the throne. Which is when the fun *really* started.

As far as Catholic Spain and France were concerned, Mary was the rightful Queen of England as Elizabeth, having been born into a marriage not sanctioned by Rome, was regarded as illegitimate. As Henry VIII's grand-niece, and in the absence of male heirs, it should, as far as the Catholics were concerned, have been Mary's auburn locks beneath the crown of England. The French Henry, never one to shirk the importance of needle-work in international relations, insisted that Mary's royal canopy in Paris feature the coat of arms of England as well as those of France and Scotland. If it was designed to catch the eye of the English ambassador, Sir Nicholas Throckmorton, it worked, for before long he was hitching up his doublet and hose and har-rumphing off to tell his queen, and the first clouds of a stormy relationship between the cousins began to gather.

When Henry II died in a 1559 jousting mishap, Francis became King of France and Mary the queen consort, with a suitably ostentatious coronation, but within a year Mary would suffer the double blow of the deaths of her mother and her husband. She was still barely eighteen years old. She had never truly loved Francis – it had been a marriage of convenience, given its potential for political expediency – but Mary mourned both him and her mother at considerable and harrowing length, displaying behavioural traits that today would be diagnosed as clinical depression. After the death of Francis, Throckmorton arrived with a letter of condolence from Elizabeth, to which Mary asked that he thank the English queen for 'her gentlesness' and commented that Elizabeth 'now shows the part of a good sister, whereof she has great need'. Mary would keep faith in her familial ties to Elizabeth, something that would largely prove to be her undoing.

Before long Mary decided to return to Scotland: there was nothing for her in France and there was a considerable mutual dislike between Mary and her mother-in-law, Catherine de Medici. While Mary had been in France her Protestant half-brother James had been in charge of Scotland and had signed a treaty at Edinburgh recognising Elizabeth as Queen of England. Mary naturally refused to abide by this, which is why Elizabeth refused her safe conduct through England to Scotland and forced Mary to undertake a long voyage by sea.

When she set off in August 1561 Mary wept as she saw the coast of France disappear into the Channel haze but, driven by a sense of duty that would never leave her, she docked at Leith and set foot on Scottish soil for the first time in fourteen years. Not long afterwards she made a triumphal entry into Edinburgh, passing along the Royal Mile to Holyrood. Scotland was in uneasy religious equilibrium at the time: it was now officially Protestant, although Mary was allowed to practise her own Catholicism as long as her faith remained private and within the walls of Holyrood. The rumbustious preacher John Knox did his best to upset that balance, however, preaching three-hour polemics against the scourge of Catholicism from his pulpit at St Giles's Kirk on the Royal Mile each Sunday. Two years earlier Knox had published an inflammatory pamphlet spitting feathers at the very prospect of what he considered the 'repugnance' of female monarchy. When she summoned Knox for a meeting soon after her arrival, Mary held her own in a ding-dong discussion.

Mary also sought to renegotiate the terms of the Treaty of

Edinburgh, finding a middle way by which she would acknowledge Elizabeth as queen as long as she, in return, was recognised
as Elizabeth's heir. It was an impressive piece of diplomacy for
such a comparatively young monarch, but Elizabeth, who lived
in constant fear of plot and assassination, would have none of it.

Mary's court in Scotland was, like her time in France, a fun
place to be, at least initially. She rode every day, enjoyed hunting
and hawking, played billiards and even played golf. She was such
a good-time girl that she employed a personal jester, a French
woman named Nichola, and kept a bunch of musicians on her
books. Even her domestic staff got together and formed a choir
for her amusement. Her parties became legendary, and
Christmas 1561 was possibly the biggest knees-up Edinburgh has
seen before or since. It would prove to be the happiest time of
Mary's adult life.

It didn't last. There was no way Elizabeth would agree to
Mary's amendments to the treaty, even though deep down she
probably agreed that Mary was the best person to succeed her.
Elizabeth was a strong believer in the monarchical bloodline, that
the royals really were God's representatives on earth, but she also
knew that in the hysterical climate of religious tension Mary
could not succeed her. Elizabeth's chief adviser William Cecil
was terrified of the consequences of a Stuart accession to the
throne and when Mary repeatedly made it known that she
wanted to meet Elizabeth to discuss the situation (the pair were
becoming regular correspondents, even exchanging verses in
Italian), a meeting looked increasingly likely, to Cecil's hopping
concern. One was even set for York in August 1562, but Mary's
uncle, the Duke of Guise, was then involved in a massacre of
Huguenots. Cecil, a spin doctor of whirling surgical proportions,
blew up the incident into an anti-Protestant crusade and succeeded in preventing the two queens from meeting. Elizabeth
would remain sympathetic to Mary's claim, but Cecil spent most
of his waking hours attempting to head off what he saw as

inevitable Catholic conspiracy. As well as fearing Elizabeth's endorsement of Mary as her successor, he was convinced that public backing of the Scottish queen by the Pope or even Phillip II of Spain would trigger an uprising among English Catholics who were still in the majority.

Increasingly paranoid about Mary's very existence, Cecil drew up an Act of Exclusion with the aim of legally barring the Queen of Scots from the English succession. Mary sought to bypass this by finding herself a husband who would strengthen her claim. She was still young, very beautiful and she came with her own ready-made kingdom. The drawback was that few English nobles would consider taking a widow as a wife. It just wasn't done. On Elizabethan dating websites, the first thing an English aristocrat would look for was a tick in the status box marked 'widowed monarch' and then scroll past, no matter how good a sense of humour she might have.

Elizabeth was determined not to let Mary marry into European power. She wrote suggesting that any potential husband should be approved by her and hinted that the 'right' spouse might be the way to retain her claim. Mary winkled out of Elizabeth the name of the person she thought she should marry, and was disappointed to learn that it was her former favourite and – probably – lover, Robert Dudley, Earl of Leicester. Not inclined towards her cousin's rejects, Mary instead set her cap at Henry Stuart, Lord Darnley, a teenage noble with the strongest claim to the throne after Mary. He was, like most of Mary's menfolk, a pretty poor choice. A noted roister-doister and almost certainly bisexual, Darnley, it seemed, would shag anything that moved and probably a few things that didn't. One contemporary account described him as 'a cock chick', a phrase that has sadly and inexplicably disappeared from the vernacular. They met for the first time in February 1565 and Mary, always a sucker for a rascal with a twinkle in his eye, described her first impressions as 'the properest and best proportioned long man' she had ever seen. Darnley's reaction isn't recorded; he was probably too busy attempting to hump a lady-in-waiting, a passing dog and a wardrobe to give an opinion. They were soon spending plenty of time together, playing billiards as a doubles team against Mary's servants, and Mary even nursed Darnley through one of his regular bouts of syphilis. And they say romance is dead, eh?

Mary requested Elizabeth's consent for marriage to Darnley, to which the English queen responded with a demand that she marry Dudley, who had already made it quite clear that he didn't fancy that prospect one little bit. Meanwhile, Mary made Darnley the Earl of Ross, which went straight to his head and removed any vestigial constraints on his behaviour. Permanently drunk and obstreperous, he was even caught in bed with Mary's secretary David Rizzio. Elizabeth recalled Darnley, but Mary ordered him to remain and, despite the fact that she'd clearly be marrying a cross between Russell Brand, Pete Doherty and Genghis Khan, Mary wed Darnley in July 1565. Her new husband immediately proclaimed himself King of Scotland, something Mary reluctantly approved even though she probably wasn't particularly happy about it. In fact nobody in the world was happy about it except Darnley himself.

At around the same time Mary was forming a not inconsiderable army, instrumental in the assembling of which was the Earl of Bothwell. A charismatic aggro merchant with a deep hatred of the English and a fierce loyalty to Mary despite his own Protestantism, Bothwell was never one to discuss things amicably when a punch in the face could bring matters to a swift and satisfactory conclusion. Bothwell detested Mary's brother James, who had been usurped from the regency by her return, and chased him across much of Scotland until he fled to England, further strengthening Mary's rule.

By Christmas 1565 Mary was pregnant but, as everyone bar her had predicted, the marriage was in poor shape as she argued fiercely and constantly with her husband, and even took away his self-proclaimed monarchical status. By a convoluted route this eventually led to the sadistic murder of Mary's secretary Rizzio, who was filleted by a group of nobles in front of Mary in such brutal fashion that he was left with more than fifty wounds all over his body. Mary, who had a pistol aimed at her head during the incident, knew Darnley was involved, but he was still the father of her unborn child. The birth of their son James did nothing to improve the domestic situation, with one observer writing that when talking about Darnley Mary used 'language that cannot for modesty nor with the honour of a queen be reported'.

Despite her marital strife, Mary's relations with Elizabeth were improving to such an extent that she appointed the English queen protector of James in the event of her death, while Elizabeth proposed recognition of Mary's claim to the throne if each mutually agreed not to bother the other. Mary, who had been in poor health – she once 'died' for half an hour before being revived by a skilful French surgeon – was elated. Finally it seemed as though, for the first time in her life, things would become a bit more relaxed, her troublesome spouse notwith-standing.

Then Darnley was murdered and things went spectacularly and irrevocably awry for the Queen of Scots. A massive amount of gunpowder was stored in the cellar of Kirk o'Fields, a house in which Darnley was recuperating from another unspeakable pox. It was ignited and the house was blown to kingdom come. Curiously, Darnley's body was found in the garden in his night-clothes, with not a mark on him to suggest he'd been caught in the blast itself.

Although Mary was implicated by some it's highly unlikely she was involved. For one thing she'd only left Kirk o'Fields an hour or so before the explosion. In fact, if she hadn't promised to attend the wedding reception of one of her attendants at

Holyrood that night there's every chance she would have still been there when Scotland's biggest-ever firework went off. Indeed, for some time afterwards she was convinced that, having been at the house for most of the week, *she* was the intended target rather than her old scabbynuts of a husband. At the time of the explosion she had advisers looking into a divorce or an annulment of the marriage – she certainly didn't want to be involved in anything dodgy, and even for Mary, who made some spectacularly bad decisions in her time, it would have made no sense to be behind anything remotely suspect, especially when things were looking up on the English succession front.

The nature of the times dictated that Mary's name featured strongly in whispers about the murder. If you think conspiracy theories are loopy today, you should have been around in Elizabethan times. Mud stuck, though, and even her own family turned its back on her, along with the Catholic Church. A month after the incident Mary received a terse letter from Elizabeth, telling her that there would be no more talk of a reconciliation and that she was to ratify the original treaty renouncing all her claims to the English throne without any more of this poetic Italian shilly-shallying.

From being tailed by her own pig's bladder on a stick-wielding jester and throwing the best parties Edinburgh had ever seen, Mary was now almost completely alone. Still not even twenty-five years old, she had already outlived two husbands and, through no fault of her own, had found herself at the head of a nation but shunned by nearly everyone she knew. She sent the infant James to Stirling Castle for his protection, not having the slightest inkling that she would never see her son again.

En route back to Edinburgh Mary was intercepted and abducted by Bothwell, who took her to his castle at Dunbar, virtually imprisoned her and, it seems, raped her too. Some argue that although Mary was kept at Dunbar for two weeks Bothwell was away for much of that time and she had plenty of opportunity to leave. Either way, they were married within a month. Mary's popularity in Scotland plummeted – many believed that Bothwell and Mary had colluded in Darnley's murder to facilitate their own relationship. A notice nailed to the gates of Holyrood read 'As the common people say, only harlots marry in May'. Mary and Bothwell had married on 15 May 1567.

Mary's reasons for marrying Bothwell remain unclear to this day. It's possible that she did love him – probably the first time she'd loved any man – but soon realised that he was only after status and power. Bothwell treated his new wife appallingly and was universally detested at court. He was bullying, controlling and jealous of Mary's power, but Mary, a stickler for doing what she believed to be the right thing however chronically misguided that thing may be, stuck to her marriage vows. There was so much opposition among the Scottish lords that civil war in Scotland seemed likely. A military confrontation at Musselburgh was averted by Mary's quick-footed diplomacy and Bothwell was allowed to escape while Mary returned to Edinburgh with the rebel lords. She'd never see him again, even though she was now carrying his child.

Although these confederate lords recognised Mary as queen they saw her as wholly unsuitable to run the country. It's likely that some of them were involved in the plot to kill Darnley too, and when Mary announced she was to conduct a full inquiry into the murder it was soon decided that she should be kept out of the way. They certainly wanted Bothwell out of the picture permanently (he would leave Scotland to eventually die a slow, painful death chained to a pillar for a decade in a Danish dungeon) and maybe hoped that they could blackmail Mary into divorcing him in exchange for her freedom. They also intended to force her abdication in favour of her useless half-brother James, now the Earl of Moray, whom they planned to install as regent until the younger James, Mary's son, was old enough to assume power.

So, back in Edinburgh, while eating her first meal in three days, Mary was ordered to pack a nightdress and leave immediately. Naively she thought she was being taken to her baby son in Stirling but instead, after an exhausting ride through the night, Mary arrived at the shores of Loch Leven as the dawn of 17 June 1567 glowed on the horizon. Exhausted, frightened and wondering what on earth life had in store for her next, Mary would have stepped, dazed and shattered, out of the boat and passed through the gateway in front of which I now stood. Mary had visited Loch Leven Castle before, in happier circumstances when touring her kingdom after her arrival from France. This time she was a prisoner, a sickly pregnant woman with three marriages behind her, separated from her son and now a captive of upstart lords whom she strongly suspected of being behind the murder in which she was being implicated. To make things worse, the owners of the castle were the Douglas family, the Dowager Lady Margaret being the mother of James, her half-brother. James had been the illegitimate offspring of a fling between Margaret and Mary's father, James V, but Margaret claimed – falsely – that they'd secretly married so she could push James forward as the rightful King of Scotland. If Mary's circumstances weren't bad enough to start with, seeing a tight-lipped, harrumphing Margaret emerging in full sail out of the morning haze can't exactly have helped her mood.

For the first two weeks Mary was very ill. She hardly ate or drank a thing, said very little and, not surprisingly, within a month had miscarried twins, nearly dying in the process. Within days three of the rebel lords were in her chamber, trying to harry her into abdicating. I walked across to the Glassin Tower in the corner of the castle courtyard, where Mary was placed on arrival. It was a small, round tower, open to the elements from top to bottom now but during Mary's stay it consisted of three rooms, one above the other. I walked up the narrow, age-worn stone steps to the level of Mary's bedchamber on the first floor.

A fierce wind whipped across the loch and the choppy water was white-tipped.

It wasn't hard to imagine Mary here, the fire burning in the fireplace and the queen maybe sitting at the window looking out across the water to the land that was rightfully hers. I could also almost picture her, weak and pale in her bed, constantly badgered by the lords – who were trying to claim that Mary had been sleeping with Bothwell before Darnley's murder and that the killing had been arranged prior to her alleged abduction – into signing the abdication document. Finally, on 24 July, Lords Lindsay and Ruthven, two of the leading scoundrels of the conspiracy, finally lost patience and stormed into the room. They forced the sickly queen to listen to the lawyers reading the deeds, placed her fingers around a pen and told her to sign or they'd cut her throat there and then. With a reluctant, shaky hand, Mary gave up her throne in favour of her son, inserting her half-brother as regent until such time as James was old enough to take over. As I thought about those events, which took place right in front of where I now stood, the wind blew stronger through the glassless windows and the cloudy, scudding sky seemed to grow a little darker. Mary's despair was almost tangible.

Five days later, the infant James was crowned in a damp squib of a coronation. Mary's captor, Sir William Douglas, celebrated by lighting bonfires and setting off the castle's cannon. When Mary asked what all the fuss was about he took great delight in telling her, and advised that she should be as cock-a-hoop at the news as he was.

In the months following her abdication Mary's health improved greatly. Perhaps the removal of the day-to-day pressure of being a beleaguered monarch helped, but certainly she grew stronger and healthier, was heard to laugh with her attendants and, although her captors wouldn't have known it to look at her because of her outwardly relaxed appearance, was fostering a burning desire to regain the crown. No doubt about it: Mary was intending to escape.

I was only on the island for a short while, but I could feel the confinement. It must have been far worse for Mary, as while today the castle is surrounded on all sides by trees and a small island, it's only been that way since the nineteenth-century draining of the loch. In Mary's day the water would have lapped up against three sides of the castle, and with just a small courtyard for exercise within the walls, Mary's prolonged stay must have been a wholly dispiriting and claustrophobic one for a woman used to having space around her to ride, to play golf, or just to take long walks.

Mary had won over George and Willie Douglas, two of her captor's sons, and they secretly discussed plans for Mary's escape. One idea was to spirit Mary away from the island in a big box of documents; another to have a supportive band of soldiers commandeer a coal boat en route for the castle and storm the place. A plan for Mary to jump down from the walls was abandoned after a dummy run left one of her maids with a badly injured ankle.

One attempt at the end of March 1568 nearly succeeded, when Mary was disguised as a washerwoman and sent from the castle in a boat with the laundry. Unfortunately, halfway across the boatman realised that the soft, delicate hands he could see weren't used to wrenching textiles about in cold water and the plan failed; fortunately the boatman was persuaded to keep the escape attempt to himself. Word reached Sir William, however, and George was banished from the castle and the island.

The setback was temporary and within weeks Mary's flight from the castle would be secured. Every Sunday the whole troop of guards dined with the Douglases in the keep. After all the doors had been locked the keys were placed on the dining table, next to Sir William Douglas, for the duration of the meal. Young

Willie Douglas, who would have been around seventeen at the
time, worked as a page and waited on the tables on these occasions. Having first ensured that all but one of the island's boats
had been scuttled, at dinner on Sunday 2 May Willie seized his
chance. With Sir William firmly in his cups, Willie dropped a
napkin on top of the keys and swiped them from the table. His
bravery was extraordinary, his sleight-of-hand one of the major
turning points in Mary's already turbulent life. Swiftly he collected Mary, snuck out of the gate and led her to a boat already
containing one of her attendants, locked the castle gate behind
him and set off rowing across the loch where help was waiting at
the other end in the form of his brother George and the sympathetic Lords Seton and Hamilton. Halfway across, Willie
dropped the keys into the water where, when the loch was part-
drained nearly three hundred years later, they were found lying
in the mud.

I walked down to the modern jetty where the tourist boats
normally arrive. It wouldn't be the exact spot from which Mary
departed thanks to the draining of the loch, but the view out
across the water would hardly have changed at all since Mary's
day. I wondered how she felt as she crept out of the castle and
quietly stepped into the boat. During her time in Edinburgh she
was well known for escapades such as dressing herself and a maid
in men's clothing and walking the streets. The stakes were a
little higher this time, but she would probably have been feeling
a mixture of nervous anticipation at the uncertainty of what lay
ahead and relief at being out of the confines of the castle and the
island where the twin babies she miscarried lay buried. It's possible that she felt as free as she ever had – no longer a captive, no
longer a queen, no longer having to put up with a violent
drunken buffoon of a husband. Friends were waiting for her at
the lochside, people she could trust, people who wouldn't be
part of any plot against her. As the oars sploshed quietly on the
moonlit water, she may have looked up at the sky and felt the

freedom of the birds whose silent shapes soaring in the darkness made the stars wink.

The wind was blowing up quite fiercely now. Duncan appeared behind me and said that we'd better get a move on before the loch got too rough for the boat. Back at the jetty he wrapped himself into some formidable waterproofs that left just his eyes visible, ushered the dogs and me into the boat, untied the rope, gunned the engine and set out into the wind. The dogs curled around my feet as I sheltered in the front of the boat facing astern where Duncan stood, proud and defiant against the crashing, wind-whipped waves.

We don't know how long it took until the castle garrison realised something was amiss, but it must have been hilarious when they did – Sir William Douglas reaching for the keys and finding them gone, lifting his dish, moving his tankard around, pushing his chair back and looking on the floor, the realisation that they'd gone slowly dawning. By then someone would have tried the door and found it locked, and chaos would have ensued. Soldiers running around, crashing into each other, knowing that something was wrong and that they had to do something about it but not being entirely sure what. Battering at the door handle with a chair, trying to jemmy it open with a ladle until the lock was splintered and they all spilled out of the room, scurried one by one down the ladder outside the tower and found the courtyard gate locked too. Someone would have checked on Mary and found her gone, and Douglas would have experienced a cold, creeping sensation as he realised that he'd been hoodwinked and his captive had escaped. Boy, was he in trouble.

As we arrived back at the pier the heavens opened as if Scotland had just taken delivery of a monsoon. It was as fearsome a cloudburst as I'd see on any of my journeys, yet Duncan still had to help put the castle's other boat, which had just arrived from Arbroath on the back of a truck, on the water ahead of the imminent summer season. Four men pushed and grunted and cursed the rain as I stood and watched from the doorway of a tower built, Duncan told me, as a watchtower to survey the cemetery on the other side of the wall during the time of the notorious grave robbers Burke and Hare. Eventually the boat was free of its trailer and, given the weather conditions, I accepted Duncan's offer of a lift as far as Dunfermline, just the other side of the Forth from Edinburgh, to where he was heading home. From Dunfermline it was a relatively short journey to North Queensferry and the Forth Bridge, and before long I was in Edinburgh.

Edinburgh is one of my favourite cities in the world. It's beautiful just to look at, for one thing, and its tiny, steep nooks and walkways between the shadowy majesty of the buildings, dimly lit at night, promise mystery, intrigue and cases for Inspector Rebus. Although Mary hadn't reached Edinburgh on her journey – having briefly stopped at Dalmeny Castle, close to where the southern end of the Forth Bridge now stands – I was keen to see the place where she had spent her years openly ruling as Queen of Scots and wanted to walk the Royal Mile just as she had done on her triumphant entry into the city. The castle dominates the centre of Edinburgh from its craggy perch and it was there that I began my retracing of Mary's procession – an occasion as far removed from the journey I was following as it's possible to be. The entrance arch is flanked by statues of two of Scotland's greatest historical heroes: Robert the Bruce on the north side, who defeated Edward II at Bannockburn in 1314 and drove out the English, and William Wallace to the south, who'd also given the English the run-around a few years earlier before settling into the public consciousness as Mel Gibson with a blue face and an accent from just the far side of nowhere. I looked out past Wallace across Edinburgh to the horizon, where fast-moving dark clouds approached with determined intent. Far below me a suburban train eased into Waverley Station with a lazy click-clack, click-clack. Statues line the wide cobbled expanse outside the castle gates – as I walked past a small boy was trying to shin up the leg of Earl Haig. I'd only progressed a few yards further when a squally cloudburst suddenly pelted the city, sending tourists blundering into kilt shops to a soundtrack that combined squealing with the snapping of anorak hoods in the wind. By now well used to being targeted by the weather gods to the extent that I suspected a personal vendetta, I pressed on, passing Brodie's Close on the right, named after Francis Brodie, whose son William led a bizarre double life of respectable businessman and deacon of trades guild by day and drinker, gambler, cock-fighter and robber by night, a dichotomy that inspired Robert Louis Stevenson's *Dr Jekyll and Mr Hyde*. Deacon Brodie was hanged in Edinburgh in 1788 after an attempted robbery of the Edinburgh Customs and Excise building went badly wrong, and – get this – the gallows he swung from were of a design he had created a few years earlier. It was around here that Mary's escort of fifty men dressed as moors, wearing yellow taffeta and black hats, took the lead in the procession until they reached Lawnmarket, where she heard a choir sing from the gallery of a specially constructed wooden arch and was presented with a key to the city.

Further along, past the kiltmakers and cafés, the pubs and fudge shops, I passed the large and slightly incongruous statue of the eighteenth-century philosopher David Hume who, clad in just an off-the-shoulder toga, looks absolutely freezing. On the right, set into the pavement, is the mosaic of the Heart of Midlothian that marks the former entrance to the old Tolbooth prison, just by St Giles's Cathedral, and a little further on, on the left as I walked, the City Chambers. Mary spent her last night in Edinburgh here, before being taken off to Loch Leven, and a bronze plaque on the wall confirms that 'On this site stood the lodgings of Sir Simon Preston of Craigmillar, Provost of the City of Edinburgh 1566–67; in which lodging Mary Queen of Scotland after her surrender to the Confederate Lords at Carberry Hill, spent her last night in Edinburgh 15 June 1567. On the following evening she was conveyed to Holyrood and thereafter to Lochleven Castle as a State Prisoner.' As I read the plaque there was a rumble and roar in the sky as two fighter jets passed overhead. Scotland were playing England at rugby on the other side of the city, and the singing of the national anthem, 'Flower of Scotland', at Murrayfield is always accompanied by the flypast that thundered above me.

A few yards beyond the city chambers is the house where Mary's Edinburgh nemesis John Knox lived for a while on the third floor, the ground floor having been occupied by Mary's jeweller James Mosman. Mosman's initials are gilded in the brickwork, and along the top of the shopfront is the message LYFE GOD ABVFE AND YI NYCHTBOUR AS YI SELF.

The Royal Mile itself becomes decidedly less regal the further down the hill towards Holyrood you go: the souvenir shops begin to shed any pretensions of distinction, and when I saw a poster in a shop window advertising Celtic clairvoyant gatherings I knew it was time to hasten my step, not least because it looked like it was going to rain again. When I reached the bottom of the Mile, big blue gates barred me from visiting the Palace at Holyrood, where a whole bunch of religious allegorical plays were being performed as Mary passed, so I crossed the road to a modern, glassy building opposite. A kindly security guard coaxed me inside on the grounds that the Scottish Parliament building was worth seeing. It wasn't really, to be honest, and parliament wasn't in session. I didn't want to leave straightaway as the security guard had been so keen for me to experience the wonders of Scottish democracy, so I spent a respectable amount of time aimlessly wandering around the reception and gift shop reading leaflets in English and Scots

Gaelic while resisting the urge to buy a bottle of Scottish Parliament whisky.

When I tried to leave a cursory push of the revolving door had no effect whatsoever. I tried again, a bit harder. It didn't budge. There was a wheelchair access door next to it and I tried that, at which a security guard on the other side of the glass gestured at me to use the revolving doors. I gave them another shove and again nothing happened. I looked back at the guard and shrugged my shoulders, giving him a look that in a cartoon would have been represented by a wavy line instead of a mouth. He tried to push from the other side – no joy there. I'd entered the bearpit of Scottish politics and it didn't look like I'd be allowed to leave. Eventually the security guards admitted defeat and allowed me through the wheelchair access door, while jabbing frantically at a panel of buttons that were probably setting off sirens and alarms in a control room somewhere leading to the imminent arrival of a SWAT team crashing through the windows and my being carted off whimpering to Guantanamo Bay or, worse, a Celtic clairvoyant gathering.

Once I'd extricated myself from the Scottish Parliament and left the security guards attempting to shoulder the recalcitrant revolving door into action I soon realised that I needed to steady my nerves from the trauma and found a pub. Inside, the whole place was rapt by the television screen in the corner: Scotland's rugby team was beating England. Scottish rugby has not been at its peak in recent years but, to use that hoary old sportswriting chestnut, the form book goes out of the window when they play England. As the blue shirts and white shirts heaved and hauled each other around the screen in what was clearly an exhaustingly physical encounter, the Scots around me roared their encouragement with a substantial national pride. This wasn't just about Scotland winning; it was about Scotland winning and England losing. It was centuries of oppression and occupation, bloodshed and politics. I'd just left the gleaming symbol of Scottish devolution, but such progress has not dimmed the desire to see England dumped on her backside at every opportunity, and international sporting encounters were the best place to do it. As the cauliflower-eared colossi in blue shirts heaved against the English pack close to the Scottish line, every inch that the grunting, steaming mass gained was greeted with roars of approval. The tension was as palpable here, in this half-full, modern, largely characterless pub, as it was at Murrayfield Stadium across town, and the clock in the corner of the screen seemed to tick slower with each passing second. Finally, a couple of shrill parps on the referee's whistle signalled the end of the game and a deserved win for Scotland. Enormous smiles on muddy faces made toothless by gumshields filled the screen, hundreds of saltires waved in the crowd and my fellow drinkers caught each other's eyes and punched the air in a celebration of Scottishness.

That Edinburgh night was a memorable one. The pubs were filled with joyful Scots in kilts and rugby shirts, while forlorn bunches of English fans in their white replica shirts mooched stoop-shouldered, hands thrust in pockets, through the cold Edinburgh night. From somewhere out of sight the skirl of the bagpipes speared the chilly air, swirling around the old walls of the Royal Mile in celebration of yet another blow struck against the old enemy.

I was up and out early the next morning, the fierce wind stinging my face with bullets of drizzle, heading west out past Edinburgh airport to Winchburgh, in search of Niddry Castle, where Mary spent her first night of freedom. It was a pleasant walk along the Union Canal until the pedal-bin monolith of the castle loomed up against the dark green background of the Pentland Hills, punching its way up from the landscape on a small rocky outcrop. It was as austere and unwelcoming a castle as I had ever seen. I'd clocked up a few on my travels, but none had been as charmless as Niddry.

A sign overgrown by weeds and grass announced the approach to the building, which sits at the edge of a golf course, a brooding pile of dark stone without a single flourish save for an ugly gable at the top of one wall which was clearly added long after construction. What windows there were were slitty and thin; a huge crack meandered down the middle of one wall. The presence of a garden off to one side, fenced off and containing a swing hammock and some children's toys, showed that the castle is now somebody's home but it looked a fairly bleak place to live, at least from the outside. A huge net was ranged between the castle and the golf course and I wasn't sure whether it was to protect the castle from stray golf balls or vice versa. Given that it was a private dwelling I didn't get too close, but then even if it hadn't been I'd most likely have kept my distance. It had obviously lain neglected and derelict for some time before the present occupiers arrived, and there's clearly still some work to do, but I'd say it'll take more than a few scatter cushions and tealights in the fireplace to make Niddry a welcoming place. The last thing castles are designed to be is welcoming, of course, and many were built in haste and for purely military and strategic reasons, but it must have presented a fairly bleak vista for Mary as she arrived there and, as the sun went down, looked out through a narrow window at a landscape that was no longer her responsibility, officially at least. She would have been cheered, however, that her passage to Niddry had seen her greeted warmly by the Scottish people as she passed. Indeed, when supporters gathered outside the castle in the morning Mary greeted them with her auburn hair loose around her shoulders: she was so pleased to see friendly faces that she didn't wait until her attendants had put it up.

I squelched around the edge of the golf course and headed back to Winchburgh before heading further west to Linlithgow, a much more pleasant prospect. Linlithgow is a town that's quietly pleased with itself, and with pretty good reason. Hunched around the southern side of its own loch, it's a peaceful, laid-back place with the atmosphere of somewhere that's done very well for itself, thank you. Indeed, its patron saint is St Michael, he of the quality clothing and swanky food stores. In addition, Linlithgow positively bubbles with history, not least because it's the site of Linlithgow Palace, a beautiful old place subtly hidden from the town by its lower position by the loch, and the place where Mary was born. It also has a strange link to the, er, history of the future inasmuch as it is the home town of Scotty from *Star Trek*, who will, apparently, be born into a world of tight-fitting clothing and planets with wobbly landscapes in Linlithgow in 2222.

A light drizzle was falling as I passed Linlithgow Cross and walked up towards the castle past a line of plaques commemorating every English monarch since James. I walked into the courtyard, the focus of which is the oldest working fountain in Britain according to the enthusiastically helpful man in the ticket office (it apparently ran with red wine when Bonnie Prince Charlie passed through in 1745. If it did, it's remarkable that Charlie, who liked to take a drop or two, ever left.) Although much of the castle is open to the elements it's not difficult to gain a sense of how grand it must have been in its heyday. Mary, historians believe, was probably born in a room on the second floor of the south-west tower. It's just four walls now, but I stood at the bottom and looked up towards the grey sky, blinking away the raindrops that flew at me from above. Nearly half a millennium had passed since these shiny, wet stone walls had reverberated to the cries of the child born into one of the most turbulent lives in history; a life that began here and ended on an executioner's block in Northamptonshire. It was here, in this tower, that Mary knew innocence for the only time in her life. Within six days she was queen, and then her troubles began. This tower was the only place in the world where Mary, newborn, was totally free of trouble and worry. And it didn't even last a week.

I stopped for lunch at the Four Marys pub, named after the Queen of Scots' loyal attendants, which is undoubtedly one of the finest inns in Scotland and not just because they have a wall full of certificates that say so. Pictures of Mary cover the stone walls inside, and the warmth, the sense of history and a startlingly good pie made me reluctant to leave.

Mary and her advisers were making for Dumbarton Castle, a fortress held by her supporters. The open support she was receiving on her travels would have encouraged her, and she knew that once at Dumbarton she would be able to assemble an army more than capable of wresting the throne back from her brother, the Earl of Moray. Her itinerary fixed, Mary's next halt was Cadzow Castle on the outskirts of Hamilton, to the south-east of Glasgow. Today it's in the swanky surroundings of the Chatelherault Country Park, close to the seventeenth-century hunting lodge of the long-demolished Hamilton Palace. The castle is now little more than a few chunks of stone and some eighteenth-century additions designed to make the ruins look like *grander* ruins, when having a dilapidated castle in your grounds was as de rigueur as decking is today. In Mary's day the castle was fairly new, its building having been finished in 1550, but it was destroyed by the English in the late sixteenth century and never rebuilt. What's left is fenced off and covered in scaffolding; a sign announcing that renovation work is in progress has been there for some considerable time. The stumps of stone that are visible are smeared with ivy and look as though they should be the subject of a late eighteenth-century etching, where in the foreground a man in a top hat points at something for the benefit of a woman with a parasol. Alas, today the only hats in the foreground are yellow and hard and worn in conjunction with high-visibility vests rather than frock coat and cane.

The castle would probably have been a more welcoming prospect for Mary than Niddry had been, situated as it is on a gorge over Avon Water, just across from the cobwebby peace and ferny brown carpet of a coniferous forest. The fact that the sun now shone from a cloudless blue sky probably helped, as did the fact that, unlike at Niddry, nobody had sloshed 'RANGERS' over the stonework in white paint. I peered between the grey steel bars of the fence surrounding the site in the forlorn hope that one of the workmen would invite me in, but gave up before too long and retired to the park's visitor centre for a cup of tea and a bowl of soup. Some of the best mannequins I've ever seen populate the centre: all Georgian men and women who look almost real even when placed in incongruous locations, like next to a fire exit or, in one case, regarding half a dozen piles of stacked plastic chairs with a benevolent smile.

It was possibly while at Cadzow that Mary realised some kind of military conflict was almost inevitable. The rebel lords were closing in and they had a substantial force of men with them. As word had spread of Mary's escape – she'd sent out messages notifying her supporters that she was back in business that first night at Niddry – some six thousand troops had been assembled in her name and they would meet the forces of the lords and her brother at Langside: then a village, now a suburb on the southern side of Glasgow. Mary had been hoping to make it as far as Dumbarton without conflict, but James and his supporters headed her off here.

It was a strange kind of skirmish on the face of it, more like a family quarrel with weapons: a woman fought her half-brother, who in turn was fighting in defence of his nephew, her son. Today they would have slugged it out on a mid-morning television chat show, but in the sixteenth century armed conflict was the only way and on 13 May 1568 the two sides met. Unfortunately for Mary, in less than an hour of fearsomely intense battle her well-meaning but inexperienced military commander the Duke of Argyll was outwitted and outfought, and the battle was lost. It was a crucial turning point in Mary's life and in the history of Scotland itself. In the space of about forty-five minutes Mary had gone from being an ousted monarch with a genuine grievance and a terrific chance of crippling the cause of those responsible for removing her, to even more of a fugitive whose cause was now in big trouble.

Langside has been long swallowed up by the spread of Glasgow and the battlefield itself is now an area called Battlefield. I knew there was a memorial to the battle, close to Queen's Park, and on a blustery morning I set out to find it. I passed along the outside of the park, past some of the Victorian era's most stentorian architecture, and came to a busy roundabout. At its centre, largely unnoticed by the drivers snaking past, was a plinth and pillar, atop which sat a rampant stone lion. Beyond the memorial was the bright red and yellow façade of a tyre centre, and peeping out from behind the pillar was a big cartoon of a tyre giving me a smiling thumbs-up. Even with the memorial it was nearly impossible to imagine this as the site of one of the major conflicts of Scottish history. It made me a little sad, for some reason. Maybe it's because I'd grown to like and sympathise with Mary so much that I felt so deflated I felt like popping over to the tyre place and replacing my mojo with a remould. It certainly had much to do with the fact that history seems to have been erased here. Even the austere Victorian-ness of the memorial looked inappropriate, let alone the fact that it was now the centrepiece of a measure to keep traffic flowing.

I wasn't sure where the hill from which Mary watched the Battle of Langside might be, but I headed towards Mount Florida anyway. Its name suggested height, and it is also the location of Hampden Park, Scotland's national football stadium, which was good enough for me.

Within twenty minutes I was climbing the steps to the entrance of the recently rebuilt home of Scottish football and, with nothing better to do, signed up for a stadium tour. As I waited at the meeting point for the tour guide, a small, grey-haired man with a limp approached and asked whether I was going on the tour. I was, I replied. He said he was too, and then asked me who my team was. Now, in Glasgow, where Celtic and Rangers are, generally speaking, divided along religious lines, that seemingly innocuous question can sometimes be a risky one to answer. Celtic was set up by a Catholic priest as a way of raising money for the poor – mainly Irish immigrants – in the 1880s. Inevitably they gained a strongly Catholic following and became hugely successful on and off the field. Glasgow Rangers then adopted a strongly Protestant stance – including a policy of never signing Catholic players – and a religious as well as sporting divide was created, one that has subsequently been propagated by Glasgow's specific socio-economic situation. When the two clubs play each other, as they do at least four times every season, there are usually violent incidents across the city and deaths have resulted. From the stabbing of youths for wearing the wrong colour jacket to Rangers removing eggs benedict from their corporate hospitality menus when Pope Benedict XVI succeeded John Paul II, there is a constant tension between the clubs. Hence I was relieved to be able to reply 'Charlton Athletic' to my inquisitor. I needn't have worried, as he then revealed himself to be a Partick Thistle supporter, one of the city's smaller clubs that doesn't carry the baggage of the big two.

Fred, who would be the only other taker for the tour, was a Glaswegian native but now lived in Peterborough. Such was his devotion to Partick Thistle that he'd travelled up on the train. He was terrifically sprightly despite walking with a stick, and proved to be a fascinating companion on the tour which was, I regret to say, a bit of a disappointment. So recently was the stadium refurbished that it was like being shown around a municipal sports centre; there was no real feeling of the history of the place where some of Scottish football's most significant games have been played. Even as we walked up the players' tunnel towards the pitch there was no sense of the passion, the mixture of jubilation and broken dreams that settle invisibly on a football field. Thank goodness for Fred, who kept me rapt with his tales of his playing days in Scottish junior football, the memories making his eyes sparkle as he recalled darting down the wing evading the lunging tackles of ponderous, lurching full backs. He seemed visibly to grow younger as he recalled the cup finals and big matches, how he'd played regularly in front of crowds of several thousand, so much so that the walking stick supporting him seemed to bear less and less of his weight the more he reminisced.

At the end of the tour we moved into the Scottish Football Museum where the real history of the game lies, rather than in breezeblock dressing rooms with anonymous pine fittings. Whether you like football or not, the Scottish Football Museum is a terrific example of what a museum should be, with just the right mixture of artefacts and information. Its exhibits have been carefully chosen and thoughtfully displayed. And what exhibits they are: priceless items of football memorabilia gathered from around the world. There's a ticket for the world's first football international, played between Scotland and England in Glasgow in 1872. There's also a ticket and the match ball from the first match at Hampden Park, between Queen's Park and Celtic in 1903. Fred and I, who had the place to ourselves, wandered spellbound between the displays of old shirts, footballs, tickets, programmes, caps and mementoes from times far removed from the modern commercial game.

Eventually Fred looked at the time. 'They'll have had the pitch inspection at Partick by now,' he said. 'I'll give them a ring. Er, if you've nothing planned for the evening, would you be up for coming to the game?'

I've been a football addict for as long as I can remember. I would watch football in one of the world's greatest stadia or in the park at the end of the road. In recent years, however, the rampant commercialism of the game has, for me, taken the soul out of it to a great extent. Yet here, on this rainy afternoon in Glasgow, the combination of some startling memorabilia and the stories of an old amateur footballer had reminded me why I fell in love with the game in the first place. I could think of nothing I'd rather do than join Fred and a couple of thousand other hardy souls watching Partick Thistle play Stirling Albion. I agreed without hesitation. Fred prodded at a few numbers on his phone and settled it against his ear. After a few seconds, he said, 'Ah, yes, hello. Is the game on this evening, please?' There was a slight pause. 'Oh really? Ah well, that's a shame. Thanks anyway.' He snapped his phone closed and said, 'It's off. Waterlogged pitch.'

Now that is devotion. For a man of advanced years, limited mobility and not in the best of health to travel all that way to see a match of no consequence in the knowledge that it might not even take place took some level of passion for the game, and for Partick Thistle in particular.

Fred didn't seem too downhearted, though, and wandered off to look at some old pennants in a glass case as a stout grey-haired attendant came over to me and asked if I'd missed out the trophy room. I was ashamed to admit that I had, on the grounds that once you've seen one trophy you've pretty much seen them all. How wrong I was. Kenny was one of the museum's curators and, I deduced, was mainly responsible for the trophies. For the next twenty minutes he held me spellbound with his passion for the glinting silver cups and shields behind the glass. They ranged from the beautiful to the bizarre to the out-and-out bling. The centrepiece of the collection is the Scottish Cup, the oldest trophy in the world still being played for. It's a tiny, intricately decorated little thing on an incongruously heavy-duty plinth, with the names of every winner since 1874 engraved either on the trophy itself or, when space ran out, on the base.

'How much is it worth?' I asked.

Kenny puffed his cheeks. 'Well, you just can't put a price on it, but it's insured for two million pounds,' he said.

'Whoa!' I replied articulately. 'And you let the winning team get their sweaty muddy hands on it and wave it about?'

'Aye. It's taken out of the case on Cup Final day itself and is presented to the winning captain at the end of the game. They get to parade it around the pitch, but as soon as they leave the field I'm waiting to whip it out of their hands and give them the replica. It comes straight back in here, fingerprints on it and all, then on the Monday the experts come in and polish it back to the state you see it in now.'

We walked back through the display cases to a section devoted to the Wembley Wizards, the 1928 Scottish team that travelled south to Wembley and thrashed the English 5–1 with one of the best displays of football ever seen. There was an original shirt worn by one of the players and the match ball too, arguably the holy grail for any Scottish football supporter. I asked Kenny, whom I had already decided had the greatest job in the world, what his ultimate prize to acquire for the museum might be. He thought for a moment.

'I'd say it would have to be an original Scotland jersey worn in the very first international in 1872. It won't happen though. The reason Scotland play in blue isn't because of the national flag; it's because that first ever team was made up entirely of Queen's Park players. Queen's Park played in blue back then so they used their own shirts and attached a Scottish crest to them. In those days they used the shirts over and over again, not like today when players are given brand new kit for every match, so there wouldn't have been a special shirt for that game. Hence even if one came up now it would be absolutely impossible to confirm if it had been worn for the England game. Aye, one of those would make me a very happy man, but I can't see it happening.'

I asked where that game was played, and whether the ground was still there.

'Yeah, it's still there all right,' he replied. 'They played at the West of Scotland Cricket Club in Partick. I've been there myself. The original pavilion is still used and you can see exactly where the football pitch had been.'

I told Kenny about my historical odyssey and decided I had to go and visit this footballing shrine before rejoining the Mary trail. I pulled out my OS map and opened it out on a glass case containing a collection of nineteenth-century international caps won by R. S. McColl, the man behind the chain of Scottish newsagents of the same name. Kenny ran his finger over the map and tapped a spot to the west of the city centre.

'It's there,' he said. 'You come out of the station and head straight on, you can't miss it. By the way,' he added, 'you know Mary, Queen of Scots was a football fan, don't you?'

I laughed.

'No, I'm serious,' said Kenny. 'Come with me, I'll show you.'

I followed him out of the museum and then through several doors until we arrived in a huge warehouse-sized space somewhere in the depths of the stadium. Floor to ceiling racks of shelving creaked under piles of boxes, some with a flap open to reveal old programmes and photographs. There was a single desk in the corner, covered in papers and mouldy coffee cups, and Kenny was rifling through the drawers. He caught sight of me looking around the room.

'The stuff we have on display is barely a quarter of what we've actually got,' he said, before adding, 'here we are – found it.'

He began leafing through a glossy, colourful booklet. 'It's all in German,' he explained. 'We helped put on a history exhibition at the World Cup, and we took the Mary, Queen of Scots ball out there. Tell you what, let's go and ask Richard: he'll know all about it.'

Back we went, through several more doors, until we emerged in a little office, its raked ceiling revealing that it was directly beneath the seats nearest the pitch. Richard, a young, serious-looking man with a floppy dark fringe, looked up from a computer screen and Kenny asked him to tell me about Mary, Queen of Scots the football fan. Remarkably, the incident he would tell me about occurred at the end of the journey I was making.

'It happened not long after the Battle of Langside,' he told me, at which I squeaked excitedly about just coming from the memorial. 'As you know, Mary ended up in England hoping to seek help from Elizabeth. When she was seized on arrival she was kept at first under house arrest at Carlisle Castle under Henry Scrope, the governor of Carlisle, and Sir Francis Knollys, one of Elizabeth's privy counsellors. Given how close Carlisle is to the border, these two kept a close eye on Mary and her activities, worrying that she'd be sprung by supporters, and kept William Cecil informed of her every move.'

He turned to his computer, clicked a few times and found what he was looking for. 'Here it is: a letter dated 15 June 1568 from Knollys to Cecil that says, "Yesterday she went out at a postern to walk on a playing green towards Scotland waited on by Scrope with twenty-four of Read's Halberdiers, and some of her own gentlemen etc, where twenty of her retinue played at football before her for two hours very strongly, nimbly, and skilfully, without foul play – the smallness of their ball occasioning their fairer play."'

I was agog. I was already a Mary fan but this made me want to marry her, high mortality rate among her spouses notwithstanding.

'Now, the Stirling Smith Museum features within its collection what is reckoned to be the world's oldest surviving football,' Richard continued. 'It was found during conservation work in the queen's bedchamber, among the roof beams in the royal palace at Stirling Castle, and has been dated to the mid-sixteenth century, bringing it very close to the lifetime of Mary herself.'

This was amazing stuff. I already knew that Mary was keen on outdoor pursuits in her younger days, and after her long incarceration at Loch Leven she must have been dying to get out into the open and indulge herself again. For someone to spend two hours watching a bunch of blokes kicking a ball around shows some level of enthusiasm. And a football in her bedroom? I might be getting carried away here, but the fact that the ball was found among the roof beams of her bedchamber suggests to me that it was the result of an over-exuberant miskick in a game of three-and-in with her attendants. As someone who has lost countless balls thanks to gutters, chimneys and impenetrable undergrowth, and knowing Mary's boisterous character, it's a theory that holds water if you ask me.

Kenny showed me out. 'You know they've found Henry VIII's football boots, don't you? A pair of boots turned up that belonged to him which were designed specifically for sport, and we know that he enjoyed playing an early form of football.'

This historical *Match of the Day* was becoming too much for me. I was starting to suspect it might actually be a really brilliant dream. Fired up, I headed out of Hampden and into the purple-skied Glasgow evening. My deflation at the Langside memorial had been negated by the chance discoveries I'd made as a result of a whimsical detour. To cap it all, Mary, on whom I had developed a bit of an historical crush, was a football fan. All I needed to find out now was that she played the ukulele and had a penchant for whiskery English blokes in waterproofs and historical perfection would be mine.

I was up early the next morning: I had one last thing to see in Glasgow. I took the Subway out to Partick and emerged just as big, heavy dollops of rain arced out of a blustery sky. I followed Kenny's directions and soon came upon a rusting green fence, at the end of which, in whitewashed iron letters, were the words 'West of Scotland CC'. I was disappointed to find the first couple of gates bolted, gates that would have admitted the couple of thousand spectators who witnessed that first-ever international. Thankfully, however, a dustbin propped the last one open and I went inside.

I emerged right by the pavilion, the one Kenny said was the original building. A flight of steps led from the central doors to a gate in a white picket fence, and beyond it was the expanse of cricket outfield where the first international football match was held. It was here that the eleven Queen's Park players stepped on to the turf to take on England clad in the shirts for which Kenny, despite trying to convince himself it would never happen, is still searching. I thought of the massive cavalcade of the World Cup, with its billions of worldwide television viewers. I thought about the international matches I'd seen over the years – eating sunflower seeds in oppressive heat while Uzbekistan played Bahrain in Tashkent, sitting in a freezing and deserted stadium in Zenica watching Bosnia thrash Liechtenstein – and realised that I was standing exactly where it had all started. Standing there, on a drizzly, blustery morning in Partick, looking at a neatly trimmed expanse of turf, the detritus of a cricket ground surrounding me, the scorebox, rollers, sightscreens, exactly where it all began. The players and spectators can't have had any inkling of the future significance of what they were watching. They would have melted away into the neat Partick streets talking about the curiosity of it all, maybe how dull it had been, what with neither side scoring a goal, and whether they'd go again if the opportunity arose. I've been to hundreds of football matches in my time but that was THE one to have seen: arguably the most historically significant football match ever played. I walked back through the gate and joined the trickle of commuters grimacing in the cold wind as they headed towards the station.

After the Battle of Langside Mary and her advisers realised that their original plan of making for Dumbarton was too risky.

Instead they decided to head south-west towards Dumfries. France was still an option, and a boat could probably be found somewhere down in south-west Scotland. In addition, it was a Catholic stronghold at the time, with strong support for Mary. It was, in the circumstances, a wise move.

A couple of days after my football indulgence I pitched up at Sanquhar, in whose castle Mary stayed after an exhausting sixty-mile journey on horseback. I held out little hope of Sanquhar throwing up much of interest beyond the grassy ruins of the old castle, not least because the weather had worsened. Gusty winds flew in from the hills, flinging squally showers at the little town, and I expected to do little more than saunter up to the castle, have a cursory look around and continue on my way to Dumfries. My anticipation wasn't boosted by an encounter at a map of the town. An elderly man called out, 'Where ye making for?'

'The castle,' I replied.

'Och, there's not much to see there,' he replied.

'Mary Stuart spent the night there, apparently,' I said.

'Really? Well I've been here seventy year and I've not heard that before.'

My heart sank a little, but Jim fell into step beside me and we chatted about Mary and, once he'd clocked my accent, Anglo-Scottish relations.

'Of course, every time someone talks about Queen Elizabeth II up here it's an insult, you know,' he said, looking at me side-ways. 'They forget that she's not Elizabeth II here. When the previous Elizabeth was Queen of England, Mary was the Queen of Scotland. So she's Elizabeth II of England, but Elizabeth I of Scotland. That's why it's an insult: it implies that England and Scotland have always been under the same banner, but the Act of Union wasn't until 1707.'

I could have slapped my forehead. Of course, he was absolutely right. Despite being born and raised in England I'm always careful to try to avoid the Anglocentric bias that has become almost second nature. British national radio and television stations referring to English sporting teams as 'we', for example, absolutely make me wince. Yet it had never occurred to me that Elizabeth I wasn't Elizabeth I north of Hadrian's Wall, despite the hefty clue in the fact that I was following Mary, Queen of Scots.

I liked Jim immensely. I'd spend the best part of the next two hours covering about three-quarters of a mile listening to Jim giving me probably the best historical guided tour I've ever had anywhere. He lifted his stick and pointed at the chimneys of the surrounding buildings. 'Look,' he said, 'they're all different. You won't find two the same.'

He was right.

'See? That one's just a can, that one's a can with lugs. That one over there, it's about as tall as you, and look how small the building is.'

How on earth had he noticed this stuff?

'Och, when we were kids at school they'd send us out to draw the chimneys. That was the school there.' He indicated a large, low building to our right, now derelict and surrounded by metal fencing. 'It's closed now. We used to get sent out to draw chimneys while the rich kids learned the proper stuff. The kids of the bankers and lawyers, they got favoured. Us miners' children . . .' He trailed off and shook his head.

Jim had the most observant eyes I think I've ever encountered. I learned much about the history of Sanquhar that day, but I also learned that I walk around most of the time with my eyes practically closed.

'See that building there?' he said as we reached the end of the road from the station. 'How old is it?' The date 1893 was clearly carved into the lintel, but Jim wasn't trying to catch me out.

'Right, now look closer, look at the bricks.'

They were red, I noticed, and . . . well . . . in pretty good condition.

'Exactly,' said Jim, swinging his stick around to point it at me triumphantly. 'Look at it: that building's well over a hundred years old but looks as though it could have been built last week. Local brick, terrific stuff – lasts for ever even in the weather we get here.'

Sanquhar was a mining and weaving town, he told me. 'The price of wool for the whole of the south of Scotland was set here, and in the eighteenth century the gloves that were made here were famous through the whole of these islands.

'It's a proud town, quite parochial. A few years ago they brought a load of families down from Larkhall, near Glasgow, because the mines were doing so well and there weren't enough men to work them. Some of them are fourth generation now,' he said with a chuckle, before dropping his voice a little and adding, 'but we still call them the Larkies . . .' and screwing his eyes up with laughter that turned into a wheezy cough.

A few yards further on we stopped outside the Post Office. 'It's Britain's oldest,' said Jim proudly. '1712 it was when the Post Office opened here. Doesn't bring me much these days though.'

He pointed out an old building across the street that looked nearly derelict. 'That used to be a pub, years ago. Robert Burns used to go in there when he worked for the Revenue; the land-lord was a friend of his. He scratched some lines on the window pane once. It's not there now, though, the original's in New Zealand.'

Before long I'd seen the house Jim was born in, met half the population of the town who all, young and old, knew him and clearly liked him, and had the covenanter's cross pointed out to me, where in 1680 Scottish Protestants and Presbyterians dissociated themselves from Charles II with the Sanquhar Declaration, a move that would eventually lead to the end of the Stuart dynasty. As we neared the castle Jim pointed out the old boundary of the castle grounds, his sharp eye separating the original fourteenth-century retaining wall from more modern building work in what looked, to me, like an anonymous jumble of walls between some houses.

At the far end of the high street I had to leave Jim. He was going to visit a friend just out of hospital. He told me a couple more things to look out for on the way to the castle and added with a grin, 'When you've been to the castle and head back up the street, have a look at the Old Town Hall and see if you can work out where they got the stones to build it.'

And with a cheery wave of his stick, Jim was gone, disappearing up a garden path and through the door of a little house.

The Jims of this world are invaluable. Without him I might as well have walked through Sanquhar blindfolded for all I'd have noticed. The place had come to life thanks to his accompanying me along the length of one street. I knew much of its history now, and had gained a valuable lesson in how to read a place and not just look at it. The castle, a few lumps of wall on a mound hemmed in by a steel fence, was practically an afterthought now. I spent barely a couple of minutes there. But at least I knew where the stones for the Old Town Hall at the top of the street had come from.

Considering that it was used by, among others, Robert the Bruce and William Wallace and was home to the multi-talented 'Admirable Crichton' for a while in the sixteenth century, not to mention Mary's visit that even Jim professed to know nothing of, the castle somehow seems separate from the town. It's fenced off now, and there's a cursory information board some distance away, but until relatively recently it was just a jumble of stones in a field of sheep, empty beer cans in its nooks and takeaway wrappers in its crannies. It's a shame as it's in decent nick for a ruined castle – certainly better than Cadzow – and such an historically significant place perhaps deserves a bit more acknowledgement. Mind you, as I'd just learned, Sanquhar has a lot more going for it than a dilapidated old castle as it is. It's a cut-throat world, Sanquhar history.

★

I arrived in Dumfries and it was full. Whoever makes the 'no vacancies' boards for the guesthouses of Dumfries is clearly a wealthy man to whom all the locals were presumably trying to marry off their daughters. I knocked on one door; he had no rooms but suggested his brother-in-law's place across the road. The one with the 'no vacancies' sign in the window. When I pointed this out the man said, 'Hang on, I'll give him a ring.' He retreated behind a half-closed frosted glass door and I heard the murmur of a phone conversation. The words 'Aye, he looks OK,' floated across the hallway, and eventually the man returned and said that his brother-in-law could put me up. 'They're just back from holiday so weren't going to take anyone in today, but he said to go over, it's fine.'

It was warm, quiet and cheap, the holy trinity for the long-distance walker. In addition, my host knew Port Mary, the place where my journey would end, as he fished there regularly.

'It's on MOD land, though,' he told me. 'If the flags are up you won't be able to go down there because they're shooting. If they're down you're fine.'

I was only passing through Dumfries as if Mary had come here she didn't hang around in the town, but went to explore anyway. Wherever you go you can't escape Robert Burns, and luckily for me I'm a fan. The poet spent the last years of his life, until his death in 1796, living in Dumfries. His statue stands at the town's main junction, overlooked by Argos, Poundstretcher and the enormous austere presence of Greyfriars Church. It was a beautiful day and the base of the statue spilled over with spring flowers. I headed down the street and noticed how most people were smiling. Women with shopping bags greeted each other warmly and stopped to chat. People sat on benches, faces turned up to the sun, just passing time in the warm weather doing nothing in particular. It was a happy town that day, and not just because the local football team, Queen of the South, were on their way to the Scottish Cup Final and a chance to cavort around the Hampden turf with the priceless trophy while Kenny had kittens watching them from the players' tunnel. Further down I came to Midsteeple, a tower in the centre of the high street where Burns's body lay in state while his wife Jean Armour gave birth to their son Maxwell in the house at which I arrived a few minutes later. Now a museum, the Burns house is an absolute treasure trove. Downstairs are cases full of personal effects, from Burns's gun to a nutmeg grinder. I chatted to the attendant, a pleasant Englishman, and he pointed out a patch of duck-egg blue paint in the corner of the room where the wall-paper had been scraped away.

'We were going to put a cabinet there,' he explained, 'and moved some old bookshelves. When we started scraping off the wallpaper we found this old paint behind it. There was a time when the Brontë sisters were in the area and came to the house to see Burns. He wasn't at home, but Jean invited them in and in later correspondence they mentioned the decoration. From the description we think that that patch of blue is contemporary with when the Brontës were here.'

I couldn't help but chuckle at the thought of the Brontë sisters calling in on Burns and finding he wasn't in (most likely he was in the pub). There's many a literatus that would have given anything to be present at a meeting of behemoths like that, but you know what? I don't think they'd have been talking about high-falutin' literary things. I prefer to think that they'd have talked about the dreadful state of the roads ('How's a girl to read when you're being thrown about a coach like that? And as for that bloke who got on at Carlisle with the wandering hands . . .'), the best place to get a decent pork pie in town and where to find paint in this delightful shade of duck-egg blue. As I'd seen at Dylan Thomas's Boathouse in Laugharne, genius often springs from mundanity. Burns himself, having spanked all his poetry earnings on booze and fast living, was working for the Excise at this point, so the chances of them all sitting there discussing poetic form or the state of the great British novel were, I reckon, pretty slim. He was much more likely to be sharing anecdotes about duty evaders and contraband whisky.

I went upstairs to the bedrooms, in one of which Burns died. 'We don't know for certain which room it was,' said the attendant, 'but given that Jean was about to drop it's likely that she would have had the main family bedroom at the time. The other children were away so Burns probably died in the other room, the one they usually slept in.'

I went first into the main bedroom, off which was a tiny study just big enough for a table and chair where Burns would have written. I squatted to look at where he'd engraved his name into the window pane (after Sanquhar and other instances of lines engraved into windows in his collected verse, it seems there was barely a pane of glass left unmolested by Scotland's national bard). This may not be the person I was following on this specific journey, but this is exactly the kind of thing I was looking for; one of the reasons I was making these journeys was to find tangible links to the past. For all the Burns poems I'd studied at school, the Burns suppers I'd attended with friends in Scotland, the book of his poetry on my shelf, here I was, in the broom cupboard of a room where he wrote, on the exact spot where, one day, while gazing out of the window, he'd decided to reach out and scratch his name into the glass. Who knows why he did it? Did he know why he did it? Was it some heart-felt cry for the immortality he hoped for but doubted his verse would give him? Or did he do it absentmindedly and immediately think, bloody hell, Jean's going to kill me when she sees that? Either way, for all the meticulous reconstructions of rooms, for all the carefully assembled artefacts in the cases on the other side of the wall, here I was looking at real, living history. The mark left by one of the greatest poets, indelible and timeless. For me it's even more remarkable than an original draft of 'Tam O'Shanter' – that was Burns the poet. The name scratched on the window gives us an insight into Burns the man, the everyday Burns, the bored Burns, sitting at his desk waiting for inspiration, doodling on the window pane wondering at what time he could reasonably get away with heading up to the pub.

I stood for a good while just looking at that window, until the people in the building opposite were probably starting to get a bit unnerved. Eventually I left and crossed the main road to St Michael's Church and visited Burns's grave. The churchyard contains some of the most ostentatious examples of sepulchry you're likely to see. Neoclassical constructions, some of which were so big they must have needed planning permission, that detailed at great and florid length the achievements of the grave's occupants. Some stretched so far into the sky that they possibly even needed lights to warn passing aircraft.

I found Burns's mausoleum. Even among the temples to posthumous self-aggrandisement a white marble mausoleum among the brown, mossy colonnades is hard to miss. Even so, I was bit disappointed. Perhaps it was the fact the grave was closed inside the white domed construction with a fence around it, meaning you couldn't get close to Burns himself – a strangely incongruous situation for the poet who wrote 'A Man's A Man For A' That'. After all, in Laugharne I could crouch over Dylan Thomas's grave. Perhaps it's because I'd just come from the house and the window pane. There was nothing of Burns here except his bones, fenced off reverentially but divisively. There was a Burns family pew in the church, but otherwise this wasn't a place with which he was associated. The wreaths and flowers may lay here, but his historical presence is in that house, engraved in that window, and soaked into the inns of Dumfries.

From Dumfries I walked on to the picturesque village of Kircudbright and booked into the Selkirk Arms, where Burns wrote the famous Selkirk Grace:

Some hae meat, and canna eat,
And some wad eat that want it,
But we hae meat, we can eat,
And sae the Lord be thankit.

There was a warm welcome all right: when I told the owner I was going to walk out to Dundrennan Abbey, where Mary spent her last night in Scotland, and then on to Port Mary, he appeared at my door ten minutes later to offer me a lift. I declined and set out for Dundrennan on foot the following day. It was a glorious morning as I walked in the leafy shadow of trees and the warm spring sunshine. A couple of hours later the ruined abbey hove into view on a plain below the road.

Mary couldn't have known that the single night she spent at Dundrennan would be the last she'd spend in Scotland. She'd made up her mind that Elizabeth, despite a wobbling tower of evidence and hints to the contrary, would see her right; would look after her and would help restore her not only to the throne of Scotland but also to her place as Elizabeth's heir. Mary's advisers and confidants were wholly in favour of a return to France to build support there, but Mary herself would not be swayed: her blood ties to her cousin Elizabeth would supersede any political or religious differences. It was the biggest miscalculation of her life – which, as we've seen, is saying something – and one that would lead directly to her unfortunate end.

Mary arrived at Dundrennan at night; I arrived in the late morning of a beautiful spring day. The gate was open but there was nobody at the ticket office, and nobody around but me. Then I became conscious of the sound of a two-stroke engine and saw a woman astride a motor mower through an archway in a wall. A minute or so later she went back the other way. Then the other way. After about five minutes she caught sight of me standing by the little wooden building that serves as a gift shop and ticket office, killed the engine, dismounted the lawnmower with the aplomb of an experienced horsewoman and walked over to me, smiling a greeting. I paid my entrance fee and we got chatting about Mary and her time at Dundrennan as we walked among the vaulted ruins.

'We think we can hazard an informed guess as to where she stayed,' said the curator. 'The apartments had been refurbished not long before Mary arrived, so it's almost certain she would have stayed over there' – she indicated a raised, gravelled area with a bench on what would have been the first floor – 'and in fact she sent a letter to Elizabeth from here, asking for her help. She must have been convinced that it would work as she left for England the next morning anyway.

'You're going down to Port Mary? I've not been there myself, but apparently there's a boulder there with what looks like a footprint in it: it's supposed to be where she boarded the boat – the last step she took in Scotland.'

I bought a postcard of Mary, crossed the courtyard and climbed some wooden stairs up to the site of the apartment where it seems Mary spent her last night in Scotland and, effectively, her last night of freedom (if her fugitive status counted as 'free', but at least she wasn't under lock and key). I crunched across the gravel and sat on the bench for a while, trying to picture her at her desk writing to Elizabeth. She must have presented a pretty pathetic sight: she was in dirty, borrowed clothes and had had her head shaved as her famous auburn hair made her instantly recognisable. At nearly six feet tall, she literally stood out in a crowd anyway.

Such was her conviction that Elizabeth would come to her aid, Mary probably felt nothing but excitement as she sat there writing. Soon her ordeal would be over, soon she'd be enjoying the trappings of royalty again and would no longer be an outsider. Soon she could also get hold of some clean clothes. So excited was Mary that once the letter had been dispatched she saw no reason to wait for a reply. In the morning she told her chaperones to prepare the boat: she was setting sail for England.

It's possible that I was sitting on the exact spot where Mary laid her head that night, dreaming of an end to the running, the fighting and the plotting. Dreaming of being reunited with her son and of being accepted into the English royal family and anointed as Elizabeth's successor. Dreaming of riding again, pushing a horse to the limits, testing the boundaries of her skill. No more remote, draughty castles, no more talk of murders, no more hiding and fleeing.

I set off down the single-track road alongside a babbling burn, the same way Mary had come with hope in her heart. I passed three children playing pooh sticks on the bridge over the stream and bore left down a track that would skirt the MOD land and take me down to Port Mary. At the end of the track, however, was a gate. 'Port Mary House', it said. 'Private.'

Bugger.

Now, I'm not one to trespass – being permanently convinced that the moment I step on to private property a man with a blunderbuss will appear and empty a volley of grapeshot into my behind – but I'd come all this way. I was barely two hundred yards from the end of my journey, the two-hundred-odd miles I'd walked since Loch Leven. I could hear what sounded like very big dogs barking somewhere in the distance. Considering my options, I mooched back up the road to a gate in the wall where the house's land met the MOD land. I stood innocently by the metal gate for a while, as if I was taking in the scenery, placing my hand on the gate in an apparently harmless gesture when I was actually gauging how sturdy it was. Any MOD personnel who might have been observing me through their field glasses, or maybe even lining me up in their crosshairs, could only have been impressed by my convincing subterfuge. I may have looked about as threatening as Private Godfrey from *Dad's*

Army, but my beady, steely eye was taking in everything around me. Eventually I plucked up what courage I had, hopped over the gate and scuttled across the field as quickly as I could. On the other side was an ancient rusty gate that clearly hadn't been used in donkey's years. I put one hand on top and one foot on a rung, heaved myself up and then fell face first into the long grass on the other side as the whole thing gave way under me with a grinding, metallic sigh. I spat out the grass and bugs and stopped, listening out for gunfire, attack helicopters and the excited panting of approaching dogs, but there was nothing. I'd got away with it. The rocky beach was some way below me and I scrambled down a steep slope to reach sea level, looked out across the water and took in the last view Mary saw from Scottish soil. There, in the haze, was the faint grey outline of the Cumbrian coast.

I made a cursory search for the boulder with the footprint, but couldn't find it. Naively I'd imagined that the beach would be sandy with one great big wave-teased, footprint-branded boulder smack in the middle of a big yellow expanse, but the whole area was a mass of near-identical dark grey rocks. I parked myself on one for a while, alone with the rocky beach, sea and sky, and pulled out the postcard portrait of Mary. She was dressed in an elaborate red dress spattered with pearls, a high white collar framing the lower half of her face, her auburn hair neatly arranged and decorated with more pearls. She looked wistful, her eyelids heavy, no hint of a smile and a definite air of sadness about her. As I held the picture she was looking over my shoulder at Scotland, a kingdom that was rightfully hers, a place in which she'd been involved in more emotional turbulence and upheaval in just seven years than most people endure in an entire lifetime: murdered husbands, miscarriages, servants filleted before her eyes, imprisonment, abdication, accusation – you name it, it happened to Mary. Once the boat was crossing the Solway Firth she apparently had second thoughts and asked to go to France instead, but by then it was too late – the winds and tides, like those of history, had set their course and nothing Mary could do would change that.

She landed at Workington and within days found herself under effective house arrest yet again. For eighteen years she was ferried between various English castles in the keep of a number of nobles until, in 1585, she was implicated in the Babington Plot to overthrow Elizabeth. It seems likely that the damning letters purportedly from Mary were forged or at least heavily altered by Sir Francis Walsingham, who had succeeded William Cecil as secretary of state. Mary was tried and found guilty of treason, and executed by a clumsy beheading at Fotheringhay Castle in Northamptonshire on 8 February 1587. She told her executioners that she forgave them for 'you are about to end my troubles'.

I sat for a while at Port Mary as the haze cleared and the Cumbrian hills grew sharper against the sky. When Mary left this place it was probably the last time she felt real, genuine hope. She would have looked to the future with optimism. A short time into the four-hour crossing doubt had crept in, however, and, although she didn't know it at the time, the shifting, twinkling shards of sunshine on the water that she watched from the boat and followed to England paved the road to the executioner's block.

I looked at the portrait again, put it on the ground, anchored it with a stone and began the ascent back away from the beach.

Chapter Six

1746: Bonnie Prince Charlie and Flora MacDonald

Accordions. Everywhere. I can't turn a corner without seeing one; I can't escape the sound. Wherever I go there's at least one free-reed, bellows-driven aerophonic contraption being pushed, pulled, caressed, squeezed or any combination thereof. It's been like this all day. I think I am going mad. Yes, that's what's happened. After months of constant plodding in the rain, wind, sun and hail on the trail of long-dead itinerants I've gone ga-ga. There are bats in my belfry, a kangaroo is loose in my top paddock and there are jam doughnuts in my buttery. I go into a pub: there are accordions. I walk across the square: there are accordions. I open the window of my hotel room and accordion music drifts up from below. Surely I have flipped. I am a milk float short of a dairy, I am knitting with one needle.

Actually, I'm not mad. Nor am I dead and paying for my sins by being sent downstairs. I've not been blown off a windy ridge and gone to the other place because everyone knows that there are no accordions in hell, only banjos. No, I've merely been following the journey of a prince who came this way more than two hundred and fifty years ago, having spent a significant part of his journey dressed as a woman and insisting on being called Betty. See? All perfectly sane.

I've hit Accordionville having just followed Bonnie Prince Charlie's flit across the Minch from the Hebridean island of Benbecula disguised as Flora MacDonald's maid, and arrived in the postcard-perfect town of Portree on the eastern side of the Isle of Skye. It's where Charles and Flora said their farewells, and the inn which stands on the spot is just one of many venues hosting the Portree Accordion Festival, into which I have just blundered.

It's one of history's greatest romantic yarns: a well-documented story of bravery, daring, selflessness and one very good dirty joke. I sit by the harbour watching the boats bobbing on the deep blue water, look out to the islands beyond and reflect on the journey I've just taken with my namesake. Well, namesake as far as the Charlie bit goes – in the bonnie and princely stakes he had me licked. Moonfaced Peasant Charlie doesn't quite have the same ring, accurate though it may be.

So just how did Charles Stuart come to be clumping around the Hebrides trying to pass himself off as an Irish maid with hairy legs and a five o'clock shadow? How did a handsome, charming man of excellent breeding and with a fairly good case for being addressed as 'Your Majesty' wind up here, in drag and coming out with falsetto 'begorrahs' and 'to be sures'?

I tried to blot out the accordions – there's no bigger respecter of and enthusiast for the indigenous music of a place than me but, be fair, there are only so many free-of-dynamics renditions of 'Loch Lomond' a man can take – and thought back over one of history's most ripping and gripping yarns.

Charles Edward Stuart was born to great rejoicing in Rome on New Year's Eve 1720 and, like his great-great-grandmother Mary, Queen of Scots, embarked upon a life of turmoil and unfulfilment caused by royalty and religion. He was the grandson of

James VII of Scotland and II of England, who had been nudged from the throne on account of his Catholicism in 1688 and replaced by William of Orange and his wife Mary, James's daughter. A quarter of a century later one of those periodic crises of succession arose, the kind of thing that blows up regularly in history and never seems to be resolved without leaving at least one religious faction with a sense of grievance and the chance to hunker down for some good, hard, ingenious plotting.

When William and Mary's successor Queen Anne died in 1714 (so swollen by gout that she was buried in Westminster Abbey in a square coffin), having become ruler of both England and Scotland thanks to the Act of Union of 1707, Charles's father James Stuart, son of the deposed king, was regarded by many as her natural successor. Poor Anne had had seventeen children, of whom eleven were stillborn and of the rest none survived to see their second birthday. Despite the Jacobite support, James's Catholicism counted against him and when Parliament voted on the issue a majority of one decreed that the throne should be given to George of Hanover despite the small matter of fifty-six Catholics being ahead of him in the regal pecking order – or would have been, had the 1701 Act of Settlement not prohibited Catholics from ascending the throne.

James relocated to the Pope's protection in Rome, where the young Charlie grew up. By the age of six he could converse in Italian, French, English and Latin, and was receiving a fairly balanced religious upbringing, with James being sure to employ Protestant advisers as well as Catholic. Most of Europe regarded James as the rightful King of England and Scotland, something Charles himself was certainly aware of and a position he was keen to fill himself eventually. Hence in 1744, when his father had named him Prince Regent, he set sail across the Channel with a French fleet that was thwarted by a combination of the

English navy and some awful weather. The failure didn't seem to daunt Charles and in July 1745 he set sail again in a hired trading ship, the *Du Teillay*, the French having cooled in lending practical support after the failure and cost of the previous attempt.

Bonnie Prince Charlie, the Young Pretender, set foot on Scottish soil for the first time on 23 July 1745, on the Hebridean island of Eriskay. He planned to raise an army to support the Jacobite cause and once he'd arrived on the mainland a couple of days later he met with local clan chiefs and succeeded, after initial scepticism, in winning their support. At Glenfinnan on 17 August he raised his standard and declared to anyone with a vested interest in the English and Scottish monarchy that he meant business. He marched his army around the south of Scotland, gathering troops and cementing support as he went. He visited Scone, where for centuries Scottish monarchs had been crowned, and the old family seat at Linlithgow – when the fountain ran with red wine – before he managed to secure Edinburgh and win a ruthless victory inside fifteen minutes at the Battle of Prestonpans on 21 September. In that short time around seven hundred redcoats were killed or wounded and a further fourteen hundred taken prisoner in one of the most convincing victories ever achieved on British soil. It was also a victory that boosted Charles's cause inasmuch as his army doubled in size once the news of his success was out, and the Young Pretender began the march south to London. And march he did, showing commendable solidarity with the clansmen by choosing to walk with them rather than go on horseback.

Charles expected to find further practical support in England but was disappointed when few English nobles and their military forces joined him on the road, despite the country's large Catholic population. Backing Charlie's cause over pheasant and port at your own dining table is one thing, but lacing up your best walking boots and digging out that old musket to march to an inevitable battle where people would get, you know, killed and stuff, was quite different. This lack of support caused the march to falter and doubt itself until, when they had got as far south as Derby, the Jacobite progress juddered to a halt. Word had reached them that the notorious military leader the Duke of Cumberland, the son of George II, had twelve thousand troops stationed a mere twenty-five miles from Derby and there was a strong (but unfounded) rumour that a massive English army had assembled at Finchley, then north of London. Charles's advisers, perhaps conscious of Mary's error in going to England when unprepared for the consequences, anxiously advised him to turn back. Reluctantly, he did.

If only Charles had known that London was, even as he and his generals gathered around the table with maps in a Derby inn and traced their route back north, in a state of total panic at his imminent arrival. George II had even taken the precaution of loading his possessions on to a boat at the Tower of London, ready to hot-foot it back to Hanover before you could say 'Knockwurst'. It was one of those moments that, ever since, has had historians purring over what might have been, but back to Scotland they went to regroup and build further support another attempt at securing the English throne for the Jacobite succession. They fought and defeated the redcoats at the Battle of Falkirk on 17 January 1746 in weather so foul that neither side was initially certain who had won. Instead of bolstering Charles's support, however, with many of his men having been away so long and finding themselves close to home large numbers went back to the Highlands. In addition, a number of Highland chiefs suddenly found other things to do when they heard the news that the Duke of Cumberland was massing a considerable army to set about the Jacobite forces once he'd caught up with them. 'Good God, have I lived to see this?' was Charles's reaction once he saw large chunks of his army disappearing over the hill.

Three months later came the decisive confrontation at Culloden, just outside Inverness, on 16 April 1746, and things couldn't have gone more wrong. The Jacobites were heavily outnumbered, they were tired, the terrain of the battlefield didn't suit them in the slightest and the weather was again appalling. They were routed; comprehensively and mercilessly so. Cumberland ordered the massacre of all the Jacobites the red-coats could find, including the wounded, an atrocity that earned him the nickname 'Butcher', and has never been forgotten north of the border.

In less than an hour not only the course of Scottish history had been changed, but the very social structure of the nation too. Culloden set in motion the terminal decline of the clan system and led directly to the notorious Highland Clearances. It also triggered one of the most dramatic, romantic and downright exciting journeys of all time, the period of Bonnie Prince Charlie's flight from the battlefield known as the Prince in the Heather.

At first, Charles and a ragged handful of supporters headed south, their intention being to reach France and solicit support for an invasion. Turning west, the prince then headed for the Isle of Skye, unaware that he'd been given a few days' breathing space by Cumberland's conviction that the Young Pretender had been spirited away to St Kilda, way out in the north Atlantic, one of the most remote island communities in the northern hemisphere. Cumberland took several warships and headed out to sea, eventually frightening the bejesus out of the poor St Kildans who had absolutely no idea what was going on.

Meanwhile Charles had managed to secure a boat to the Western Isles thanks to some supporters in Arisaig and he made the seventy-mile crossing to Benbecula in a single, stormy night, during which he was copiously seasick. Then followed five months of hiding in various bothies and caves around the

Western Isles, often barely one step ahead of the Hanoverian troops combing the islands and in the knowledge that, with a thirty thousand-pound bounty on his head, he could be betrayed at any moment. That he wasn't – and in the mid-eighteenth century thirty thousand pounds represented undreamed of riches – says a great deal about the Hebrideans and Highlanders, and their senses of hospitality and loyalty. There was even a three-week period in which Charles stayed in a bothy near Corrodale on Benbecula, enjoying boozy nights with local clansmen (whom he consistently drank under the table), resting and recovering his strength, and nobody betrayed his whereabouts.

In addition, Charles had adapted to life on the road (or, rather, off it) remarkably cheerfully. For a man who grew up in the more salubrious parts of Rome, roughing it in the Outer Hebrides must have been like living on the moon yet he seems to have remained in extraordinarily good spirits despite the sore feet, filthy clothes and constant assault by midges and foul weather that blighted his time in the Highlands and Islands. When he had first arrived on Eriskay (it must have seemed like a lifetime ago by then, but it was barely nine months), Charles spent his first night in a crofter's hut and had to keep bolting outside for air because of the smoky atmosphere inside. Despite this unpromising start, he seems to have adapted admirably and despite the straitened circumstances frequently exhibited a defiant, twinkly-eyed wit: when he learned of the bounty on his head, for example, Charles responded by placing a bounty on King George's head – of thirty pounds.

After several weeks of covert shuffling between remote bothies, and with a loyal and ingenious network of locals ensuring that the prince stayed one step ahead of the troops combing the islands (sometimes even with the collusion of members of the militia themselves), it was decided by his advisers that he should leave the Western Isles for Skye. Which is where Flora MacDonald came in, and one of history's favourite tales began.

An educated, musical and, according to Dr Johnson (who met her in the 1770s during his tour of the Hebrides), 'uncommonly well-bred' woman of twenty-four, Flora was the stepdaughter of Hugh MacDonald of Armadale, who happened to be in charge of the local militia scouring Benbecula for Charles. Despite this, Hugh was keen to help the Young Pretender escape even though he and his family were Presbyterians. Among the Gaels in the Highlands and Islands there was a strong sense of hospitality and protection, and the MacDonalds would not only eschew the potential thirty-grand reward but also actively help Charles to escape at huge risk to themselves and their property.

On the night of 20 June, Flora was sleeping in a bothy where she was tending the family's cattle when she was woken by Neil MacEachen, a local tutor known to her who was assisting the prince on the island. Hugh MacDonald had come up with the idea of asking his stepdaughter to assist Charles in his escape, but when MacEachen and Charles's other companion, a Captain O'Neill, explained the situation to Flora she was reluctant to risk the lives of her clansmen. Eventually, when Charles had been brought into the bothy and Flora had set a dish of cream in front of him, the Prince managed to convince her to change her mind.

Hugh MacDonald had realised that things were getting too hot for Charles. More troops than ever were searching the islands and the net was closing fast. MacDonald's idea was to use Flora to take Charles over to the Isle of Skye where his wife, Flora's mother, was staying at the time. If Charles was disguised as a maid, Hugh could arrange the necessary paperwork as Flora visiting her mother was a plausible reason for the journey. Her links to the leading militiamen of the region were impeccable – what could possibly go wrong?

Once Flora had agreed to help she immediately set off for the family home at Nunton on the western side of Benbecula, having arranged to send further word to Charles as he hid on the slopes of Hecla, on South Uist. However, on her way there she was picked up by soldiers and taken for questioning. As time passed and no word came, Charles sent MacEachen down from the mountain to find out what was happening. He too was arrested but a potentially grievous situation was avoided by the fact that they were both presented to none other than Hugh MacDonald, who promptly set them free.

Flora returned to Nunton and began preparing Charles's costume. He was to pose as Betty Burke, an Irish maid whom Flora, as far as anyone else was concerned, was taking with her to use her spinning skills. Disguising the prince as a woman was a stroke of genius: uncommonly tall and with a French accent, he was the most unconvincing Highlander ever to wear plaid. But with the bonnet that Flora made for him, and with his slight frame and faintly feminine features, there was more chance of him evading capture if he was giggling coquettishly, hiding his face and swishing around the place in petticoats. First, though, he had to make the agreed rendezvous at a cottage near Rossinish, but when he, O'Neill and MacEachen arrived there they found soldiers camped just a matter of yards away. A cowherd ushered them into a bothy but early the next morning had to advise them to leave as the soldiers were coming to buy milk. For three hours Charles hid behind a rock that offered no shelter from the hammering rain, uttering what a later account by MacEachen called 'hideous cries and complaints'.

But then the Jacobite luck seemed to change: when, a couple of days later, Charles, Flora and their co-conspirators arrived at a bothy by Loch Uiscebhagh on the eastern coast prior to departure, most of the soldiers seemed to have moved on from Benbecula. The mood was as relaxed as it could have been in the circumstances and the fugitive group cooked a fortifying meal of heart, liver and kidneys. Then a messenger arrived with news that at least two thousand troops were landing on the island, some barely three miles away, which triggered a sudden panic of preparation.

'The company being gone,' wrote MacEachen of when everyone not travelling across the Minch had left, 'the Prince, stript of his own cloathes was dressed by Miss Flora in his new attire, but could not keep his hands from adjusting his headdress, which he cursed a thousand times. The gown was of calico, a light coloured quilted petticoat, a mantle of dull camlet made after the Irish fashion, with a cap to cover His Royal Highness's whole head and face with a suitable headdress, shoes, stockings etc.'

Charles wanted to tuck a gun inside his undergarments, but Flora protested, saying that if he was searched a pistol in the petticoats was a bit of a giveaway. The prince answered, 'Indeed, Miss, if we shall happen with any that go so narrowly to work in searching me as what you mean, they will discover me at any rate.' Which, as eighteenth-century dirty jokes go, isn't a bad 'un, especially under duress. With Charles dolled up like a drag queen fallen on hard times the group waited for darkness – scattering into the heather when a warship briefly hove into view around the headland – before setting out to sea on one of history's most famous journeys, one that more than 250 years later I flew in to Benbecula to emulate.

Benbecula airport is one of the jolliest in the world. As a handful of passengers descended from the propeller plane that had brought us from Glasgow, a tubby man in fluorescent overalls and ear defenders on top of his head like Mickey Mouse ears smiled a cheery hello from the bottom of the steps. As we entered the terminal building a woman wearing a high-visibility jacket marked 'security' did exactly the same. Inside there were squawks of delight as people were reunited amid the rattling of the small baggage carousel. Such was the air of bonhomie that as I heaved my rucksack on to a chair to adjust the straps a thin, grey-haired man came over and said, 'Excuse me, I'm not waiting for you, am I?', to which I reluctantly had to reply in the negative. I quite liked the idea of people turning up just in case there was someone to wait for.

It was a beautiful early-summer's day as I set out to walk to my hotel from the airport, a two-hour journey that was among the most pleasant of my entire amble through history. I took the road around the west coast of the island where the Atlantic lapped gently against the shore and the next landfall was New York. The sea was so calm you could almost hear it sigh, and under the sunshine it was the deepest blue imaginable. I passed the odd house, a medieval burial ground and a collection of buildings at Nunton that may well have been where Flora MacDonald assembled Betty Burke's outfit all those years earlier. Further along there was a more modern landmark, a giant silver tube that looked like a huge aerosol can lying on its side. It must have been at least sixty feet long and about fifteen feet high, and was, I learned later, a container that had been lost from a ship in the English Channel about six months earlier and had washed up on Benbecula three weeks later. On the side of the container someone had sprayed in large letters the word 'DUFF', the beer of choice of Homer Simpson and the regulars of Moe's Tavern.

Benbecula is by far the flattest of the hilly Western Isles, as if someone had once gripped the edge of the island and given it a bit of a shake to get rid of the bumps and humps. The hills of North and South Uist loom on the horizons in contrast to the flatness of the sea to the east and the west. The number of green vehicles with big tyres that passed me on the road betrayed the fact that Benbecula is an important military base, and certainly the soulless grey houses of Balivanich, a village close to the airport, suggest that they were erected by the military when the airport was the base for the missile testing on the Uists during the Cold War. The further I went from Balivanich the less overt Benbecula's military heritage became, until I finally reached my hotel on the south side of the island. I took to my bed as the sun reluctantly went down, the silence outside the open window broken only by the odd rodent squeak from the long grass outside.

In the morning I set out for Loch Uiscebhagh, hoping to find the bothy where Charlie, Flora and the crew spent their last hours on Benbecula before setting out for Skye. In the couple of hours it took for me to walk out to the inlet just two cars passed me, both of their occupants giving me a cheery wave. There was a smattering of houses, one of which was derelict yet surrounded by cars of a range of vintages. A stocky man with red cheeks and short red hair worked on a fence while bagpipe music played from a radio inside his nearby caravan, a sound that followed me over the next hill and was occasionally brought on the breeze for a good while afterwards. Other than that, my walk east was in total silence beneath a deep blue, cloudless sky. I eventually left the road and cut across country to the rocky edge of the inlet of Uiscebhagh. I poked around for a little while, wondering where the bothy was, until I found a small rectangle of stones in the long grass. There were several of these shielings around the bay, so it wasn't definitely the one used by the Young Pretender, but it was as likely as any. Ever the optimist, I even toed around in the grass looking for some kind of evidence that this had been the place – some ancient animal bones still bearing royal teeth marks perhaps, or the pistol Flora forbade the prince to shove down his petticoats. Finding nothing I sat on a rock and looked out across the water, possibly at the same angle from which the escapees saw the warship nose around the headland, sending them pelting for cover after quickly kicking out their campfire. I imagined them huddled back in the bothy, waiting for the sun to go down – which, if the previous night was anything to go by, would have taken an age – as they half-expected the militia to come tramping over the hill at any moment. It must have been a nervous few hours despite their passports and the letter from

Hugh MacDonald to his wife commending 'Betty's' skills as a spinner – anything more than a cursory inspection of the tall, quiet, faintly butch maid with her face turned away and the game would probably be up. It was a tremendous risk, and the bravery of Flora, Neil MacEachen and the others was extraordinary. Eventually the time would have been right and the little party scuttled down to the boat, pushed it into the water and heaved away on the oars. My own journey across the Minch wouldn't be as laborious or secretive, nor would it feature an unconvincing drag queen. At least I presumed it wouldn't. I hopped off my rock and headed back the way I came.

Charles suffered unseasonably bad weather throughout most of his flight from Culloden but it would have worked in his favour. It's easier to conceal yourself in mist and rain, and the searching soldiers would have been thoroughly miserable and less thorough if soaked to their goosepimply skin, but for once my journey wasn't blighted by rain, wind, sleet, hail or any of the biblical weather I'd suffered elsewhere on my travels. Also, the main part of the journey I was following wouldn't even be on foot. Instead it would be on a hefty, warm and comfy Caledonian MacBrayne ferry stocked with snacks, sandwiches and souvenirs. For once history was not going to leave me footsore.

The next morning I waited outside one of the island's two schools for the bus that would take me to Lochmaddy on North Uist and the ferry across to Uig on the Isle of Skye, a short distance south from where the little boat made landfall with its strange, apparently female passenger. As I waited for the bus I saw a different type of vessel pull up, this time with a genuinely female passenger. It was a mobile bank, a high-top van driven by a portly man with grey hair, with a young woman in uniform and perfectly applied make-up in the passenger seat. It pulled into the forecourt of the school, the engine died, they waited for a while, attracted no customers, started the engine again and chugged off into the distance until the babbling sound of the diesel engine had vanished completely. For a remote area this is a terrific idea, as long as you could resist the urge to ask for two 99s and a strawberry Mivvi when you got to the hatch.

Soon an ancient wheezing coach pulled up and I boarded, passing between front seats that contained a man with a dog on his lap on one side of the aisle and a big sack of potatoes on the other. After an hour or so we arrived in Lochmaddy, a small town – a village really – clustered around a pretty harbour. I bought my ferry ticket in the little terminal where a bookshelf heaved with dog-eared thrillers and romances. A sign taped to the wall above advised that it was a kind of one-in, one-out library – as long as you left a book of yours, you could swap it for one from the shelves, which is another delightful idea.

Before long the ferry eased its way around the headland and pulled up at the jetty, yawning emphatically as the bow opened to allow the vehicles out. About a dozen or so foot passengers boarded and I sat in a comfy chair in a lounge high at the front of the superstructure. This wasn't just a far cry from the original journey I was following; it was a full-throated Tarzan yodel.

There'd been no wind at first and the four oarsmen had had to row for hours, then a strong wind blew up around midnight. It started to rain and the sea began to swell but, according to Flora's later account, the prince sang loudly to keep everyone in good spirits. Flora herself grew tired and slept in the bottom of the boat, Charles gallantly crouching over her in case any of the men inadvertently stepped on her in the darkness. As it became light the wind and the sea calmed but a morning mist came down and, without a compass, the crew had little idea of where they were. Fortunately it wasn't long before the mist rose and they found themselves on course and close to the tip of the Vaternish Peninsula in the north-west of Skye. The wind turned against them and they paused at an inlet to rest and eat bread and cheese. Once they'd set off again a pair of sentries clocked them and ordered them to pull in, but the boat kept going and, according to some reports, was fired upon from the shore. Despite this hairy moment they made landfall at about two o'clock in the afternoon, at Monkstadt on the Trotternish Peninsula, and found no militiamen awaiting their arrival.

Although I wasn't making the journey dressed as a woman, I did feel a pang of guilt at the comfort of my journey compared to that of my quarry. I moved to the rear of the boat and sat in the bar for a while, where a couple of lads sculled pints of lager while three or four people were laid out asleep on the long seats. I was still restless and feeling as though I wasn't making enough of an effort so moved outside to the rear observation deck, where the wind pulled at my clothes and buffeted my ears. I wasn't getting soaked, for once, unlike the knot of seabound folk I was following, but at least I wasn't sitting in the lounge in a comfy chair eating crisps and reading the *Herald* any more.

I sat on a red plastic bucket seat and watched the Western Isles disappear into the haze. The sea was calm, flat and featureless save for the arrow-straight wash that we left foaming in our wake across the Minch. The Vaternish Peninsula loomed into view, dark against the yellow-grey sky above. The red-coated sentries must have stood out like two radishes on a snooker table and I could picture them running to the edge of the cliffs, shouting and waving, one priming his musket, the puff of white smoke followed a second later by the crack of the shot, the rhythm of the oars in the water getting faster, the breathing of the rowers more laboured, Charles and Flora lying low in the boat.

I left the ship at Uig, walking up the jetty towards the town as the cars slowly drove off with the 'clank-clank' of disembarkation. Uig is a village of less than four hundred people but, spread as it was around a large horseshoe-shaped bay, I found it was a good half-hour's walk to the hotel past tidy whitewashed houses where the accents seemed to be, despite being here on the Isle of Skye, anything but Scottish. In the shop I was sold an egg sandwich and a tube of toothpaste by a woman with a broad Yorkshire accent. Two men were lifting something from a car, with one admonishing the other in broad cockney. I was checked into the hotel by an American receptionist.

After dumping my pack on my bed I walked back around the bay and tacked up a steep road that veered back and forth up the hillside before emerging on the plateau of the island. I was look-ing for the point where Charles, Flora and the exhausted rowers would have landed, a place now known as Prince Charles's Point. The view looked spectacular in the late afternoon sun. There were few houses scattered across the plateau and I could see the Point from some way off. Eventually leaving the road for a track, I passed a couple of houses, went through a gate and tramped across some spongy heather towards the inlet, watched by some disinterested sheep and, I was sure, several pairs of eyes from the houses behind me, who I presume owned the land I was sloshing through and the sheep whose attention I was failing to capture. I couldn't get right down to the Point but I was close enough to gain a good impression of where Charles had arrived.

They had landed close to Monkstadt House, the home of Sir Alexander MacDonald, a leading Hanoverian, and his wife Margaret, a Jacobite who had aided Charles on the Western Isles by having newspapers sent to him and preparing some of her (absent on the mainland) husband's shirts for his arrival. Flora had gone to the house only to find that Lieutenant MacLeod of the local militia, and the man responsible for checking every boat that arrived on the island, was there. Fortunately Charles had been persuaded to stay at the boat, where he sat, grumpy and sulky, still dressed as Betty and with the rest of the company prepared to denigrate him as a useless, cantankerous and lazy maid should anyone approach asking questions. Flora kept MacLeod busy with small talk: when he found out who her stepfather was he would probably have been reassured, and he didn't insist on searching or even seeing the boat she had arrived in. Even with such family connections it must have taken quick thinking and nerves of steel on Flora's part not to arouse any kind of suspicion in the lieutenant. In the meantime, Lady MacDonald and her fellow local Jacobites, including Donald Roy MacDonald, who had been wounded in the foot at Culloden and was still suffering, decided that Charles should make for Portree, some eighteen miles to the south-east. They spent the night at the house of MacDonald of Kingsburgh, Charles having gained unwelcome attention from Kingsburgh's staff for the ungainly way he walked and for the 'indecent' height to which he lifted his petticoats when crossing a stream. Despite the predicament and the near-encounter with Lieutenant MacLeod, Charles, still dressed as Betty, spent the evening in good spirits, behaving, according to MacEachen, 'not like one that was in danger, but as cheerfully and as merrily as if he had been putting on women's cloathes merely for a piece of diversion'.

Before setting off on the road to Portree the next morning, I stopped for a cup of tea at a guesthouse close to the harbour. I'd been served breakfast at the hotel by a very pleasant South African, bought my newspaper from an Englishwoman at the shop and been greeted by a distinctly West Midlands accent when I popped into the Skye Brewery shop next door to the tearoom. The man serving me spoke in broad Yorkshire tones. There didn't seem to be a single Scot in the place – when I'd nipped into the pub by the jetty the night before, the barmaid and the only other customer were bonding over the fact they were both from Luton. I asked why there were no Scots here.

'It's the same pretty much all over Skye,' the proprietor told me. 'All the Scots have gone south to earn the money and the English have come up here for the quieter life.'

It's a curious place, Uig, and not just because its name sounds like someone swallowing a peach stone. Although it's postcard picturesque there's a sense of transience about the place. That's possibly understandable given its reason for being these days is as a ferry port that relies on passing trade for survival. The soulless, ugly grey warehouse building that houses the passenger and freight terminals is the focus of the town; you can see it from everywhere, yet somehow it doesn't look particularly out of place among the whitewashed cottages. Nothing seems to belong there: even the hotel I stayed in, which certainly looked as though it was long-established and an Uig institution, felt as though it was separate somehow. Maybe the geography of the place – the buildings are all well spread around the bay – helped give the rootless, unfocused impression that I took away. This isn't to say Uig was in anyway disagreeable, but I did leave with a curious feeling that nothing of the past had really stuck there, and not much of the present either.

My walk to Portree, a good eighteen miles, was beautifully uneventful and not worth dwelling upon. When you're on the Isle of Skye the picturesque becomes commonplace and, particularly when it's bathed in sunshine beneath a cloudless blue sky, description soon becomes redundant. Charles, of course, had a different experience – he walked through the night in the customary pouring rain. At least his temporary transvestism could come to an end: at the edge of a wood not far from Monkstadt he divested himself of the women's clothes and resumed being a Highlander. Most of the clothes were later burnt, although his gown was made into a bedspread by Flora MacDonald's mother, while Flora herself kept his apron.

I arrived at Portree in the late afternoon and gravitated towards Somerled Square, the main focus of the town aside from the harbour, and my first encounter with the massed accordions of the festival. A small stage had been set up, a canopy more than anything, and an accordion band was in full swing in front of an appreciative crowd. I stopped for a while, standing by two men talking.

'They need to tighten up the tempo a wee bit,' said one.

'Aye, maybe, but it's a bonnie tune,' replied his companion.

'Oh aye, it's a *braw* tune,' said the first, 'only I'd have taken it a wee bit faster masel'.'

Everyone's a critic, even in the world of the piano accordion.

I'd booked into the Royal Hotel, which stands close to the harbour on the site of MacNab's Inn, where Flora, MacEachen and Donald Roy MacDonald had met to discuss plans to get Charles to the island of Raasay, from where they hoped to organise a rescue ship from France. Flora asked Donald Roy to wait outside for the prince, but in the cold and wet his Culloden injury forced him back inside until the small boy who'd walked with Charles as a guide came in and said that the prince was waiting outside. Donald Roy fetched him and the prince, dripping wet, gladly accepted a whisky. Almost immediately word came to the inn that Captain Malcolm MacLeod was outside, another Culloden veteran who was to sail the prince over to Raasay. MacLeod suggested leaving immediately as the rain gave them cover. Donald Roy persuaded him to let the prince dry out and eat a little and, with clothes given to him by Kingsburgh, Charles changed out of his sodden attire. When told that the inn served only whisky and water, Charles was handed the latter in a bowl that the innkeeper used to bail out his boat. Having just seen Donald Roy take a big swig out of it himself, Charles initially reluctant until his companion whispered to him that if he refused it now he would arouse suspicion. Hence the prince took an enormous gulp.

Having just got out of his wet clothes, eaten and warmed up, the last thing Charles wanted was to head back out into the storm, but Donald Roy was insistent that he should go. The prince employed his rarely used stubborn streak and called for a roll of tobacco to stall a little. The tobacco cost fourpence ha'penny; Charles handed over sixpence but didn't pick up his change. Donald Roy, realising that such profligacy could cause suspicion, asked for it himself, much to Charles's amusement.

I walked into the hotel and announced that I'd booked a room. The receptionist smiled, tapped away at her computer keyboard and then frowned. 'You have,' she said, 'but . . . it's for tomorrow night.'

I knew things had been going too well. I rummaged in the depths of my pack, among the half-eaten cereal bars and socks of dubious vintage, looking for the booking confirmation I'd printed out. My hands closed around a piece of paper. I pulled it out and handed it to her.

'This, er, appears to be a leaflet about York Minster.'

'Oh, sorry.'

I rummaged again and pulled out another piece of paper. The booking confirmation. I unfolded it and found that it was true. I'd booked the wrong night.

'I'm afraid we're completely full tonight, Mr Connelly, what with . . .' She gestured behind me at the stalls the accordion vendors had set up around the lobby, where earnest men purred over mother-of-pearl inlays. The door to the bar opened and a burst of accordion music escaped before it closed again. I'd been accordioned out of a bed for the night.

'I'll try a few other places for you if you like?' she offered, which was very kind of her considering that she was faced with a fuckwit. She rang half a dozen numbers at least, all of whom were completely booked out by people arriving with trolleybags and big square instrument cases that promised untold squeezebox delights within. I developed a sudden and virulent hatred of the piano accordion, blaming it squarely and wholly inappropriately for my predicament. I was tempted to run amok among the vendors, hurling accordions through hotel windows like some folk-music Keith Moon. Then, finally, the lovely receptionist struck gold. It was a hotel back on Somerled Square for a rate that, even when considering the deposit I'd lose on the following night's erroneous booking, still left me up on the deal. I went back to the square, checked in, went up to my room and found that it faced out on to the square itself. My ill-conceived accordion antipathy still lingered. As I opened the window and accordion music drifted in, filling every nook and cranny of the room, I pondered for a moment how with a good, strong catapult I could take out the band leader with a golf ball. I immediately felt guilty, so lay on the bed for a while, closed my eyes and tried to lose myself in the music. I've heard – and enjoyed – music from accordions of all kinds around the world, from the foot-tapping, nasal sound of the Cajuns to an English melodeon accompanying traditional Morris dancing in a Dorset village one chilly Boxing Day. In the hands of a Creole zydeco musician, the piano accordion becomes a honking, snarling beast of a thing, almost a natural extension of the musician as the dancers whirl around the dancehall, sweaty and ecstatic as condensation runs down the walls. I've heard a plaintive traditional Scandinavian melody drifting across a frozen lake in central Finland and thought it was among the most beautiful sounds I've ever heard. But here, I just couldn't get it. The plinky plonky piano accompaniment, the rat-a-tat-tat of the snare drum, the limited dynamics of the accordion itself . . . no matter how I tried, however much I wanted to like it, it wasn't getting past my musical armour.

I spent the rest of the afternoon wandering around the town. It's a delightful place, Portree, never more so than on a warm sunny day when the water in the harbour is a deep blue complemented by the greens of the islands and headlands. There's a calmness about the town, a sense of reassurance that whatever else might be going on in the world, everything's all right in Portree and that's all that matters. No wonder Bonnie Prince Charlie was so reluctant to leave, and that was on a rainy night, let alone a summery evening of lengthening shadows and the gentle lap of the water in the bay. Finally, as darkness fell I went into the pub next to the Royal Hotel. There is a MacNab's bar around the corner but it's a modern construction – as far as I could tell, this pub was the spot on which Charles and Flora MacDonald parted company. He also bade farewell to Neil MacEachen and Donald Roy MacDonald, despite pleading with the latter to accompany him to Raasay – but Donald Roy's injured foot would have made it impossible for him to do so. It was a traumatic and emotional parting. It also became protracted, with MacEachen and Donald Roy getting through a whole bottle of whisky between them before leaving.

I ordered a whisky myself. A small PA system and a primed but dormant accordion indicated that more music was inevitable, but as I took my seat there was just a low murmur of conversation from the people gathered at the bar. I thought about the room from which Charles would have left his friends, those extraordinary people who had risked – at the very least – their liberty for him. Flickering candlelight would have lit his face in the low-beamed, dark oak room. Donald Roy was accompanying him to the waiting boat, so he would have clasped the hand of Neil MacEachen, probably silently, no words being necessary, the only sound the rain on the road outside. Finally he turned to Flora. Saluting her, he said with a formality that hadn't hitherto been a feature of their relationship, 'For all that has happened, I hope, Madam, we shall meet in St James's yet.'

With that he was gone, looking as unlikely an occupant of St James's Palace as you could imagine. His borrowed clothes were ill-fitted, there was a bottle of whisky tied to his belt, a bottle of brandy in his pocket, four shirts in a cloth bag, and he had a cooked chicken for the journey. As he passed through the door his silhouette would have been framed briefly, and then he was gone.

Flora and Charles would never meet again, not in St James's nor anywhere.

He would be in hiding for another three months, the Raasay plan having come to naught, before leaving Scotland, never to return, on the French ship *L'Heureux*. Charles left from Borrodale, where he had first landed on the mainland fourteen months earlier. He departed into an unfulfilled exile of torrid affairs, alcoholism and depression, during which time the merest mention of Scotland was enough to send him into a tearful funk, until his death in 1788. He was expelled from France following the Treaty of Aix-la-Chapelle between Britain and France in 1748 and had to be forcibly deported to Rome, while his lowest moment came when, after the death of his father in 1766, the Pope refused to endorse his succession. One can only wonder at what might have been had he not been persuaded to turn back at Derby that day in 1746.

Flora was arrested after the boatmen who had rowed them to Skye were captured and revealed the details of the escape. She was sent to London and initially imprisoned in the Tower of London, but was soon transferred to a messenger home – effectively house arrest. Under the 1747 Act of Indemnity, however, she was released and went north to Edinburgh. Eventually she returned to Skye, being shipwrecked en route and nearly drowning. She returned to a Highlands being devastated in the aftermath of the Jacobite rebellion. Among other things, the Disarming Act and the Unclothing Act – which proscribed the wearing of plaid and tartan – filleted the clan system. Flora married Allan MacDonald in 1750, and in 1774, when Allan's father had died and their herd of three hundred cattle had been entirely wiped out by a brutal winter, they emigrated to North Carolina. Within two years the MacDonalds were caught up in the American War of Independence, Allan was taken prisoner, their lands were seized and, on his release, the couple emigrated to Nova Scotia but the cruel, hard winters proved anything but welcoming. Flora's health was poor by this point, and she was in constant pain from a badly set broken arm. When Allan sent her back to Scotland for the benefit of her health, the ship was attacked by a French privateer. Instead of hiding below deck, Flora insisted on helping to repel the invaders and in the course of the struggle she fell, breaking her other arm. Again it was poorly set and would cause her problems for the rest of her life.

The deaths of two of Flora's sons served to diminish her health further, and by the time Allan returned, penniless, from North America he was in time to be present when one of history's great heroines died, in 1790.

Both Flora and Charles endured lives of tremendous hardship: she suffering prison, exile, pain, illness and bereavement; he never coming to terms with a life of unfulfilled promise defined by those forty-five minutes at Culloden. As I sat in the bar and thought back to that rainy June night in 1746 when on this spot, their faces illuminated orange in the candlelight, they made plans for a meeting in better times in a better future that would never arrive. The fugitive monarch and the island girl, bound together by historical circumstance, sharing a moment of hope that would gutter and die like the candles that lit the scene in brief, warm candescence.

Chapter Seven

1849: The Doolough Famine Walk

I'd come a long way since the Norwich Travelodge. I'd broken two toes for a start, not to mention wrenching a knee and growing several beards of variable success and advisability. My thighs had definition for the first time in years and as for my buttocks, well, pert didn't even begin to do them justice. Most of all, though, my time on the road had fleshed out my history books, added a third dimension to some of history's greatest yarns and allowed me a deeper understanding of some of the past's great and not so great, famous and not so famous, figures. Then sitting at home one day, emptying some of the accumulated rubbish from my pack (I discovered that I appear to be some kind of deity to every half-eaten flapjack in the world – they all seemed to have made a pilgrimage to the depths of my rucksack), something struck me. And for once it wasn't one of the elasticated toggles on my pack twanging its plastic nodule into my eye. No, I realised that each and every quarry I'd pursued so far had been a monarch of some kind. All of them, from the Queen of the Iceni to the Young Pretender, every footstep I'd taken had been behind a royal. Owain Glyndwr had proclaimed himself a prince, granted, and Bonnie Prince Charlie had spent his whole life either in exile or fighting in vain for what he thought was his by birthright, but they were all, without exception, regal.

I was long, long overdue in following the faceless. The people unnamed. Those whose identities don't even make a footnote to an appendix but whose contribution to history is equally as significant as the most important, ermine-shrouded king. I thought of all the traders, the soldiers, the minstrels, the labourers, the messengers, the tinkers, the refugees, the vagrants, the peddlers – all the people whose lives helped to shape the world we live in today, whose every journey changed something, even if it was at the most parochial level.

The nature of recorded history means that it's the powerful and privileged who have gained the celebrity. Olaf the Dwarf may not have put his head above the parapet of history (he'd have needed a chair to stand on for a start) but he's there, recorded, in a glass case at the British Library. But what about the regular soldiers of Sky Hill? Of Hastings? Of the Carreg Cennen siege? Of Langside and of Culloden? They all had stories to tell, stories that probably never made it past the family hearth, the harvest field and the inn, but which contributed in a small way to some of the most significant moments in history.

I'd thought long and hard about the best way to follow the unrecorded. Accounts, certainly detailed accounts, of specific journeys are rare for those of the lower orders and I looked largely in vain, but a chance conversation with a friend put me on to the 1849 Doolough tragedy, way out in the western reaches of Ireland.

'The story goes that the people in my home town of Louisburgh in County Mayo, around six hundred in total – women and children included – were starving as a result of the potato famine and a rumour started that if they walked to Delphi Lodge, where the landlord and council of guardians were, then they'd be given food,' Anna told me. 'It's about fifteen miles – very beautiful – by the shores of the Killary and Doolough lakes but bleak and freezing that night. So they set out and walked and died from starvation on the way: they found corpses with grass in their mouths by the side of the road. When they eventually got there, they were told that the guardians couldn't be disturbed during lunch so they had to wait. When they were able to see them, they were sent away empty-handed and most of them died on the way back.'

She went quiet for a moment, gazing into the middle distance. 'It makes me very sad and very angry.'

The Great Hunger, *An Gorta Mór*, is one of the biggest tragedies ever to afflict these islands. Between 1845 and 1850 an estimated one million people died in Ireland as a result of the potato famine. Add emigration figures to that and Ireland's total population reduced by around a quarter as a direct result of the famine. Ireland had endured famines before, but nothing on this scale. The potato crop was blighted in 1845 and failed completely in 1846. By 1847 the country was in disarray and although the crop didn't fail, little had been planted as desperate people ate seeds rather than risk planting. The blight returned in 1848 and by then diseases such as typhus had exacerbated the gravity of the situation. The British government, which had brought Ireland into its empire with the 1801 Act of Union, was keen to let the free market solve the problem, while absentee landlords continued to collect rents and on many occasions forcibly evict starving families from their homes even at the height of the famine.

There was an horrific attitude to the Irish prevalent at the time, which may have also made any relief efforts cursory. In March 1847, for example, as the famine took its firmest grip, *The Times* opined that the Irish were 'a people born and bred from time immemorial in inveterate indolence, improvidence, disorder and consequent destitution'. The previous September a letter to the newspaper pronounced of the Irishman that 'the great object of his life is to rent a miserable piece of land, to build himself a hovel or burrow in the earth, to marry, and if possible to live as well as his pig. The word "improvement" does not appear to be in his vocabulary.' To some landlords the people were expendable, and frequently a nuisance. In 1846 Major Denis Mahon of Roscommon realised that the 2400 tenants on his lands produced only a third of the food necessary to support them. Hence he spent four thousand pounds on sending them by ship to Canada as that was cheaper than keeping them as paupers. A quarter died on the journey across the Atlantic and the rest arrived in a dreadful state, shocking even Canadian immigration staff well used to seeing the effects of the long voyage on already desperate travellers.

Relief efforts were put in place but the man in charge of them, the Assistant Secretary to the Treasury Charles Edward Trevelyan, was a firm believer in market forces: he would only release imported Indian grain gradually and then only in order to control the price (at first he attributed the high demand for grain not to famine but to low prices). He was also of the opinion that relief efforts would make people too reliant on handouts and thus introduced a scheme of public works – in a country that was largely subsistence-based – by which the people could earn money to buy food. This, he thought, was the only way forward, the best way to snap the Irish out of their indolence. Hard work and organisation, not charity and handouts, were the only way to cope with the famine. When in 1846 the Inspector-General of the Coastguard Service gave out food supplies to a desperate, pleading, half-starved group of villagers he encountered somewhere on the west coast he was publicly rebuked: according to Trevelyan, he should have instructed the people, who had been reduced to eating whatever nettles and berries they could find, to form a public works committee and set about raising funds for food through private subscription. Indeed, Trevelyan was on record as having a low opinion of the Irish in general. He had even written that 'the real evil with which we have to contend is not the physical evil of the famine, but the moral evil of the selfish, perverse and turbulent character of the people'. In reality, even if the grain stocks had been released the complete failure of the 1846 crop meant that it would not have been anywhere near enough, but the shocking fact is that throughout the famine Ireland remained a net exporter of food.

Nowhere was the effect of the famine more marked than in the west. Nationwide, one third of the population of Ireland subsisted on the potato alone. In County Mayo, on the western coast, the figure was 90 per cent. Arguably no county in Ireland suffered from the famine more than Mayo: in 1841 it was one of the most populous counties in the land with 389,000 people. A decade later – a decade that included the famine – that had shrunk to 274,000, and by 1911 Mayo's population was almost exactly half what it had been seventy years earlier. Even today there are people in Ireland who, on hearing the very name Mayo, add 'God help them', and the journey that Anna had implored me to make was in the heart of the country.

There are a number of versions of the Doolough story, in which the numbers involved and the circumstances vary wildly. At the heart of the tale, though, is a letter published in the *Mayo Constitution* on 10 April 1849 that first drew attention to the incident. Signed 'A Ratepayer', the letter detailed in an understated, matter-of-fact way the dreadful events at Louisburgh, a small town in the south of the county, practically in the shadow of Croagh Patrick. It described how, at the end of March, a Colonel Hogrove, a member of the Board of Guardians (who administered the poor relief), and Captain Primrose, the local Poor Law inspector, arrived at Louisburgh to inspect those claiming relief. People came to the town from all over the surrounding countryside, only to find that the colonel and captain had gone, heading some sixteen miles south to Delphi, the

Marquess of Sligo's hunting lodge on the shores of Doolough lake, leaving instructions for the poor to gather there for the inspection instead.

'In obedience of this humane order, hundreds of these unfortunate living skeletons, men, women and children, might have been seen struggling through the mountain passes and roads to the appointed place,' said the letter. 'The inspection took place in the morning and I have been told that nothing could equal the horrible appearance of those truly unfortunate creatures, some of them without a morsel to eat, and others exhausted from fatigue having travelled upwards of sixteen miles to attend the inspection.'

The letter called for an inquiry into the 'melancholy affair'. It's impossible to say for sure how many made the journey, although six hundred is a figure that crops up in many sources. It was an awful night: the people had been told to attend inspection at Delphi Lodge between seven and eight in the morning or be struck off the poor relief register. This meant that the starving had to make a sixteen-mile walk through the night in snow, sleet and hail, and when they got there the inspectors didn't emerge from the lodge until noon. No food rations were distributed, so those who had made it were forced to make the return journey empty-handed. It's no wonder that some estimate four hundred deaths, with many frail bodies so lightweight that they were washed or blown into the lake, and other corpses lying on the road for days before being buried.

Louisburgh is a small, friendly town based around a crossroads. I arrived and checked into the only hotel, where a family birthday party was getting underway: red-faced men with hair plastered down by determined combing looking uncomfortable in their suits; little girls in party frocks pelting in and out of rooms with excited squawks; balloons and banners taped to the walls. Earlier I'd stopped around four miles from the town at the foot of Croagh Patrick, Ireland's busiest pilgrimage site, to see the National Famine Memorial. It's an extraordinary sculpture of a three-masted emigrants' ship of the sort that took desperate folk from Ireland to North America and became known as coffin ships. Interlinked around the ship, starved skeletal souls sweep like an endless web of the dead. But here, in the very heart of the tragedy, as another wave of noise washed through the briefly opened door to the function room and two children – a little girl with ringlets and a small boy in a bow tie and a waistcoat – rocketed past me the atmosphere was a raucously happy one.

The next morning I set out on the road south towards Delphi Lodge, now a country house hotel popular with fishing enthusiasts. I followed the route taken by the starving wretches, many of whom died because, as one theory has it, the colonel and captain had received a dinner invitation from Delphi and didn't want to miss it because of a headcount and the need to estimate the authenticity and extent of the locals' degradation.

My last day's walk through history was through the most ruggedly beautiful countryside I've ever seen. It was a warm day with the odd smudge of cloud the only blemish against the blue sky, and was probably the most pleasant day's walking I'd had. In the early afternoon Doolough, the black lake itself, came into view. The mirror-calm water was flanked by two huge steep hills with a third in the distance, all dark brown and hazy in the sunshine. On the nearest slopes it was possible still to make out the scratchings of what must have been pathetic little potato patches carved into the hillside. Along the route I'd passed the familiar sight of derelict cottages that had in all likelihood remained empty since the famine. The road followed the edge of the lake and as the sun glinted off the water I could barely believe that this was the location of one of the worst episodes of a dreadful era. Two memorials confirmed it, though, one a simple stone cross engraved with the words 'Doolough Tragedy 1849, erected to the memory of those who died in the famine of 1845–1849', around which passers-by had placed stones, slowly forming a cairn that will one day swallow up the monument itself. The second monument had a more elaborate inscription: 'To commemorate the hungry poor who walked here in 1849 and who walk the Third World today,' it said. "How can men feel themselves honoured by the humiliation of their fellow beings?" Mahatma Gandhi.'

This was what had convinced me that in choosing the Doolough Famine Walk I'd found the best way to illustrate the power of history, even the history of the nameless. Since 1988 there has been an annual walk along this route to commemorate both the victims of Doolough and the suffering and starvation of the world's poor. Archbishop Desmond Tutu has done it and there have been visits from Chernobyl children, refugees from Zaïre, the cellist Vedran Smailoviç, who played his instrument in the streets of Sarajevo during the siege of the early nineties, and Kim Phúc, the woman made famous by the photograph of her as a little girl, running naked and burned raw by napalm during the Vietnam War.

Perhaps most notable of all, however, is the regular presence on the walks of Choctaw Americans. When they learned of the Doolough tragedy in 1849 the Choctaw tribe collected $710 and donated it to Irish famine relief because the episode chimed with their own recent experience. In 1831 they were forcibly moved from their native lands in Alabama, Mississippi and Louisiana by the US government and made to walk to modern-day Oklahoma, a distance of roughly five hundred miles. Around fifteen thousand Choctaw set off; more than 2500 never made it and the journey has become known as the Trail of Tears. In 1992, a group of Irish people returned the gesture by walking the Trail of Tears route, raising $710,000, exactly one thousand times the amount donated by the Choctaw in 1849, for famine relief in Africa. From a terrible incident in the remote west of

Ireland via the centre of the North American continent to relief camps in Africa, history stretched a considerable way.

I reached Delphi Lodge, the scene of, and indirectly the reason for, this dreadful tragedy. It's a happy place today, ill-deserving its association with the tragedy. It has an atmosphere reminiscent of a dinner party rather than a hotel – everyone eats together at a large dining table and there are no room keys or televisions. There's no mobile phone signal and the rest of the world is far away. It's a thumping great L-shaped building of two storeys looking out on to the lake and the mountain beyond; another mountain rises behind it, dwarfing the place with the sheer intimidating scale of nature. It's almost as if the ground itself rose up in indignation at the terrible thing that happened here. After arriving and being shown to my room I was told that I'd be served tea in the library in ten minutes – a bit of a contrast to the temperamental vending machines and pork scratchings in back-street pubs I'd been used to at the end of a day's walk. In the library, surrounded by glass-fronted bookcases containing ancient tomes on hunting and fishing, I couldn't help looking out of the window and picturing the starving people gathered outside, many collapsing where they stood, others on their hands and knees, pathetic, skeletal people dehumanised by hunger, sallow skin hanging from their bones, their eyes dark and sunken, and wondering just how nobody could have been moved enough – no, *human* enough – to at least try to alleviate their suffering even slightly. If there's one thing Delphi Lodge has in abundance it's windows; there's just no way the people inside could have missed the gathered waifs looking pleadingly at the austere walls and firmly closed front door. Then they sat down to lunch.

As the sun prepared to drop behind the hills I walked a short distance out of the lodge to a little bridge over part of the lake, then turned and looked back. There was total silence. I thought again about the tragedy here and realised that although we know barely a handful of the names of the people who died that awful day in March 1849, the annual commemoration ensures that history won't forget any of them. Not only that, they have become a focus for suffering worldwide, the threads of their history intertwining with those of the Choctaw, the victims of the Bosnian wars and Chernobyl, and even a little girl whose village on the other side of the world was bombed forty years ago, who had never even heard of Doolough but whose plight was captured and sent all around the world.

I thought too of the people I'd followed and the people I'd met on these journeys. I'd grown to like all of them; I'd found a dignity and nobility in all my quarries, even the priapic Olaf. I'd walked miles in their shoes, and there'd been no better way to gain a sense of their plights, their hopes and fears, the motivations behind their actions that would ring down the centuries to the extent that we still talk about them today.

I'd met some fantastic, inspiring people too. The couple at the Gwenllian monument, the woman's eyes burning with patriotic pride and a fervour that the tragic fourteenth-century nun should never be forgotten. Old Jim in Sanquhar, who had pretty much taught me more about history and how to regard the world about me in the space of three-quarters of a mile than I'd learned on the entire journey. The history group in the pub in rain-soaked Llanidloes, passing the evening hours in the fire-light discussing some of the more ancient niches of the Welsh past. Duncan tarting up Loch Leven Castle ready for the thousands of tourists that would chug across the water in the coming summer months to see where Mary carried out her daring but ultimately futile escape. The fresh flowers on the purported grave of King Harold at Waltham Abbey. Kenny, constantly on the lookout for the next priceless piece of Scottish football history to preserve for the nation. Even Anna, still sad and angry enough about Doolough a century and a half after the events to practically plead with me to go there. It's all uplifting, gratifying evidence that history is irrefutably alive. It's not just in the textbooks and the soulless cabinets of museums, it's in the passion of its patrons. Journeys are still being made all across these islands. My footsteps have already disappeared from the mud and gravel of England, Scotland, the Isle of Man, Wales and now Ireland, but others will follow them. My journey had taken me from a no-frills motel above a bathroom shop on a busy ring road to here, a beautiful, peaceful hunting lodge as far from anywhere as you can get, and I felt that Boudica's oppressed, angry followers would have identified with the famine poor here. I felt a definite contentment that the nameless victims of the Doolough cruelty had not vanished into the wispy caverns of obscurity but had drawn together oppressed people across the world, people from wildly different cultures and centuries who had suffered themselves and were determined that these things should not be forgotten; that some basic human good should come out of it all. I looked down at the water. I saw the scuffed, well-worn uppers of the boots that had propelled me here and, beyond, my reflection shifting slightly on the surface of the lake but still enough to betray the smile tugging at the corners of my mouth. Some of the Doolough victims would have drunk from this water, probably from this exact spot. History may not know their names but their journey and their story now reached way beyond the closed doors of Delphi Lodge.

The sun dropped slowly behind the mountain and the air grew colder as twilight settled upon the peace of Doolough. I walked back across the grass and saw a match flare through one of the dining room windows before it lit a candle on the table within.

Acknowledgements

I am grateful to the following fine people for their advice, encouragement, company, support, assistance and occasionally towels in the researching, travelling and writing of this book. Lizzy Kremer, Sarah Shrubb, Zoë Gullen, Jenny Fry, Richard Beswick, Mum and Dad, Pete Howls, Jen and Brian Miller, Lorcan and Una Leavy, Polly Evans, Anna Rafferty, Kylie Jenkins and the Isle of Man Tourist Board, Jonathan Manning, JR Daeschner, Kez Piper, David Prest, the Ukulele Cosmos, Mick Collins, Paul and Emma s'Jacob, Laura Keenan, Melissa May, Steve Morgan, Margaret Daly, Kevin Dawson, Russell McKay, Jon Edwards, Giulia Liside, Donna White, Douglas Wilson and Paul Spence at Historic Scotland, Kenny Strang and Richard McBrearty at the Scottish Football Museum, Michael Grant, Simona Aversa, Richard Else, Jessica Pratt and Mia Ylönen. I am also grateful to Messrs Hood, Galliver, Condren, Walters and Brown for sparking in me a passion for history from primary school to university.

Finally, much love and thanks to Jude for her boundless inspiration, faith, yokes and presses.

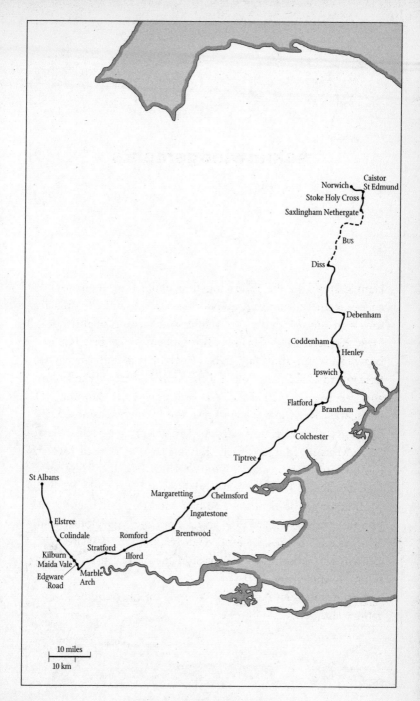

AD60–61: Boudica's revolt

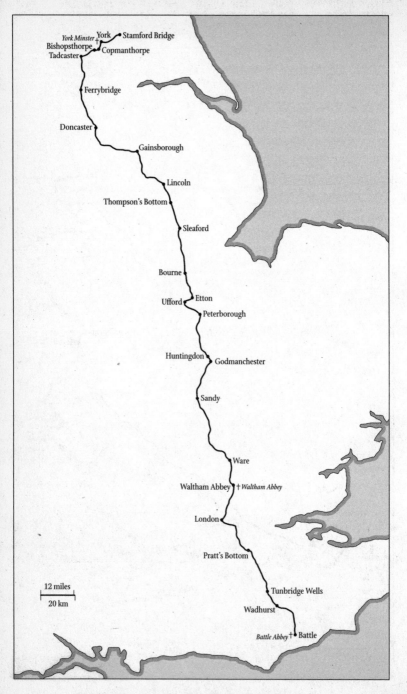

1066: King Harold, Stamford Bridge to Hastings

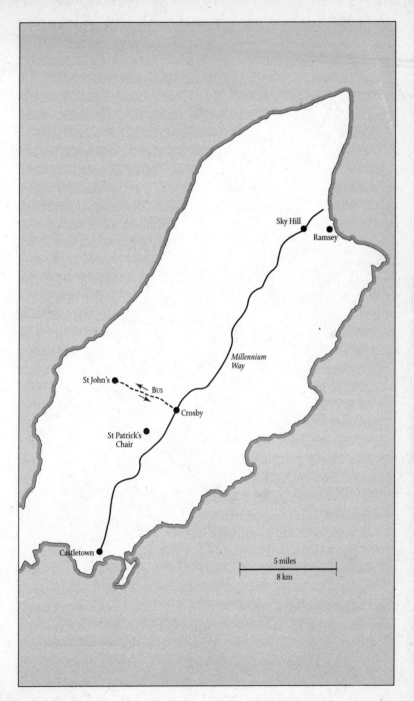

c. 1150: On the trail of Olaf the Dwarf, King of Man

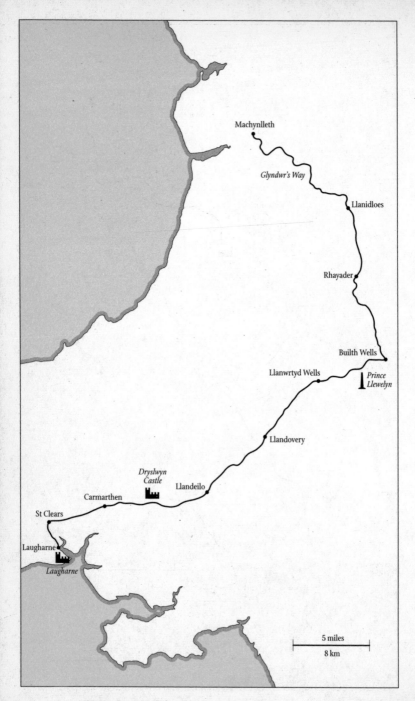

1403: Owain Glyndwr rises up against the English

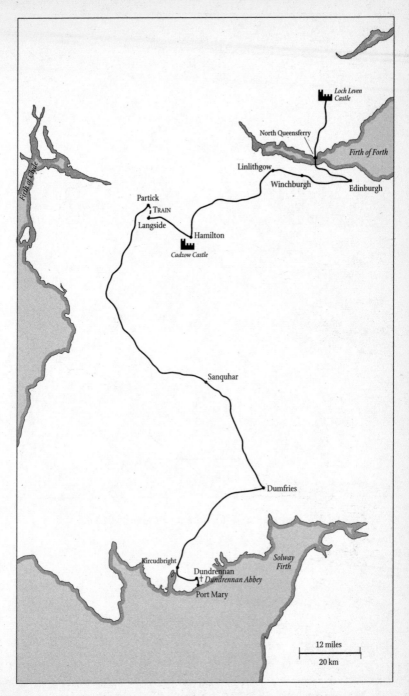

1568: Mary, Queen of Scots escapes from Loch Leven

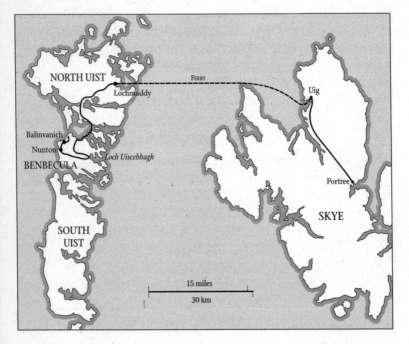

1746: Bonnie Prince Charlie and Flora MacDonald

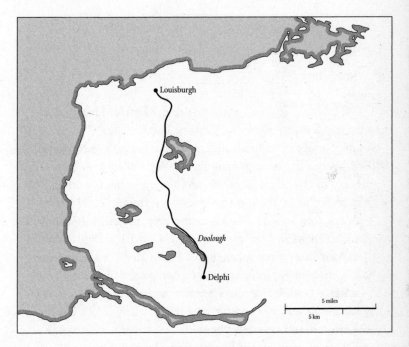

1849: The Doolough Famine Walk

Further Reading

I didn't sleep away my entire time in the British Library during my early training period. Oh no. I spent a considerable time reading books, tutting at undergraduate students messing with their phones and having arguments with people pushing into the queue while waiting for the doors to open in the morning. The first proved to be the most productive of the three.

I consulted a range of texts in the preparation of this book. I won't list them all here, partly because I can't remember most of them, but there were a handful of books that I consulted more heavily than others; some of which accompanied me on my travels.

Vanessa Collingridge is a terrific writer about history. Her *Boudica* is a lively and entertaining read packed with a wealth of background and research about the enigmatic warrior queen, and it accompanied me on the first journey. I also consulted *Boudica Britannia: Rebel, War-Leader and Queen* by Miranda Aldhouse-Green, which was heavier going but still very useful. The 2003 film *Boudica* was useful inasmuch as it reassured me that I had some idea what I was talking about by my triumphantly spotting the glaring errors and anachronisms that litter the thing.

Ian W. Walker's *Harold: The Last Anglo-Saxon King* travelled with me from Stamford Bridge to Battle, and provides the best and certainly most readable account of the life of a man I came to admire very much. *Harold II: The Doomed Saxon King* by the appropriately named Peter Rex was also a useful resource. Both books are excellent at the forensic dissection of the Godwines and their contemporaries from the labyrinthine original records.

My copy of *Cronica Regum Mannie et Insularum: Chronicles of the Kings of Man and the Isles* was produced by Manx National Heritage and proved to be agreeably hard-wearing on my two-day yomp across the Isle of Man, despite the inexplicable curry sauce stain on the cover. In addition, and arguably more importantly, it provided me with what little we know about Olaf the Dwarf. I also carried G. V. C. Young's highly useful *A Brief History of the Isle of Man* across the island.

For the Owain Glyndwr journey I couldn't separate the merits of two large and weighty paperbacks and took both with me which, given the need to travel light, serves I hope as testament to them both. *The Revolt of Owain Glyn Dwr* by R. R. Davies is a detailed and very readable account of the rebellion, its roots and its consequences. Alongside Chris Barber's *In Search of Owain Glyndwr*, in which the author visits just about every place associated with the Welsh prince, Glyndwr emerges from the mist of history as a tangible character. George Borrow's *Wild Wales* also proved to be an enjoyable travelling companion. He was some character. And boy, he could walk. The Princess Gwenllian Society has an informative website at www.princessgwenllian.co.uk.

My Heart is my Own: The Life of Mary, Queen of Scots by John Guy is probably the most accessible of the many biographies of Mary available, while Antonia Fraser's *Mary, Queen of Scots* is also a good resource. The book that went into my rucksack, however, was *On The Trail of Mary, Queen of Scots* by J. Keith Cheetham, which combines simple and useful biography with information about the locations associated with the queen.

In the same series, *On The Trail of Bonnie Prince Charlie* by David R. Ross was invaluable for the same reasons, while Frank

McLynn's *Bonnie Prince Charlie: Charles Edward Stuart* is a riveting biography. I also drew on Eric Linklater's *The Prince in the Heather* and John Ure's *A Bird on the Wing: Bonnie Prince Charlie's Flight From Culloden Retraced* when researching the journey. In a gift shop in Uig I picked up *A Wee Guide to Flora MacDonald* by David MacDonald, a slim but useful biography of the heroine of the tale who is sometimes overlooked given the focus on the Young Pretender.

The account of the Doolough tragedy that appeared in the *Mayo Constitution* I found in *The Irish Famine: A Documentary* by Colm Tóibín and Diarmaid Ferriter, which offers a perceptive analysis of the famine and its legacy as well as reproducing some fascinating and horrifying contemporary reports and documents. Cecil Woodham-Smith's classic, *The Great Hunger: Ireland 1845–1849*, is a harrowing account of the famine and is probably the pick of the general histories of the tragedy.

There are relatively few general books about walking, but three that I found invaluable were *Byways, Boots and Blisters: A History of Walkers and Walking* by Bill Laws, *Shanks's Pony: A Study of Walking* by Morris Marples and *The Vintage Book of Walking*, edited by Duncan Minshull.

Finally, heave off your walking boots, hang your waterproofs in front of the fire and settle in in front of www.charlieconnelly.com where you'll find further information about the journeys, the chance to sign up for e-mail updates as well as photographs from the walks, some of which, be warned, feature alarming facial hair. It's a whole big bumper bunch of fun.

ATTENTION ALL SHIPPING

Charlie Connelly

The shipping forecast is a curious piece of broadcasting; at once impenetrably baffling yet at the same time reassuringly familiar, and most of us have grown up with this sonorous gazetteer firmly planted in our subconscious. But where are these places, and what secrets do they conceal? Charlie Connelly sets off on a journey around the forecast to find out. From North Utsire to FitzRoy, South-east Iceland to German Bight, Connelly brings to life the places behind the mysterious names and unearths the history and culture behind one of Britain's best-loved broadcasting institutions.

More than simply a hilarious travel book, *Attention All Shipping* ensures that the evocative stanzas of the shipping forecast will remain a mystery no more.

Abacus
978-0-349-11603-7

IN SEARCH OF ELVIS

Charlie Connelly

August 2007 was the thirtieth anniversary of the death of Elvis Presley, yet he remains the biggest cultural icon of our time. His influence has spread across the globe, but he left the USA only twice in his lifetime. Charlie Connelly sets out to explore the worldwide legacy of the king of rock 'n' roll – and in the process uncovers some unlikely characters in deeply unlikely places.

In Search Of Elvis takes Charlie to Finland to meet a literature professor who performs Elvis songs in Latin, while wearing a kilt. In Canada he finds the Jewish Elvis impersonator Schmelvis, and then addresses the congregation of an Elvis-themed Anglican church alongside its minister, Elvis Priestley. And in Uzbekistan Charlie finds himself performing on national TV alongside the country's biggest pop star while wearing dreadful trousers. But the heart of Charlie's journey is to the places Elvis knew best: Memphis, Tupelo, Las Vegas and Hawaii.

Not just a hilarious travel book, *In Search of Elvis* is a timely exploration of the global reach of the hip-wiggling, guitar-slinger from Tennessee.

Abacus
978-0-349-11900-7

Now you can order superb titles directly from Abacus

☐ Attention All Shipping   Charlie Connelly   £8.99
☐ In Search of Elvis   Charlie Connelly   £8.99

The prices shown above are correct at time of going to press. However, the publishers reserve the right to increase prices on covers from those previously advertised, without further notice.

Please allow for postage and packing: **Free UK delivery.**
Europe: add 25% of retail price; Rest of World: 45% of retail price.

To order any of the above or any other Abacus titles, please call our credit card orderline or fill in this coupon and send/fax it to:

Abacus, PO Box 121, Kettering, Northants NN14 4ZQ
Fax: 01832 733076   Tel: 01832 737526
Email: aspenhouse@FSBDial.co.uk

☐ I enclose a UK bank cheque made payable to Abacus for £ . . . .
☐ Please charge £ . . . . . . to my Visa/Delta/Maestro

Expiry Date | | | | Maestro Issue No. | | |

NAME (BLOCK LETTERS please) . . . .

ADDRESS . . . .

. . . .

. . . .

Postcode . . . . Telephone . . . .

Signature . . . .

Please allow 28 days for delivery within the UK. Offer subject to price and availability.